The HISTORY of

CYCLING in FIFTY BIKES

First published 2013. This paperback edition published 2014.

The History Press
The Mill, Brimscombe Port
Stroud, Gloucestershire, GL5 2QG
www.thehistorypress.co.uk

Conceived, designed and produced by
Quid Publishing
Level 4 Sheridan House
114 Western Road
Hove BN3 1DD
www.quidpublishing.com

Book design by Lindsey Johns

British Library Cataloguing in Publication Data.
A catalogue record for this book is available from the British Library.

ISBN 978 0 7509 6060 1

Printed in China by 1010 Printing International Ltd

The HISTORY of

CYCLING in FIFTY BIKES

TOM AMBROSE

Contents

Introduction

The late eighteenth century saw the coming of two inventions that were to change human lifestyle dramatically. One was the railway steam engine, which allowed people, goods and materials to be carried freely on a continent-wide scale. The other was the first practical bicycle, which was to revolutionise personal travel and end the dependence on horse power when travelling short and medium distances.

This book tells the story of the development of the bicycle over more than 200 years in 50 cycles that were fundamental to the progress of bicycle technology. It starts with the early prototypes that were little more than two-wheeled sections of farm machinery made almost entirely of wood.

T*he History of Cycling in Fifty Bikes* also shows the controversy often associated with the early bicycle. Some thought it the machine of the devil, careering dangerously along and threatening the lives of passers-by and the rider. Others thought it a threat to public morality, encouraging young men and women to ride out to isolated spots together. In particular, the need for women to ride in less bulky and, as it happened, more revealing clothes badly shocked social conservatives. In fact, the bicycle was seen by many women as the chariot of female emancipation and was taken up by forward-thinking young women for that very reason. Social progress became associated with practical progress along the road.

There is no doubt that the bicycle improved the physical fitness of both sexes. It also encouraged young men to go further afield in the search for a partner, so improving the genetic quality of future children that would be born.

Undoubtedly, bicycle travel helped broaden the mind. The ability to ride out of the industrial nineteenth-century towns and explore the countryside

The early years of the bicycle was a time of great uncertainty in design. No one was sure whether it would be the bicycle or the tricycle that would triumph.

Racing bike design was revolutionised by the development of carbon-fibre technology.

became the prerogative of the many rather than the preserve of the few. An interest in nature and the history of the country was no long confined to scholars or the wealthy who could afford a horse or a horse-drawn carriage.

What this book also shows is the fascinating and steady evolution of cycle design; not just the slimming down of the basic frame but the accessories that went with it. This included pedals, used to drive the front and later the rear wheel. Almost as important was the inflatable tyre, which transformed cycling from mild torture to a pleasurable experience. So, too, with the coming of gearing systems that helped the rider to conquer gradient.

All these progressions led to the cycle being seen not just as a means of transport, but as a sporting machine, too. The early races in cities such as Paris and London show how the public, even those without a bicycle themselves, became entranced by watching cycle races. This would lead to such events as the Tour de France, one of the greatest of all sporting contests. Conquering distance in the one-hour race, as well as cycling events in the Olympic Games, helped to raise the popularity of the sport.

Crucially, the cycle also proved a great testing ground for new industrial materials, not least with carbon fibre. Lighter-weight and more powerful machines have improved the performance that can be expected from a simple bicycle. This has helped more adventurous types of cycling to develop, such as mountain and BMX biking.

With ever more advanced bicycle designs appearing, together with the possibilities of electric power as in the e-bike, development continues to be as healthy as ever. But perhaps the most interesting aspect of the future of cycling is the way that the cycle is colonising cities throughout the world. In the near future, it will take not just 50 bikes to do justice to the history of cycling, but hundreds.

1: Proto-Bicycle
The Search for the People's Horse

Until the eighteenth century, the only means of transport on land remained the horse. Without an animal to ride or pull a vehicle, travel by road or across country was the preserve of the very few. The ordinary man walked everywhere – to work, to church, to meet his girlfriend. The distances covered were tremendous. In the Middle Ages, most of the crusaders walked all the way from Northern Europe to the Holy Land, and those who survived walked back again. For centuries, people dreamed of some kind of machine that could transport them along roads and, even more improbably, across country.

Year: 1779

Inventor:
Blanchard

Location:
Paris

A t the start of the Industrial Revolution, when technology was first harnessed and the possibility of steam power was revealed, it finally seemed that the dream of a new means of transport that could bring freedom to the ordinary person could become a reality.

When it did come, the bicycle would affect the course of history in unforeseen ways. Not only would a person be able to travel freely and cheaply; the coming of the cycle changed much else. Not least would be a vast improvement in the quality of road-building. The development of bike technology would even help man take to the air. Before they built the first powered flying machine, the Wright Brothers ran a bicycle repair shop at Dayton, Ohio, where they used bicycles to carry out their first wind-tunnel experiments. The world's first true aeroplane was built in their cycle workshop using the tools and materials of that trade.

It would take the bicycle a long time to challenge the position of the horse as the principal means of travel throughout Europe.

Like something from the notebooks of Leonardo da Vinci, designs for the first bikes were more vague and fantastic concepts than working drawings for a practical and achievable machine.

The Quest for a Human-Powered Vehicle

The first attempt at making a bicycle had started centuries earlier. Even early tomb paintings from ancient Egypt suggest a distant ancestor of the bicycle. How and where this began is a mystery, although one story concerns the Renaissance artist Gian Giacomo Caprotti. A pupil of the great Leonardo da Vinci, himself a prolific inventor, Caprotti is said to have drawn a sketch in 1493 that bears an uncanny resemblance to a primitive bicycle, although scholars such as Hans-Erhard Lessing later claimed it was a fraud. Professor Augusto Marinoni, a lexicographer and philologist and an expert on the writings of da Vinci, insisted that it was authentic.

The quest for a human-powered vehicle was indisputably described in detail by French mathematician Jacques Ozanam, who in 1696 published his *Récréations mathématiques et physiques*. In it he describes the advantages of 'a device in which one can drive oneself and go wherever one pleases, without horses'. With such a machine, a person could wander freely along the roads

TWO WHEELS ARE BETTER THAN NONE

The use of the bike would strengthen the gene pool of rural workers by helping them escape from in-breeding. It would lessen the crowding in the houses and tenements of towns and cities, because people would now be able to commute to work from the suburbs over distances that had never been possible before. As they would soon discover, bicycles are three times as efficient as walking and three or four times as fast.

without having to care for an animal and might even enjoy healthy exercise in the process. Moreover, this type of self-propelled moving vehicle would need neither wind nor steam, as it would be powered by that most abundant and accessible of all resources – willpower.

With this suggestion, Ozanam urged the scientific and engineering community to come up with a solution that would lead almost two centuries later to the invention of the first practical bicycle. He also produced some practical ideas of his own that featured in the frontispiece of his book. This showed a massive four-wheeled carriage designed under his direction by a Dr Elie Richard, a physician from La Rochelle. Richard's plan shows the rider seated comfortably in the front, steering the front axle using a pair of reins. Behind him stands his servant, propelling the vehicle by stepping up and down on two reciprocating planks tangential to the rear axle. The planks are spring-loaded and suspended by a rope-and-pulley system so that when one is pressed down, the other rises up. Each plank, in turn, activates a gear fixed to the rear axle, causing the axle to turn, thereby rotating the wheels. The entire driving apparatus is neatly concealed within the body of the carriage.

Richard's carriage, despite its questionable technology, served for more than a century as the contemporary reference point for a human-powered vehicle. Other inventors' attempts on the theme were built in various European countries in the following years. Then, in 1744, a London journal

Early cycling may have
been a cumbersome
process but at least a
man could still take his
servant with him as on
a horse-drawn carriage.

celebrated a local invention by a Mr Ovenden, declaring it to be, 'the best that has hitherto been invented'. This wondrous invention was reportedly capable of cruising at 9.6 kilometres (6 miles) an hour, or faster if the footman was prepared for 'particular exertion'. Nor was it confined to the flat, as it could climb 'considerable hills', as long as they had a 'sound bottom'. This was probably a reference to a solid terrain surface.

Not to be outdone by the British, a French inventor, Jean-Pierre Blanchard, with the help of a M Masurier, came up with a similar machine. In celebration, Blanchard, together with his servant, mounted the carriage and in 1779 rode it around Place Louis XV in Paris. Soon they were surrounded by an excited crowd, curious to see this new marvel of travel. Flushed with his success, Blanchard then set off on the 19-kilometre (12-mile) journey to Versailles. This was probably the first recorded long-distance journey made by a human-powered vehicle in history. The French press became just as enthusiastic as the Paris crowd at the news, with the *Journal de Paris* reporting approvingly that the vehicle was cheered wherever it went. Blanchard, it insisted, should take his invention to a greater audience. The inventor certainly took the hint and gave regular displays of the machine in a courtyard close by the Champs-Élysées. Sadly, the enthusiasm for the cycling machine soon diminished and M Blanchard turned to another and more profitable pursuit by becoming a famous French balloonist.

Jean-Pierre Blanchard attempted to make the newly invented sport of cycling the fashionable pursuit for young men in pre-revolutionary Paris, with the help of an enthusiastic French press.

While Europe and France in particular had led the way in these early experiments in making a practical bicycle, an American now entered the field. News of M Blanchard and his exploits had reached New York, inspiring a little-known engineer named J. Bolton to patent a four-wheeled carriage in 1804. This vehicle must have been large, for it was designed to carry up to six passengers. They all sat in comfort on three upholstered benches while a two-man crew operated the contraption. While one crew-man sat in front and steered the smaller front wheels, the other stood in the middle of the riding platform facing the rear. This man supplied the power by using both hands to rotate a lever bar. This in turn activated a series of four progressively larger interlocking cogwheels on either side of the vehicle. The last of these were connected directly to the rear wheels, which measured about 1.2 metres (4 feet) in diameter, and rotated them in a forward direction. Bolton had produced an early form of a gear drive powered by the arms, not the feet, with the final cogwheels being almost as large as the rear wheels themselves. Yet the machine was far too cumbersome and unwieldy ever to be practical – the search for an efficient form of bicycle would just have to continue.

2: The Draisienne
An Early French Two-Wheeler

Throughout the late eighteenth century, engineers and blacksmiths in Europe were fascinated by the prospect of a man-powered machine that could carry a passenger along a road. How this could be done remained a mystery for decades. The biggest problem was to discover the basic technology that would be needed. Would such a machine, for instance, need two, three, four or even more wheels? How would it be propelled? Could it be driven by using cranks or foot treadles, and most importantly, how safe would the rider be if the machine could ever achieve the speed of a horse?

Year:
1817

Inventor:
Karl von Drais

Location:
Vienna

The Draisienne. Arguably the most important development in the early history of cycling.

At that time, a two-wheel machine seemed the least likely option for a man-powered machine. Surely the inherent instability caused by the lack of proper balance would rule out a two-wheeler from being the way ahead? And yet that was precisely the route that developments took.

The Célérifère

One day in 1791, a young man known throughout Paris for his eccentricities was seen riding through a park on a strange mechanical machine rather like a child's giant scooter. While seated on his 'horse' he propelled the two-wheeled machine along with his feet, making excellent progress. The only problem the bystanders noticed was that the machine had no form of steering.

The young rider was a French aristocrat, the Comte Mede de Sivrac, and his machine was to be the first properly recorded bicycle in history, the Célérifère. In many ways it was like a modern cycle, with two wheels, a central frame and a seat for the rider. De Sivrac's inspiration for the machine, he claimed, was the famous and controversial drawing by Leonardo da Vinci's pupil Gian Giacomo Caprotti. Made entirely of wood, the massive Célérifère had a wheel in front and a smaller wheel at the back. A very crude device, it had neither pedals, handlebars, nor any other parts that would be recognisable in a modern bicycle. With these limitations, the bicycle had to be driven in a straight line. When a turn was required the rider had first to dismount, then lift the machine, rotate it and put it down facing in the new direction of travel.

These procedures always attracted a crowd when de Sivrac rode his invention through the Bois de Boulogne in Paris. Soon others began to imitate his invention and the craze of cycling became a passion for the fashionable young men of Paris, who began to gather to ride their new Célérifères in the gardens of the Palais-Royal or even to race each other along the Champs-Élysées. It did not take long, however, for this new-found enthusiasm to fade as many riders suffered injuries from falls and groin strains from having to manoeuvre the cumbersome machines to change direction. Furthermore, these early Célérifères were proving very expensive to acquire, costing just as much as an ordinary riding horse.

The popularity of the early cycle led to many variations, such as customised handlebars, but as yet no one could overcome the basic problem – a lack of pedals.

The Running Machine

The first big advance on the Célérifère came in 1818 when a German, Karl Drais from Karlsruhe, took out a patent on a more advanced bicycle. It was said that Drais's interest in finding an alternative to the horse resulted from his disgust at the starvation and death of horses that resulted from the crop failure that occurred in 1816. Drais had studied architecture, agriculture and physics at the University of Heidelberg and had also experimented with an early form of the typewriter. When he was suspended on full pay from his post as a chief forester to the Baden court, he devoted himself to research on a cycling machine, inspired, perhaps, by the need to find a new way to carry out his tours of inspection in the forests.

His first attempt at a solution had occurred in 1813, when he had produced a four-wheeler that could carry up to four passengers. One or two of the passengers supplied the power by working a cranked handle using both arms and legs, while a third manoeuvred the crude steering handle. It was not a success and the patent offices in Baden and Austria rejected his patent application. In a last desperate attempt to gain international support, Drais turned up with his machine at the 1814 Congress of Vienna. Virtually ignored, he went home totally disillusioned. Nothing if not resilient, Drais refused to give up and returned to experimenting with a new form of the horseless carriage. The result was the Laufmaschine, or running machine, that would later be known as the 'draisine' or 'velocipede'. It was a two-wheeled cycle with wheels of equal size but, like its predecessor the Célérifère, without

An illustration of Karl Drais riding his famous invention in Germany.

pedals. This slender vehicle was limited in design by the carriage-building technology available at the time. Except for its iron tyres, the machine was made almost entirely of wood and had two miniature carriage wheels arranged in line. These were connected by a perch that supported a single cushioned seat. The rider sat nearly erect on the seat and propelled the machine along by pushing on the ground with one foot and then the other, as if walking or running. A long pivoting pole at the foremost end of the frame allowed the rider to swivel the front wheel to steer the machine. A small padded board was placed at waist height in front of the seat on which the rider could rest his arms or elbows as he shifted his weight to keep the vehicle from tipping to one side or the other. It weighed about 22.6 kilograms (50 pounds) and cost four Carolins.

Karl von Drais, an eccentric German baron who was to play a fundamental role in the development of the early bicycle.

Drais's first reported ride on his new invention was from the centre of Mannheim to a popular coaching inn outside the city. A more ambitious second trip took him from Gernsbach to Baden-Baden through crowds of curious spectators. As a reward for his ingenuity in creating the Laufmaschine, Drais was awarded the title of baron by the local ruler and appointed an honorary professor of mechanics. His invention had also caught the public imagination and Drais's fame soon spread. He was invited to give lectures and demonstrations of his Laufmaschine in Frankfurt and later in Paris and Nancy; in France his invention became known as the Draisienne.

THE ACCELERATOR

According to Drais, the Laufmaschine merely helped and accelerated the natural acts of walking and running but used up much less human energy. As he strode along, the rider gave a new velocity to the machine that remained even when the rider was between steps and not normally progressing. As an early enthusiast explained, the rider 'pushes the wheels along when they won't go alone – and rides them when they will'. Those who took advantage of this machine thus covered extra ground with every step, routinely advancing four

or five yards with each impulsion, about twice the distance of a normal stride. This, Drais insisted, made his velocipede not just a pedestrian 'facilitator' but also an 'accelerator'. On a good road with minimal effort, Drais found that he could bowl along at 8–9.5 kilometres (5–6 miles) an hour, about twice a normal walking gait. For, as Drais discovered, once the machine reached a certain velocity as a result of gravity, the rider could safely lift their feet up off the ground and let the machine roll along on its own.

Convinced that he had finally met the challenge of the horseless carriage, Drais now had the confidence to seek public approval. Several journals dutifully published accounts of his invention, and some foreign dignitaries offered their approval, most notably the Russian tsar, Alexander I. But despite Drais's success, the patent offices of both Baden and Austria swiftly rejected his pleas for patent protection. The examiner from his native Baden, Johann Tulla, issued a particularly harsh evaluation of the carriage and even denied that Drais had gained any ground whatsoever. Man, insisted Tulla, was ill-equipped to apply his motive powers in any context other than the God-given means of walking.

Keen to prove the military and commercial potential of his invention, Drais drove his Laufmaschine from Karlsruhe to the French border in the short time of just four hours to prove how swiftly it could carry messages across battlefields. Then, in a series of races against a conventional stagecoach, it proved to be significantly faster. Others saw the commercial potential of the cycle; the local German postal service commissioned several machines from him but failed to buy more when it saw what damage the Laufmaschine did to the postmen's shoes!

Drais's attempt to establish a factory to make the cycle eventually came to nothing and his invention became an object of ridicule, with cartoonists poking fun and people laughing at it in the street. The controversy came to a head when Drais himself collided with a visiting Englishman riding a horse. A fierce argument broke out that eventually culminated in a fist fight.

Drais's machine was more like an agricultural implement in construction than a bicycle; extremely heavy and made of wood. This 1820 model was built with cherry tree wood and softwood.

Early riders were often mocked for their insolence in setting themselves up to challenge the much-loved and traditional horse in their means of transport.

Some locals, however, maintained an affection for the eccentric inventor and whenever he drove past the city hall in Karlsruhe the sentry would invite him in for a beer in return for watching him ride down the steps outside on his Laufmaschine. Drais died poor and disillusioned in December 1851, but his invention was to live on in other countries. Louis Dineur, who became Drais's French agent, Johnson in England, and Clarkson in the USA, had all taken out patents based on the Laufmaschine in 1819.

FACING PUBLIC MOCKERY

Those who witnessed a demonstration by Drais's servant in the Luxembourg gardens in Paris were far from impressed. The *Journal de Paris* noted that a group of children on foot had no trouble keeping up with the bicycle. When another spectator tried to outpace it he collided with the Laufmaschine and broke a bolt holding it together. This amused another bystander, who commented, 'Monsieur Drais deserves the gratitude of cobblers everywhere for he has discovered a way to wear out shoes quickly.' A further demonstration in the city of Dijon produced an equally gloomy response. In Beaune the reception was more positive, although the local newspaper warned that the machine could only perform adequately on a firm, dry road. None of this deterred Drais's agent Louis Dineur from setting up a lucrative business in the Parc Monceau in Paris, hiring out machines by the half-hour.

3: The Hobby Horse
The Dandy's Choice

Denis Johnson, an Englishman, was the most successful developer of Drais's machine in Europe. A London cartwright by trade, Johnson described his version as 'the pedestrian curricle' but it was soon given the nickname of 'dandy' or 'hobby horse' after the children's toy. Johnson's patent application grandly describes it as 'a machine for the purpose of diminishing the labour and fatigue of persons in walking and enabling them at the same time to use greater speed'. It was soon to prove very popular with fashionable young men.

Year: 1819

Inventor:
Johnson

Location:
London

Johnson's invention was certainly an improvement on Drais's idea; it was far more elegant. The wooden frame had a curved, serpentine shape instead of Drais's straight one. This allowed larger wheels to be used without having the effect of raising the rider's seat. To support the heavy frame on the hubs, Johnson used an iron fork in front and two iron stays at the rear. This was a significant improvement on Drais's bulky wooden braces.

A Dandy Way to Travel

During the summer of 1819 the hobby horse, thanks in part to Johnson's marketing skills and better patent protection, became the craze for members of London's young male society. To encourage fashionable young men to try his machine, in March 1819 Johnson opened his own riding school near his workshop at Long Acre in London. The entry charge was one shilling. After a brief instruction the bold riders were invited to venture out on the London streets. Given the state of the nation's roads at the time, hobby horse riders preferred to take their exercise vehicles on the paved city streets rather than on rough country roads. The unexpected popularity of the hobby horse inspired Johnson to produce a version specially for women, making it the first dedicated lady's bike in history. The commercial potential of such a machine had also occurred to Johnson and he then emulated Drais by organising an experiment in which the hobby horse was tested by a group of London postmen.

According to contemporary newspaper reports, the hobby horse could reach speeds of up to 16 kilometres (10 miles) an hour on good roads and this made it a potentially lethal hazard on the crowded streets of London. Inevitably, a ban by the local authorities soon followed. This, of course, made it all the more appealing to the young risk-takers of the age. It was a demonstration

'A machine for the purpose of diminishing the labour and fatigue of persons in walking and enabling them at the same time to use greater speed.'

– Denis Johnson (1819)

of how appealing sensational publicity could be to those prepared to take chances. The hobby horse was also a godsend to the satirical press, which used it to mock the selfish extravagance of the aristocracy. None of this controversy had any effect on Johnson, who persisted with his attempts to make the hobby horse acceptable to a wider public. He now took his invention to the provinces, demonstrating it at such places as the Stork Hotel in Birmingham and the Music Hall in Liverpool, where one journalist admired 'the graceful movements of which it is capable in skilled hands'.

By now, Johnson was producing 20 hobby horses a week and selling them for the princely sum of eight pounds sterling. One curiosity was that he weighed each potential owner and then built the velocipede as light as possible but strong enough to carry the rider's weight. Far from having the market to himself, Johnson was plagued by imitators trying to copy his success. As his admirers increased in number, one writer in York praised those hobby horse owners who ignored public ridicule and 'mounted and set off at once with a sense not of themselves and what others think of them but of the pleasure of so desirable an invention'. Yet the press continued to grumble about velocipedes being run dangerously along the pavements. When a speed contest against a man mounted on an ass was announced many thought it an appropriate contest. A typical hare and tortoise sort of race resulted, the sore

Young men began to attend riding schools for bicycling, where they could learn the finer points of the sport in a sociable and fashionable environment.

feet of the velocipede rider leading to him being overtaken by the ass as they neared the end of the 16-kilometre (10-mile) race. In London one bold rider found himself pursued by a hostile crowd and was forced to take refuge in a passing stagecoach after throwing his machine up onto the carriage roof.

There was further condemnation when the Royal College of Surgeons pronounced against the infernal machine. Riding a two-wheeler, they claimed, was as dangerous to the rider as it was to pedestrians. All manner of hernias and ruptures could result, as well as serious injuries caused by accidents.

At best, the hobby horse remained a primitive and very uncomfortable means of transport. The wooden or iron-clad wheels, the rigid frame, together with the potholed roads of the time, combined to make for a rough and unpleasant ride. Constant movement by the rider, shifting his body as he encountered bumps and depressions in the road, could cause excruciating pain as well as minor injuries. The need to constantly use the feet to maintain balance and propulsion only added to the rider's pain. Yet for its time, the hobby horse did provide a relatively fast, if unpredictable, means of transport.

IMPROVED STEERING

Over the years, Johnson added other refinements to his basic machine. In particular, he attempted to provide it with some form of steering. Instead of his conventional wooden frame he produced a lighter version in metal. The new primitive steering was controlled by an iron bar perpendicular to the frame with wooden handgrips at either end. A metal tube bore the axis of the steering front wheel and could be more accurately positioned. The friction caused by the turning wheel could also be greatly reduced so that the steering mechanism could also be used to keep the vehicle upright. This was a fundamental advance that is still used on cycles today. Best of all, it allowed the rider to raise his feet off the ground and still keep his balance while steering.

By Denis Johnson's time the hobby horse had become a far more elaborate creation, much cherished by the fashionable elite of London.

The First American Cycling Craze

Meanwhile, in America, W. K. Clarkson had patented his own version of the velocipede in 1820. He called it the 'swift-walker' and it became a popular sight in the New York City parks. As with Johnson's machine, it aroused some controversy and led to the creation of several new by-laws in the city. While they successfully increased walking speed, swift-walkers were still too heavy and inefficient, especially on hills and bumpy ground, to become a permanent attraction. This did not stop Clarkson setting up riding schools to teach new owners the art of riding his machine. Hundreds of young men bought a Clarkson machine in what was the first American cycling craze in history.

'The bicycle ranks among those gifts of science to man, by which he is enabled to supplement his own puny powers with the exhaustic forces around him. He sits in the saddle, and all nature is but a four-footed beast to do his bidding. Why should he go a foot, while he can ride a mustang of steel, who knows his rider and never needs a lasso?'

– *San Francisco Chronicle*
(25 January, 1879)

Not everyone was convinced about its merits; one American journalist dismissed it as a purely foreign idea that would not catch on. He deplored the fact that 'every species of transatlantic nonsense, it would seem, is capable of exciting curiosity, no matter how ridiculous'. As in Germany, the pedestrian public became enraged by these heavy machines careering along public pathways with their riders barely in control. Going downhill without brakes was the most hazardous manoeuvre for both riders and spectators. Vested interests saw the new bicycle as a threat to the horse business and some blacksmiths were reported to be attacking any swift-walker that passed through their villages. By the end of the decade, Clarkson's machine had largely disappeared.

One particular criticism was that the velocipede 'turned a man into a horse and carriage' and thus compelled the rider to do work formerly only performed by animals. Even the English Romantic poet John Keats was among those who dismissed it as a novelty, a mere 'nothing of the day'. Still others derided the design's mechanical assumptions, likening velocipede riding to 'working a passage up a canal by towing the boat'. Some even thought the riders just as bad as the machine itself and lampooned them as mere vain and idle dandies.

Indeed, one sceptic in Philadelphia went even further, condemning the velocipede as 'a mere apology for a decent man to take a race by himself'. As he saw it, no respectable gentleman would ever 'run a mile for diversion… as nature made him', since the spectacle would inevitably astonish the natives and 'bring the heads of the good people at their windows, perhaps even generating a trail of boys yelling Stop, Thief!' Yet, he concluded with a more positive comment that, 'If a man only has a wheel at his back, or appears to have some machinery on foot, he may run till doomsday, and no body will molest him.'

4: The Macmillan Pedal Bike
Both Feet Off the Ground

By the 1840s the hobby horse had had its day. Heavy, cumbersome and difficult to steer, it had no means of efficient propulsion other than by the human foot. If the bicycle was going to progress, some new means of propelling it must be found. Steam power was already in widespread use, but it was totally inappropriate for a small two-wheeled cycle. A breakthrough came in, of all places, the relative backwater of rural Scotland, where a village blacksmith named Kirkpatrick Macmillan created the world's first ever pedal-driven bicycle.

Year: 1839

Inventor:
Macmillan

Location:
Dumfriesshire

'Macmillan had tired of this crude style of propulsion, and after long and anxious thought he successfully devised a plan to get rid of it.'

– James Johnston, *Gallovidian* magazine (1899)

A s James Johnston of the Glasgow Cycling Club reported in 1899 in the *Gallovidian* magazine, 'Macmillan had tired of this crude style of propulsion, and after long and anxious thought he successfully devised a plan to get rid of it.'

With the help of a friend, it took Macmillan about a year to complete the project and it is thought that by 1839 he was happy with the finished product. When he brought the machine out from his premises, dozens of villagers gathered to watch its first run. One eyewitness wrote that, 'To get it started he found it easier – until the cranks on his rear-driven wheel began to move at a fair speed – to mount his machine and get it going by striking the ground with his feet.' As the villagers watched in amazement he then lifted his feet to the pedals and went whizzing down the rough highway.

When compared to the more complicated attempts of his contemporaries, Macmillan's solution was relatively simple but highly effective, providing a continuous drive to an adapted version of the well-established hobby horse. Macmillan's contraption had a wood frame and iron-rimmed wooden wheels. The front wheel, which provided the limited steering, measured 76 centimetres (30 inches) in diameter, the rear 102 centimetres (40 inches). The two wheels ran in-line and were driven by two treadles attached by connecting rods to the crank arms on the back wheel and were also attached to pedals through connecting rods. The greatest innovation was that the rider could now use the pedals to proceed without having to push himself along using his feet. Macmillan had produced the first proper man-powered bicycle. It was a fundamental advance in the progress of cycling that would eventually lead to the invention of the gearing system.

A Velocipede of Ingenious Design

To prove the efficiency of his new machine, Macmillan set out to thoroughly demonstrate its potential. Weighing in at an estimated 27 kilograms (60 pounds) it was a still a heavy machine to manoeuvre, but Macmillan was soon growing in confidence and gaining speed. The sight of him flying through the countryside aboard his new means of transport earned him the nickname 'Daft Pate'. Soon he was able to ride as far north as Carronbridge at the entrance to the Dalveen Pass and as far south as Holywood and travelling the 23 kilometres (14 miles) to Dumfries in less than an hour.

In 1842 he set out on a gruelling 113-kilometre (70-mile) ride from Dumfries to Glasgow. The trip to visit his two school-teacher brothers in the city took him two days. On the way back to Dumfriesshire he is said to have raced alongside the local stagecoach. Women and children were reported to have excitedly cheered him on as he progressed through the countryside, while others ran indoors in panic when they saw him approaching. Workers in the fields left their crops to line the roadsides and see this amazing man on wheels go flying by. When reaching the outskirts of Glasgow in the Gorbals area, he caused what may have been the first recorded traffic accident in history involving a bicycle.

As the excited crowd surged around this 'gentleman from Dumfriesshire bestride a velocipede of ingenious design', as the local newspaper reported, he had the bad luck to knock down a little girl. The child was not badly injured but the following day Macmillan had to appear in the local police court where he was fined five shillings. The magistrate at the Gorbals Public Bar was sufficiently impressed, however, to ask Macmillan to perform a figure-of-eight demonstration in the courtyard outside and was said to have personally slipped him the money to pay the fine.

Sadly, Kirkpatrick Macmillan's velocipede did not survive. This working replica was built in 1990 to commemorate the 150 years since the first bike was made and takes pride of place in the Scottish Cycle Museum at Drumlanrig Castle.

5: Velocipede
Front-Wheel Drive

In the middle decades of the nineteenth century it seemed that the future of cycle propulsion would be not with Macmillan's rear-drive system, but with that of the front-wheel drive. What was certain was that the velocipede, whether front or rear drive, was the way ahead. The first person to make and market such a machine commercially was Pierre Michaux in Paris, though it was his contemporary Pierre Lallement who would eventually take the invention across the Atlantic to America, where it would become the centre of the latest cycling craze.

Year:
1860s

Inventor:
Michaux

Location:
Paris

With his two sons, Ernest and Henri, Pierre Michaux was already an established maker of children's prams, invalid carriages and three-wheeled velocipedes, when, in 1861, a two-wheeled velocipede was left at his workshop for repair. Fascinated by the machine, Michaux realised that from now on, two wheels would be the future for the bicycle.

The Michaux velocipede showed, for the first time, how the modern bicycle would eventually evolve, although it still depended on a front-wheel pedal drive.

Using this original machine as his model, Michaux built another and changed the history of cycling by attaching cranks and pedals to the front wheel. After looking at the velocipede that lay in his shop for a while, Pierre and his 14-year-old son Ernest came up with an idea that would help it work better. They attached the crank handles of an old grindstone to the velocipede's front wheel, thereby enabling a rider to turn the wheel by cranking with his feet. For the rest of this new bike Michaux retained the wrought-iron frame of existing velocipedes but added a saddle mounted on a long, single leaf spring. A lever shoe brake operated on the rear wheel and was activated by rotating the handlebars and tightening the attached cord.

One of those who worked with Michaux on developing the new front-wheel-drive velocipede was Pierre Lallement. In fact, Lallement always claimed that it was he, and not the Michaux family, who had invented the front-wheel-drive system in the first place. Lallement was born near Nancy in France in 1843, where he was first employed building baby carriages. One day he saw someone riding a velocipede using his feet in the traditional manner. This, he insisted, inspired him to make a velocipede of his own, but one that had a transmission comprising a rotary crank mechanism and pedals. Moving to Paris in 1863 he met the Olivier brothers, who were also interested in the commercial possibilities of cycle manufacture and who had formed a partnership with Michaux to mass-produce the new two-wheeled

'An enterprising individual propelled himself about the Green last evening on a curious frame sustained by two wheels, one before the other, and driven by foot cranks.'

– Journalist (1866)

AN IRON FRAME

Michaux added something more to his cycle design – style. His cycle was well-engineered and attractively designed with skilful detailing of the saddle, pedals and lamp brackets. It was one of the first mass-produced bicycles ever; to speed production, Michaux used a cast-iron frame, so pointing the way ahead towards the steel frames that became common a few years later. Unfortunately, Michaux soon discovered that cast iron is very heavy and prone to breaking, so later

versions of the 'Michauline' were built with wrought-iron frames. Some believe that mispronunciation by the English of the French name 'Michauline' may be the reason why the 'boneshaker' became used to describe a Michaux-type bicycle.

Now metal had become involved in cycle manufacture, as seen in these pedals from an early Michaux velocipede.

© www.sterba-bike.cz

Perched on his veloci-
pede, the fashionable
young rider could pedal at
speed while looking down
on the world.

velocipedes. Lallement claimed that it was his own original prototype for a front-wheel-drive bike that inspired the Michaux front-wheel-drive machine. Therefore, if his story was true, it was Pierre Lallement, and not Pierre Michaux who played the key role in developing the concept of a front-drive bicycle. Clearly the Michaux family disagreed and the relationship then deteriorated so fundamentally that Lallement decided to quit France and try his luck in the USA.

Lallement Takes the Velocipede to America

In July 1865, Pierre Lallement arrived in America and settled down in Ansonia, Connecticut. With him Lallement had brought a pair of wheels, an iron saddle and wheel cranks that he now used as the basis for his first all-American cycle, which he named his 'veloce'.

He had arrived at the right time as Americans were just starting, long after the disappearance of Clarkson's swift-walker, to show a keen interest in the new velocipedes that some carriage builders had begun to make. Riding schools had been established in many eastern cities, and the sport suddenly became popular, especially among the students of Harvard and Yale. When Lallement rode the 19 kilometres (12 miles) from his home to New Haven in the spring of 1866, a local journalist wrote: 'An enterprising individual propelled himself about the Green last evening on a curious frame sustained by two wheels, one before the other, and driven by foot cranks.'

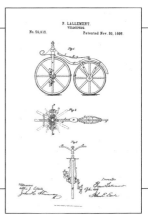

An important factor was the patent that Lallement immediately took out for his proposed new bike, one of the first of its kind in the world. With James Carroll of New Haven as his financer, he filed the earliest and only American patent application for the pedal-bicycle in April 1866. His patent drawing shows a machine bearing a great resemblance to the style of the hobby horse built by Denis Johnson of London. Lallement was ahead of the field, just, for in the latter years of the 1860s similar applications flooded into the patent offices of New York, Boston and Washington.

The craze ended as suddenly as it began. By the end of May 1869, the sport was dying. The reasons for the decline were that the cycles were too heavy and cumbersome for the average member of the public. There was no cushioning on the seat and the rider had both to steer and pedal using the same front wheel. Riding a velocipede took a great deal of strength and co-ordination far beyond the capabilities of the average man, let alone a woman. As in so many European cities where the early cycle began to appear, the American local authorities began to pass ordinances against riding on pedestrian sidewalks. This had a dampening effect on the embryonic American industry, limiting new development in the following decade.

Failing to interest an American manufacturer in producing his machine, Lallement became disillusioned and returned to Paris in 1868 just as the Michaux bicycles were creating the first bicycle craze in France, an enthusiasm that spread to the rest of Europe and then to America. Ironically, Lallement had left at the worst possible time. A group of three American acrobats toured the country racing bikes round open arenas and attracting vast crowds. The response so impressed the Hanlons that they took out their own patent on a new bike, only the second in American history.

Pierre Lallement took the detailed design for the Michaux velocipede to America and made it a success.

Soon cycling became as much an American craze as it already was in Europe, leading to young men showing off their velocipede skills in public.

6: The Boneshaker
Harsh Ride

In England the velocipede was often given the nickname of 'boneshaker' because of the jarring effect it had on riders using the roughly surfaced roads of the time. The construction of the boneshaker remained similar to that of the dandy horse, with its wooden wheels, metal tyres and bulky framework. As the name implies, it was extremely uncomfortable. However, the discomfort was somewhat ameliorated by a long flat spring that supported the saddle and absorbed some of the worst shocks from rough road surfaces.

Year: 1865

Inventor:
Various

Location:
Paris/London

At first, no one appeared to like the boneshaker. Not only was it given a bad press in its early days, but riders were often met with amusement and derision when they ventured out on their machines. Cartoons appeared in magazines like *Punch* mocking the riders as they careered along the uneven roads, scaring old ladies and startling the wildlife. Much of the problem of controlling the machine resulted from the fact that the rider had to steer and power the front wheel at the same time. Every downward press on the pedals pushed the front wheel out of line, requiring almost as much effort to steer the machine as to pedal it along.

Boneshakers had an average weight of 27 kilograms (60 pounds) and were capable of 13 kilometres (8 miles) per hour, but riding them was not easy. Mounting was always problematic; early manuals advised running alongside and vaulting into the saddle. The size of the front wheel made the pedal action unpleasantly fast; to keep them on a straight course the rider had to resist the sideways movement of the front wheel as he pressed down on the pedals. Another problem was the primitive braking system. This consisted simply of a metal lever, worked by a cord that was pulled by twisting the handlebars. This in turn caused a wooden pad to press against the rear tyre, producing a distinctive screech that warned the public of the boneshaker's approach. Some of the other mechanics were equally primitive. The front wheel axle ran in lubricated bronze bearings; some machines had small lubrication tanks that held lamb's wool soaked in oil that would pass the oil onto the bearings and so keep them running smoothly. By 1869 the first ball bearings had appeared and were used on boneshakers, as were ratchet freewheels mounted in the front wheel. The boneshaker's biggest drawbacks were its massive 27 kilograms (60 pounds) weight and wheels that were only barely 1 metre (3 feet) high, limiting the distance travelled with each turn of the pedals.

Going the Distance

In spite of its drawbacks, riding a boneshaker gave a man a sense of adventure and won him the grudging respect of bystanders. In Britain clubs were formed and members were prepared to ride long distances, even from London to John O'Groats in the north of Scotland. Given the competitive spirit of the time it was not long before members began racing against each other. The first recorded contest was held in a field near the Welsh Harp lake at Hendon near London on Whit Monday 1868. That same year the first French race was held at Saint-Cloud near Paris. This was over the short distance of 1,200 metres (1,310 yards) and was won, to great local disgust, by James Moore, an Englishman living in France.

The following year a far more ambitious race was held in France that could be seen as the precursor to the later Tour de France. The route was from Paris to Rouen, a course of over 123 kilometres (76 miles). One of the fascinating aspects of the race was that, of the surprisingly large field of 100 riders who set off, four were women. Yet the field was not confined to boneshakers, as there were cycles of all types involved including monocycles, tricycles and even quadricycles. The winner was the same James Moore who had earlier

> 'When I went down a boy watching said he would dress me up in pillows, that's what he would do.'
>
> – Mark Twain, *Taming the Bicycle* (1917)

Pedal-driven front wheel

Harsh wooden saddle

The early boneshaker soon became an unlikely sporting machine, with the first long-distance races taking place in France as young men competed against each other.

triumphed at Saint-Cloud. He completed the course in just under 11 hours at an average speed of 12 kilometres (7.5 miles) an hour. The cycling craze had really hit France and it was not confined to Paris. One maker claimed to have sold 2,000 machines in the south of France alone. The announcement of a race specifically for women attracted thousands of spectators to Bordeaux. Not least of the attractions to male spectators was the sight of the ladies' legs as they pedalled furiously along. There were four competitors and a Miss Louise overtook the field in the final strait to win.

Companions and rivals. The spirit of competition soon came to characterise the new sport of cycling, and nowhere more so than in France.

Unfortunately, the French cycling craze came to an end with the start of the Franco–Prussian War, which caused many manufacturers to go over to making armaments. The production of boneshakers ground to a virtual halt. The war had its effect on English manufacturers too. At the end of 1868, the English Coventry Machinists Company had been formed to produce 400 boneshakers for the French market. Coventry had been chosen as it had an experienced workforce with a mechanical aptitude, who were able to produce good-quality bicycles quickly. Sadly, the order had to be cancelled as so many young Frenchmen had put down their bicycles in the shed and gone off to fight for their country. Yet in England, in spite of the war, the boneshaker cult remained as popular as ever.

EARLY CYCLING FASHION

Much of the appeal of the boneshaker was due to the ability to cycle becoming an ever more desirable accomplishment for fashionable young men in both England and France. Being a good cyclist was just as important as being able to ride a horse or to dance well. Almost as important as the cycles themselves were the clothes that the rider wore. Over the early years of cycling a form of casual uniform had emerged that featured a straw boater or billycock hat. After 1870 the style had changed and a polo cap or pillbox hat become de rigeur for the fashionable gentleman rider.

Speed was of the essence and the growing spirit of competition encouraged a need for ever-faster machines, with the pedal-driven front wheel becoming increasingly larger – the shape of things to come – and the seat being placed further forwards over the front wheel to increase pedal power. One new variant of the boneshaker was the improved bicycle made by Peyton and Peyton in Bordesley, Birmingham. They produced a rear-wheel-drive bicycle, using long levers that ran backwards from two footplates and were pivoted to a rearward extension of the frame, with short rods partway along that were connected to cranks driving the rear axle.

More improvements were made during the years 1868–1870, when a step was fitted to the frame, making mounting and dismounting far easier. Machines like the Phantom also brought advances in lighter frame design, the use of rubber on the wheel rims and wheel suspension with wire spokes. In spite of all these constant innovations and improvements, by 1870 the boneshaker's days were clearly numbered. It was becoming increasingly obsolete and riders' interests were now focused on the new high-wheeler or Ordinary that had begun to appear. The problem with the boneshaker had always been that it was mechanically complicated and expensive to produce. Its place was now taken by transitional machines and early versions of the high-wheel bicycle.

7: The Ariel
Perilous Penny-Farthing

The era of the boneshaker was relatively short-lived as a growing interest in cycling led to the need for faster machines, encouraged in part by the enthusiasm for racing. Many had realised that in order to go faster, the drive wheel must be larger. It was a simple equation: the bigger the drive wheel, the faster the bicycle. This trend would lead inevitably to the development of the Ordinary, or penny-farthing, such as it was popularly known, with a large front wheel and a far smaller rear one, a distinctive shape that made the Ordinary probably the most iconic design of cycle in the nineteenth century.

Year:
1870s

Inventor:
Starley

Location:
Coventry

The problem with having a very large front wheel was that wheel technology in the 1860s had progressed little in 20 years. Then, on 11 August 1870, James Starley and William Hillman were granted a patent for improving velocipede wheels and the driving gear. The result was the Ariel, one of the first of the more efficient high-wheelers. Weighing 23 kilograms (50 pounds) it sold for £8, the equivalent of a working man's salary for eight years. The Ariel was advertised as 'the lightest, strongest, and most elegant of modern bicycles'. One of the first customers was James Moore, the famous racing cyclist. Made under licence by the firm of Haynes and Jeffries, the Ariel remained in production for nearly a decade.

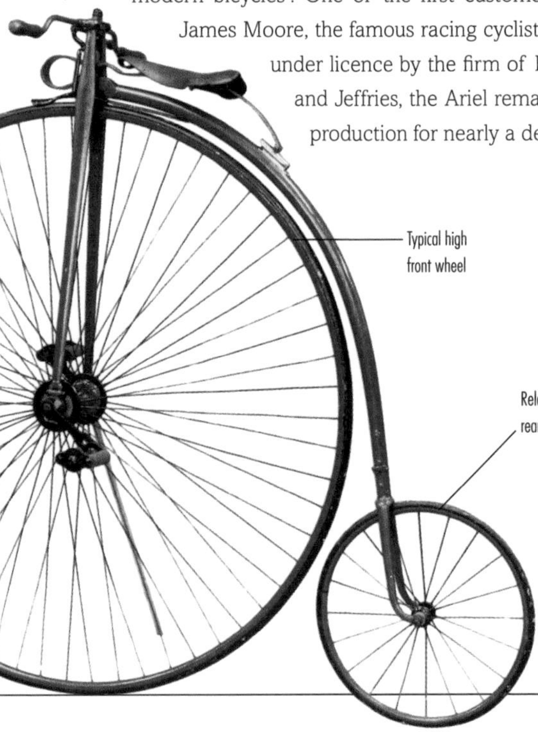

Expensive but effective. The new high-wheelers brought speed to the cycle, combined with a greater risk of injury when the rider came off.

Typical high front wheel

Relatively tiny rear wheel

Starley's Spoke: A Great Innovation

James Starley was a self-taught manufacturing engineer, typical of an era when Britons led in the expansion of the Industrial Revolution. Cycling historian Andrew Ritchie has described him as 'probably the most energetic and inventive genius in the history of bicycle technology'. Starley's cycle put the country in the vanguard of bicycle technology for 80 years and earned Starley the accolade of being the true father of the bicycle industry. It incorporated several innovative features, including a centre-steering head, but the most important advance was its robust wheels, whose design principle is still used in bicycles today. For instead of the wheels being in compression, as on the wooden-wheeled hobby horse or the boneshaker, the wheels on the Ariel were in constant tension. They relied on wire spokes that pulled the rim towards the hub, making it possible to fit larger, stronger and lighter wheels.

The spokes were arranged in pairs and hooked through a loop stapled on the underside of the rim. The other ends of the spokes were hooked into the hub flange. They were secured to the bike by two metal levers that projected from the hub and were attached to the rim using threaded spokes. When the spokes were tightened, the levers twisted the hub, bringing the rest of the spokes into tension. As long as all the spokes were exactly the same length, the wheel would tighten and remain circular and true.

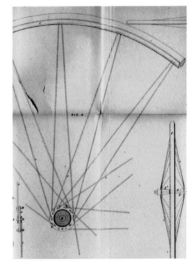

Starley continued to experiment with spoke technology. In 1874 his efforts culminated in the 'tangent-spoke wheel'. It was James Starley's greatest achievement. The tangent-spoke wheel followed the same load-bearing principles as the tension-wheel, but with cross-spokes the wheel was braced; and the force driving it was more efficiently transferred from pedal to rim. Each spoke was angled; adjacent spokes were angled in almost opposite directions, and the tangent on one side balanced the tangent on the other. Spokes were laced for strength; each spoke could be individually tensioned, and the wheel could be easily adjusted to stay true. Such was Starley's technical achievement that nearly every bicycle wheel made since 1874 had been built using the tangent-spoke method. The innovation would later be borrowed in the motorcycle, automobile and aeroplane industries, among others. It remains the most tried-and-tested method for building bicycle wheels to this day.

The spoke was one of the most simple but effective inventions that revolutionised the comfort of bike riding.

So successful was the new design that within a few years of it coming on the market there were more than 20 firms in England making versions of the Ordinary. After this major breakthrough, there were a few more evolutionary changes to be made to the original model. Where wheel technology was concerned, a more advanced wheel with radial spokes threaded into nipples loosely riveted into the rim was patented by William Grout.

THE EUGENE MEYER WHEEL

While the British were forging ahead in bike design, the French were also trying hard to improve wheel technology and with considerable success. A competing system to the British one was invented by Eugene Meyer. Regarded by the International Cycling History Conference as the true inventor of the Ordinary, Meyer's design had spokes headed at the rim, with the tension adjustment being made at the hub flange by using small nuts in radial slots. Unfortunately for Meyer, he had already sold a pair of his wheels before applying for the patent, so making his application invalid.

A classic Ordinary with its characteristic high front wheel and small rear one. Mounting was nearly always a difficult process.

Starley returned to the contest in 1874 having devised a method of building wheels where the spokes left the hub flange at a tangent. This tangent spoking resulted in a stiffer and stronger wheel that was better able to resist driving forces. The hub flange had large holes in line with the axle, through which short bars were fitted. These were tapped at either end to accept spokes. The spokes then went off at a tangent from the hub and almost at right angles to each other. This made it far simpler to replace a broken spoke than on a wheel where the spokes screwed directly into the hub flange. Suddenly, a craze for multi-spoked machines developed, with the Surrey Machinist Company advertising wheels containing up to 300 spokes, resulting in a 137-centimetre (54-inch) wheel having a spoke about every 12 millimetres (half an inch). Soon there would be more holes than actual rim! Wheels may have changed but tyres had not, with solid rubber ones still fitted to both wheels.

The Advent of Bicycle Manufacture

The success of early Ordinaries such as the Ariel brought other manufacturers into the market, particularly in England. Bicycle manufacture now became more of a business in its own right rather than an appendage to a blacksmith's forge. Larger factories were built and high bicycles were exported all over the world, many of them to the USA. One such manufacturer was the Coventry Machinists Company, whose 'Spider' cycle was considered one of the best. It was a classic touring bicycle combining good performance with mechanical beauty and with a frame of tapered oval steel. All the components on the bike, including the wheel rims, were made hollow so as to save weight.

Not to be outdone by the Spider, in 1885, at the Coventry Machinists Company in England, James Starley's nephew John Kemp Starley built his famous Rover, which had all the major features of today's bikes. Weighing 23 kilograms (50 pounds), the Rover had, unlike most high bikes, two wheels of medium size, with the rear wheel pedal-powered by chains and sprockets. The wheels were connected by a triangular frame that became known as the diamond frame. This machine's superior safety and speed spearheaded the defeat of the Ordinary. Eventually the high wheel was abandoned completely and the modern bike triumphed.

But for the moment, the high bike remained supreme, helped by the fact that the new tubular frames meant that it was easier to make lighter machines. This new technology came at a cost and the price of an Ordinary remained high, which made them mainly the preserve of well-off and athletic young men who had the time and the money to ride them around. In an attempt to broaden the market to take in the lower middle-class if not the working man, James Starley put more effort into publicising his bicycle.

CYCLING SIDE-SADDLE

James Starley also launched a version of the Ariel specifically designed for ladies. The rider had to sit side-saddle but could ride comfortably while wearing full-length skirts. The back wheel was slightly out of line with the front and both pedals were on one side of the front wheel. Because of the need to accommodate the side-saddle, the handlebars were shortened on one side and lengthened on the other. The rear wheel was mounted on an overhung axle rather than using the previous system of a spindle carried within a fork. Finally, the front wheel track was offset from that of the rear wheel to counteract the bias from the position of the side-saddle.

Cycling together. Now a respectable pursuit for both ladies and gentlemen. In keeping with social conventions of the time, the woman pictured is riding side-saddle.

As the high bicycle developed, a new form of tubular frame construction appeared, making for far lighter machines. By the mid-1880s, high bicycles weighing about 96 kilograms (211 pounds) were used for track racing, as road racing was illegal in the UK at the time. In 1889 Harry James offered a 55-kilogram (121-pound) high bicycle for sale, a difficult weight to achieve even today! The speed of the Ordinary was extraordinary for the time. Each turn of the pedal would revolve the whole giant front wheel once, gaining a distance on the road of a whole 3.556 metres (3.888 yards). This made pedalling up hills quite difficult, but guaranteed great speed on the flat.

The Days of High-Risk Racing

Throughout this period of detailed change the Ordinary bicycle remained a fast machine and its speed encouraged people to ride longer distances. It achieved great popularity among young men of means during its heyday in the 1880s. Thanks to its adjustable crank and several other new mechanisms, the average Ordinary could rack up record speeds. It also led to one of the ironic challenges of cycling that is still as popular today. This is the one-hour record – the greatest distance a rider on a cycle can achieve in just one hour. The first recorded one-hour attempt was made in 1876, when Frank Dodds of England pedalled 25.506 kilometres (15.849 miles) on a high-wheeler around Cambridge University sports ground.

The problem with the Ordinary was that, although it had achieved cult status and was fast, with a smooth and graceful motion, it could sometimes be incredibly dangerous. The high centre of gravity and forward position of the rider in the saddle made it difficult to mount and dismount, but even more challenging was the ride it gave. With its large front wheel it was always precarious, particularly when it hit a stone or a rut in the road. The whole machine rotated and would be pitched forward over the front axle. This would often leave the unfortunate rider with his legs trapped under the handlebars. He could then be catapulted forwards, coming down with his head hitting the ground. This all too frequent occurrence gave rise to the saying 'taking a header'.

None of the dangers could deter adventurous young men from competing against each other whenever they met on the road and they would often start an impromptu race as they hared along. Many took a more responsible attitude and joined the cycling clubs that had sprung up. By 1876 there were 64 such clubs in London alone, with another 125 in the provinces. At club meetings riders could exchange technical information as well as enjoy the social life that the club offered. Aside from the social life, the main attraction was the chance to watch races or to take part in them. Throughout

'The ordinary bicycle will continue as the leading machine.'

– *Bicycle World* (1881)

the 1880s the new racing tracks attracted large crowds at venues such as Herne Hill and Crystal Palace in London. Tracks were customised for racing and surfaced with ash shavings and cinders. The common distance chosen was a lap of a quarter of a mile. There were added sophistications such as a bar and some of the larger venues even provided spectator seating.

As the clubs prospered they encouraged an even greater demand for fast machines. This encouraged each of the manufacturers to produce a special racing model that was lighter and faster than their conventional road model. The appearance of these new machines became the leading feature of bicycle trade shows, which had become annual events. This was one of the great periods of cycling popularity and the high bicycle era would last until the end of the 1880s. Although alternatives had begun to appear by the late 1870s, none of them really caught on until, in January 1885, the first Rover Safety bicycle was put on display with its chain-driven back wheel. A new cycling age was about to begin.

Bringing chaos in its wake: the popular but controversial high-wheeler.

8: The Rover
Safety Bike

Throughout the period when the Ordinary dominated there was a growing awareness that a new concept of bicycle was required. Such a machine would transform the bicycle from a dangerous contraption confined to adventurous young men to a reliable and comfortable device that could be safely used by people of all ages for everyday transport. Each year the dangers of the high-wheel cycle were becoming more apparent, with *Bicycling World* claiming that, 'this country needs safety bicycles for there is a large class of would-be riders who are deterred from enjoying the sport.'

Year:
1876

Inventor:
Starley

Location:
Coventry

Manufacturers who recognised the design limitations of the current high-wheelers set out to improve the bike's basic design. The first significant attempt to produce a 'safety' bike was by an English engineer, Henry Lawson, in 1876. This bicycle represents the first step in the evolution of the modern safety cycle. Although, like the Ordinary, the front wheel remained larger than the rear, the difference in size was not so exaggerated, making it lower, and therefore safer, than its forerunner. With his machine, the rider's feet were set within reach of the ground, making it easier to stop, particularly in an emergency. In a radical departure from the Ordinary design, the pedals drove the rear wheel, not the front, so keeping the rider's feet safely away from the whirring front wheel. In fact, Lawson's original model used treadles rather than pedals. Lawson's cycle also featured the innovation of a chain drive to the rear wheel. This was an important innovation as previously it had only ever been used on tricycles.

The cycling press was full of praise for Lawson's invention, with *Cycling* praising the way that its low height meant that 'you can mount by throwing your leg over – as on a pony – and start instantly. You can go as slowly and steadily as you like, even in the most crowded thoroughfares where high bicyclists must dismount.' Sadly, Lawson's safety bicycle didn't sell well, probably due to its high cost and heavy weight and complexity compared to the penny-farthing. Lawson persisted in spite of the declining market. In 1879 he patented a revised model that he called the Bicyclette, which abandoned the treadle drive in favour of a chain and sprocket system previously only seen on tricycles. This allowed Lawson to use rotary pedals and also a smaller rear wheel. Unfortunately, the Bicyclette sold no better than Lawson's safety cycle had done. Other manufacturers now decided that the way ahead lay with modifications of the high-wheeler rather than with these low-mount machines.

The First Successful Safety Bicycle

The major breakthrough came in 1885 with John Kemp Starley's famous Rover. Starley had said that he wanted to 'place the rider at the proper distance from the ground… to place the seat in the right position in relation to the pedals… to place the handles in such a position in relation to the seat that the rider could exert the greatest force upon the pedals with the least amount of fatigue.' This he certainly achieved. Starley's first design for a Safety bicycle was introduced while his company – Starley and Sutton Co. of Meteor Works, Coventry – was still making tricycles. The first Rover Safety with a 91-centimetre (36-inch) front wheel and bridle rods (not a raked front fork) was far from perfect and Starley, with the help of his friend William Sutton, modified the design, creating the second Rover in 1885. This was a bicycle with nearly equal-sized wheels and, critically, direct-steer forks. It was introduced at the Stanley Cycle Show, Britain's main annual bicycle exhibition, held in a marquee on the Thames Embankment in February 1885.

The Rover, so called because its riders were free to rove, was to become the first commercially successful safety bicycle. Starley's design placed the rider much lower on the frame and featured two wheels of the same size. It had a chain drive that coupled a large front sprocket or chain ring to a small

> 'The Rover.
> Easy to steer, absolutely safe and very easy going even on cobblestones.'
>
> – French Reviewer
> (1885)

More comfortable saddle

Wheel sizes more similar

The safety cycle marked a dramatic improvement in the comfort and safety of bicycling.

rear sprocket that multiplied the pedal revolutions. This allowed for much smaller wheels, and replaced the need for the large, directly pedalled front wheel of the penny-farthing. Although the smaller wheel gave a harder ride, the imminent invention of pneumatic tyres that would replace the old solid ones would largely solve this problem.

A Modern Machine

Though heavier and more expensive than a high bike, the Rover was lighter and cheaper than the tricycles that were gaining sales at the time. In its original form it used indirect steering; later, direct steering was adopted and the bicycle proved to be a hit. Soon, in 1885, there were several types of safety bicycle on the market

The Rover made the sport of competitive cycling faster and more attractive to spectators in both Europe and the USA.

including seven with lever front-wheel drives, 44 with geared front-drives, and only nine with chain rear-drives. All of them were far safer than the old penny-farthing design. Chances of 'taking a header' over the handlebars had significantly diminished. The braking, too, was more effective and cycling, previously the preserve of daring young men, now became an option for adventurous young women.

By 1888, Starley's Rover had evolved to such an extent that today it would appear as a recognisably modern machine, with two equally sized wheels of 66 centimetres (26 inches), the same as a modern mountain bike, and a diamond-shaped frame. It also had pedals below the saddle that powered the back wheel through a chain and gears, handlebars to the front wheel, and forks supporting the front wheel; these elements are still part of the modern bicycle.

ROVER ROAD TEST

In the early days of the Rover Safety, the Ordinary was still considered a faster machine, whose riders looked down on the Rover both physically and metaphorically. To convince people that the Safety was here to stay, Starley organised a race on 25 September 1885. It took place on the macadamised Great North Road between Norman Cross, near Peterborough, to 1.6 kilometres (1 mile) beyond Twyford, in Berkshire. A total of 14 riders raced that day, all on Rovers, some equipped as roadsters, others as racers, and a number beat the time record for a 160-kilometre (100-mile) promotional race with the winner taking just 7 hours 5 minutes.

The Safety versus the well-established high-wheeler: a contest that would transform the history of cycling.

When Starley's new design was coupled with inflated rubber tyres, thus ending the jolting and painful ride inflicted on cyclists when hard rubber tyres were the norm, suddenly cycling was safe and fun again. Furthermore, the prices of bicycles were dropping continually as manufacturing methods improved. In the late 1890s, Starley's business became known as the Rover Cycle Company. After Starley's death the company started to manufacture and sell Rover motor cars. Many cycling historians feel that the worldwide accessibility and popularity of cycling today is due, in large part, to the work of J. K. Starley in the late nineteenth century. His Rover Safety revolutionised not just the bicycle, but the world. The billions of bicycles made since 1885 can trace their ancestry back to that original groundbreaking machine, tested on the famous stretch of London Road on the outskirts of Coventry.

Starley believed in the power of advertising to promote his products.

9: The Facile
Dwarf Ordinaries

As the Ordinary gradually gave way to the safety bike an interim stage evolved in which wheels were driven by levers, instead of by pedal cranks attached directly to the centre of the front wheel as in the Ordinary. These interim machines became popularly known as 'dwarfs' because the front wheel was not as big as that of a high-wheeler and the seat was located further back, making it safer and easier to ride.

Year:
1869

Inventors:
Beale & Straw

Location:
London

One of the three most successful of these interim machines was the Facile, patented in England by John Beale and Straw in 1869 and manufactured in London by Ellis & Co. Ltd between 1881 and 1890. It was an important step in the evolution of the bicycle from the penny-farthing to the safety bicycle. The facile had two equal-sized wheels and a rear chain drive and could be ridden just as fast as a penny-farthing. Fitted with pedals with lever extensions its pedalling action was more 'up and down' than circular, making it a better hill-climber, although it took some getting used to. It was also quite fast and won numerous road and endurance races and hill climbs organised by the manufacturers. Most importantly, it was an affordable cycle for the middle classes, retailing at between £13 and £18.

With less difference in the size of its wheels, and with the seat moved behind the front wheel to lower the rider's centre of gravity, the Facile was a much safer ride than the Ordinary.

The Facile's riding position was safer and easier than that of the Ordinary, placing the rider behind the front forks. This, for the first time, made the sport of cycling accessible for older riders; Facile advertising proudly claimed that some of its riders were well over 60 years old. Such claims were supported by fact, for in the January 1888 edition of the *Cyclists' Touring Club Gazette*, one contributor wrote a glowing endorsement for the Facile saying that he had bought a 106-centimetre (42-inch) Facile over six years ago and that, 'I have ridden it each year some thousands of miles with much pleasure. I am over 70 years of age, and there is not a mark or scratch on my person arising from riding.'

> 'The Facile might not appeal to those who have a passion for getting as high in the air as possible.'
>
> – *Bicycling World* (1883)

The Facile manufacturers sought hard to portray their cycle as a speedy machine. So popular did the model become that a specialist Facile bicycle club was established in South London with races restricted only to Facile riders. These were organised by Ellis & Co., who also promoted their bicycle with endurance races, including a 24-hour road race that covered a distance of 345 kilometres (214.5 miles). It was won by a W. Snook of Winchester. A Facile ridden by Joseph Adams also halved the 1880 record for a ride the length of Britain, 1,487 kilometres (924 miles) from Land's End to John O'Groats, which took just under seven days in 1884.

The Crypto-Geared Facile had a strangely modern look.

THE CRYPTO-GEARED FRONT-DRIVE FACILE

After their commercial success with the first Facile, Ellis & Co. went on to develop a new higher-geared version that they called their 'Geared Facile' and then followed it with the 'Crypto-Geared Front-Drive Facile.' This front-wheel-driven machine used a sun and planet gearing marketed by the Crypto Cycle Co. and in 1885 was fitted with the new pneumatic tyres. This innovation helped to extend the life of the Facile in the face of the rear-driven safety bicycle that had arrived in 1885.

© Colin Kirsch, www.OldBike.eu/museum

The Kangaroo: a successful combination of some of the best features of the dwarf ordinary and the safety cycle.

The Kangaroo

Another of the popular dwarfs in this transitional period was the Kangaroo made by Hillman, Herbert & Cooper of the Premier Bicycle Company, Coventry, England, between 1884 and 1887. Cycling literature refers to the Kangaroo as both a dwarf ordinary and a dwarf safety. It was a successful attempt to make the Ordinary bicycle design more manageable by fitting wheels of a more equal size and, more importantly, incorporating a two-chain drive, albeit of a short length, on the front driving wheel. Consequently, with every revolution of the crank the driving wheel could travel further and faster than an Ordinary bicycle.

The Kangaroo took the world of cycling by storm when it first appeared and the Premier Bicycle Company was soon selling more than 100 machines a week. So successful was the Kangaroo that almost every manufacturer at the time had a go at building something similar. The Kangaroo also proved safer and easier to mount and dismount than the traditional wheeled Ordinary. This safety feature was thought to be very important at the time and advertisements made the powerful claim that the Kangaroo was 'Safer than a Tricycle and Faster than a Bicycle'. Like the Facile, it was promoted as a fast machine and was triumphant in a number of races, including setting a new 100-mile record in 1884. This helped to bolster the machine's sporting image. The press also praised it, with the *Cyclists' Touring Club Gazette* of November 1884 describing the Kangaroo in its editorial as 'a sound and reliable little mount, likely to win its way more and more into popular favour, particularly among those who value their necks too highly to risk them upon the Ordinary bicycle'. Another magazine, *The Cyclist*, noted that a new game called the Kangaroo Hunt had become popular. Similar to a game of hare and hounds, a rider set off on his Kangaroo, and after a four-minute head start was pursued by the rest of the field on bikes.

The Xtraordinary

The third of the dwarfs was the Xtraordinary made by Singer & Co., based in Coventry. Designed more with safety than speed in mind it sold well. Like the Facile it used levers but the pivot point was located just below the handlebars. The front forks raked forward, allowing the saddle to be placed further back for extra safety. Again, like the Facile, the Xtraordinary found a good export market in the USA. This market was curtailed when America began to produce a dwarf of its own, the American Star. This bike reversed the British wheel configuration by placing a small wheel in front and a large driving wheel in the rear. It also used levers to place the rider closer to the centre of the frame, although both could be pushed down at the same time, making for a faster start. Other similar lever propulsion cycles now began to appear in the USA, the best known of which was the American Safety designed by Gormully & Teffeny of Chicago in 1885.

By the early 1880s the design possibilities of the Ordinary and dwarf had reached their limit. The future now lay with the safety bike rather than the dwarf hybrid. It would become the market leader and initiate another period of cycling enthusiasm and persuade a wider social group to take to the road.

An illustration of the Xtraordinary bicycle, a high-wheel Ordinary bicycle with geared-up transmission.

10: Salvo Quadricycle
Multi-Wheelers

In the early days of cycling it was not certain whether the future of cycling would be on two, three or even four wheels. But the great problem with the tricycle and other multi-wheelers was the difficulty of steering efficiently as the power exerted on the two rear wheels varied constantly, often making progress erratic. The solution first appeared in the Salvo quadricycle of 1877 and was an improvement on an earlier French patent of Onesime Pecquer of 1828. Both utilised a balance gear or double driving gear that would later be known as a differential system.

Year: 1877

Inventor:
Starley

Location:
Coventry

Starley's tricycles were just as popular in his day as the company's bicycles.

Many thought the tricycle would become the most popular form of cycle in both Europe and America. The earliest tricycles were little more than modified velocipedes. Driven directly by means of cranks and pedals, some had two smaller rear wheels and a larger front one. Racing helped to increase the popularity of the tricycle, with the first contests taking place in France. In 1870 there were tricycle races in London, Birmingham, Brussels and Madrid, but the great majority were held in France.

James Starley, inventor of the Salvo quadricycle, was born in the small village of Albourne, Sussex, and received a minimal education at a local school. From his childhood Starley proved to be a real inventor, producing an adjustable candlestick, a one-stringed window blind and the magic bassinette, a mechanical device for rocking a baby's cradle. After seeing a French bicycle in 1868, he immediately became fascinated by the possibilities of making a more efficient one. His first invention was the bicycle known as 'The C spring and step machine, or the Coventry Model'. The superiority of this was at once evident, with the curved spring, the small hind wheel and the step for mounting being the principal improvements. He then produced the Ariel bicycle, which became popular mainly because it was the first bicycle to have pivotal centre steering. Starley went on to produce the double-throw crank, and the chain and chain wheels to obtain rotary motion in tricycles. Still intent on improving the bicycle, he finally introduced the Tangent bicycle, and was fully employed in making Tangent wheels. In 1876 he brought out the Coventry tricycle. No similar machine is known to have existed before, and Starley may be regarded as its inventor.

Starley's Masterpiece

Starley's finest creation, however, was not a bicycle but the Salvo quadricycle. He is said to have discovered its radical differential gear literally by accident. He and his son, William, were on a cycling trip from Coventry to Birmingham on a machine made of two penny-farthings joined together – a vehicle that, if produced, was to be called the Honeymoon Sociable because husband and wife could ride together. At one point James and his son found the vehicle swerving violently. Unable to control the swerve, they careered madly off the road and tumbled into a ditch. Neither of the cyclists was hurt apart from a few nettle stings, so Starley sat by the side of the road where he had fallen to ponder the problem. Suddenly, shouting 'Why on earth didn't I think of this before?', he grabbed a pencil and a scrap of paper from his pocket and began scribbling furiously. Those scribblings were soon translated into reality when James Starley fitted a bevel-gear differential unit into the axle of a tricycle to equalise the drive. This quickly became standard equipment in all tricycles driven through two wheels and was to become an essential ingredient in the success of motor cars.

James Starley on one of his multi-wheeler cycles.

The Salvo quadricycle that resulted from this incident had two large wheels side by side and a small steering wheel in front. It was steered by a rack and pinion arrangement with a hand-brake applied by means of a lever. The balance gear, or 'double-driving gear', later known as a differential of the machine, successfully distributed the power evenly to both wheels through a bevel-gear differential mounted on the axle. The machine was a great success and agents were appointed all over Britain. Queen Victoria bought two!

NOT FORGETTING THE TRICYCLE

From 1881 to 1886 in Great Britain, more tricycles were built than bicycles, but this was primarily a class phenomenon, since tricycles were more expensive, perceived as more genteel, and the upper classes had the disposable income to buy them for the women in the family. As a result, tricycling remained popular in Great Britain long after riders turned away from them elsewhere.

11: The Columbia High-Wheeler
Born in the USA

There is no doubt that the bicycle had an important influence on the introduction of the automobile in America. Among the first bicycle manufacturers in the USA were Charles E. Duryea, Alexander Winton and Colonel Albert A. Pope. Interestingly, Wilbur and Orville Wright were bicycle manufacturers in Dayton, Ohio, before they turned their attention to the aeronautical field, and Glenn H. Curtiss, another aviation pioneer, started out as a bicycle manufacturer.

Year:
1878

Manufacturer:
Pope Manufacturing
Company

Location:
Hartford,
Connecticut, USA

In addition to introducing thousands of American people to individual mechanical transport, the bike tested the value of many materials and parts that were subsequently used by automobile designers. Ball bearings, for instance, found one of their earliest uses in bicycles. The differential controlled the spread of power from the pedals to the wheels. To do this, various forms of free-wheeling and gear-shifting devices were in use. Steel tubing, developed largely for cycle frame construction, was adopted by some early automobile builders. Pneumatic tyres and wire wheels were also in use on bicycles prior to the introduction of the gasoline automobile in America. Throughout this period of mechanical development no cycle manufacturer was more important in the USA than Albert Pope and his famous cycle, the Columbia.

The Columbia.
Albert Pope's cycle that
conquered America.

Among the first owners of Pope's new high-wheeled Columbia bicycle was the famous writer Samuel Clemens, better known as Mark Twain. The creator of Tom Sawyer and Huckleberry Finn had caught the cycling bug, a craze that had swept the USA in the decades following the American Civil War. One day in 1884 he walked the short distance from his home in Hartford, Connecticut, to the Weed Sewing Machine Company to buy one. Knowing the dangerous reputation of the high-wheeled and precarious Ordinary bicycle, Twain purchased 12 hours of riding lessons along with the machine. Sadly, he probably never mastered the skills needed for his Columbia, for two years later he went into E. I. Horsman's store in New York and bought himself a simpler machine – a tricycle!

'Get a bicycle.
You will not regret it,
if you live.'

– Mark Twain, *Taming the Bicycle* (1917)

The Columbia became the most famous all-American bicycle of the nineteenth century, the first big-selling machine to be made wholly in the USA rather than being a re-badged European import. It was the creation of a barnstorming character, Colonel Albert Augustus Pope, who had fought in the battles of Antietam and Fredericksburg during the Civil War. On discharge, Pope made a small fortune in real estate before becoming fascinated by the new sport of cycling. Visiting the Philadelphia Centennial Exhibition of 1876 he came across a display of imported Ariel cycles designed and built in Britain by James K. Starley and William Hillman. Pope was much impressed by these Ordinaries, as nothing as sophisticated had ever appeared in the USA. Starley, one of the pioneers of British cycling technology, who would later be a key figure in the creation of the safety bicycle, had used a new wheel-tensioning technique plus tangent spokes to make non-twisting wheels larger than 100 centimetres (40 inches).

Pope believed in the modern sales message and cleverly used the American media to achieve it.

Pope decided to buy a cycle for himself but instead of an Ariel he chose another rival British product, the Duplex Excelsior. Taking it back to Hartford he examined it in great detail, determined to create an even better all-American cycle of his own. What would make Colonel Pope so different from his contemporaries was the sheer scale of his ambition and his ability to harness the latest industrial methods. His Columbia would not be just another small-run, hand-built machine but a mass-produced bicycle that would sell in thousands.

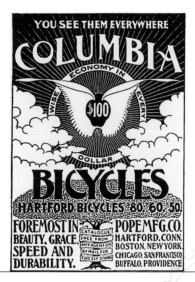

A Bicycle for America

At the time, nothing like a modern bicycle manufacturing industry existed anywhere in the USA so Pope set out to start one. By a stroke of good fortune Hartford, where he lived, was the home to the Weed Sewing Machine Company and this was a business that had the right kind of skilled metal machining experience needed for making bicycles. When approached by Pope, the Weed directors were persuaded to take on his project in return for Pope providing a generous amount of backing capital. At first the new cycles showed little technical innovation and were little more than near copies of the European Duplex. Pope, however, had no difficulty in selling the first batch of 50 machines. Orders were promising, but Pope became concerned that his success would not last and that America might soon tire of the cycling craze that appeared to be sweeping the country. A shrewd businessman, he was also wary of potential rivals copying his success and his bicycle and became obsessed with protecting his copyright. He set out to acquire as many other bicycle patents as he could find. Thus, he was able to control the USA

Along with advertising, Pope used high-quality catalogues and public-relations techniques to promote his products.

THE PRICE IS RIGHT

Much of the Columbia success had been due to Pope's ability to produce a cycle at a price that the ordinary man could afford. By manufacturing at home in the USA rather than shipping from Europe, Pope was able to save on the duty that import dealers such as the Bostonian Frank Weston were forced to pay. The reduction of price was quite dramatic. When the first Columbia was produced, the average price of other high-wheeled 'Ordinaries' was over $120. This was equivalent to three months' wages for a skilled worker and six months' for a farm hand. Naturally, such bicycles were the preserve of the relatively wealthy and played little part in the lives of the average American working man. As new manufacturing techniques and a standardised component system were introduced prices began to fall. Ownership of a bicycle now began to be a real possibility for millions of ordinary people across the USA, not only for leisure use but also as an invaluable commuting tool.

bicycle market to some degree and restrict the types of bicycle other American manufacturers could make by charging them large royalties for using his newly obtained patents.

However, in spite of Pope's initial fears, the demand for cycles continued to rise and orders for the Columbia continued to flow in. By 1888 the company was producing 5,000 bicycles a year and selling them all. Clearly America had fallen in love with the bicycle, as the soaring membership of the League of American Wheelmen showed. Other cycling clubs soon appeared including the St Louis Cycling Club, which in 1887 encouraged the commencement of professional racing in the USA with early

Racing in the USA was controlled and promoted by the League of American Wheelmen.

stars such as Arthur Zimmerman. The Wheelmen sponsored races and time trials in the European manner, sowing the seeds for American success in the Tour de France a century later. By 1900 it was recognised as the national governing body for all forms of cycle sport and recreation and its membership had reached an impressive 150,000. One of them, George Nellis, proved to the nation that cycling had finally come of age when he became the first man to cross the USA from coast to coast on a cycle, riding from New York to San Francisco in just 72 days.

Meanwhile, the Pope Manufacturing Company had grown dramatically too, becoming so successful that within a decade of starting production, Pope was able to buy out the Weed Sewing Machine Company. Eventually the Hartford Park River area became lined with five of Pope's factories. Two were frame manufacturing plants, together with a tyre factory, a steel tube mill and – with an eye to the future – even an automobile factory. Two thousand men and women were employed making variations of the Columbia – more even than worked at the vast Samuel Colt arms company on the opposite bank of the Connecticut River.

The Columbia had changed, too, as more sophisticated and reliable components such as a new head and ball bearing unit were added to the machine. The original model was now known as the 'Standard Columbia' and the improved and updated version as the 'Special Columbia'. Gone were the days when the company found it impossible to roll the wheel rims in the required U-shape and had to use a crude V-shaped substitute made from angle iron instead, recycled from a local blacksmith's shop.

Pope's success attracted other manufacturers into the cycle market, among them Ignaz Schwinn, a Germany immigrant. Schwinn was followed by many other well-known companies such as Huffy, Murray and Ross.

Power of Advertising

None of this could have happened by producing a successful product alone. An effective marketing programme was needed to ensure that the public was aware of the benefits of the Columbia. This needed the skilful use of advertising and expert knowledge of the media to create a demand for the bicycle and Albert Augustus Pope was certainly a master of marketing art. At first he presented the Columbia as a highly desirable status symbol with specific appeal to the wealthy. Then, as prices began to fall, he changed his strategy, realising that the bicycle could only achieve volume sales by being made an accessible object, first to the middle classes then finally to the man in the street. To this end he became an early master of press advertising. As one of his employees, Sam McClure, wrote of him, 'It was a maxim of Colonel Pope's that some advertising was better than others, but all advertising was good.' Once, when asked the three principles for selling bicycles, Pope replied 'Advertising! Big advertising and then even bigger advertising!' He certainly backed up his words with action, spending a fortune on promoting the Columbia and cycling in general in the press.

If possible, Pope always placed his full-page advertisements in a prime position on the back pages of magazines. He ran full-page spreads in the busy summer season and half pages in winter. All responses to the advertisement were carefully recorded and acted on. Again, as Sam McClure wrote, 'every boy in the West knew the Pope Manufacturing Company... the Pope advertisements were everywhere'. The Colonel also proved himself a talented manipulator of public relations, cultivating journalists, arranging factory tours for the press and staging promotions. One of his most audacious publicity coups involved Thomas Stevens, a young English immigrant to the USA who had bought a Standard Columbia in San Francisco and declared his intention to ride across America from California to New York. After that, he said, he would ride his bicycle around the world and become the first man ever to do so.

Stevens's ambition intrigued Colonel Pope, who saw it as a brilliant opportunity to publicise the Columbia. So when Stevens eventually arrived in Boston, Pope presented him with a smart new Columbia

In the 1870s, cycling became part of American city life.

Expert in exchange for his old machine, so publicising the company's latest model. Moreover, Pope, knowing that the League of American Wheelmen strictly forbade its members from competing for money or making a living out of professional cycling, set Stevens up as an author. His commission was to write the story of his trip across the USA, which Pope would publish, thereby neatly avoiding the charge of Stevens being classed a professional cyclist advertising Pope Company products. The book was so successful that Stevens gave up cycling and launched himself in a new career as an explorer and author that culminated in him finding the lost explorer H. M. Stanley in Africa.

Although the Columbia had been a phenomenal success for over a decade, it was rendered near-obsolete when the first of the Starley and Sutton 'Rover' safety bicycles appeared on the scene. With wheels of almost equal size and direct steering, made possible by a sloping head tube and handlebars that swept back towards the rider, the Rover pointed the way to the future. Among those to manufacture these new 'safety' machines was a Chicago immigrant, Adolph Schoeninger, whose success earned him the nickname 'Henry Ford of the Bicycle'. At his Western Wheel Works, Schoeninger used similar production methods to Colonel Pope, relying on low-cost metal stamping and other economies to produce his 'Crescent' frames. The result was that his cycles were even more affordable for the working man than Pope's. Eventually, his machines outsold those of the Colonel, with more than 2 million Crescent cycles being produced in 1897 alone. So competitive were Schoeninger's prices that his exports even managed to force down bicycle prices in Europe.

Yet in spite of his eventual eclipse, Albert Augustus Pope remained the most emblematic figure in the golden age of American bicycling. It has been said that when Pope's first Columbia appeared, the average American would have found the idea that a man could remain upright on a propelled bicycle with just two wheels ridiculous. Some early cyclists claimed that, as they glided silently along the road, country people had taken them for demons! Pope and the Columbia were to prove them all wrong.

Both men and women could now venture out together in safety and companionship.

12: Coventry Lever
The Tricycle

The problem with the early two-wheeled bicycle was that it was heavy, cumbersome and hard to control. Only a fit young man could excel on such a machine, making it difficult for lesser mortals to enjoy. Perhaps a steadier three-wheeled machine was the answer. Attempts to create a practical tricycle had begun as early as 1680, when a German paraplegic watchmaker in Nuremburg named Stephan Farffler produced a primitive machine that had both gears and hand cranks.

Year:
1884

Manufacturer:
Coventry Machinists

Location:
Coventry

The next significant attempt at making a tricycle came in 1789 when two Frenchmen, Blanchard and Maguire, produced their machine. It inspired the *Journal de Paris* to use the words 'bicycle' and 'tricycle' possibly for the first time to differentiate between the two types of machines. Interest in tricycles was apparent throughout Europe, with even Denis Johnson, the father of the English hobby horse, producing his version, the three-wheeled swift-walker, in 1819.

Looking surprisingly modern; a tricycle of the 1880s.

© www.sterba-bike.cz

Yet it was the coming of the velocipede that led to the first credible tricycles. These were adaptations of the basic velocipede but with two smaller rear wheels running free to an axle attached to the backbone. The machine was propelled by cranks and pedals. These tricycles became popular particularly when the sport of tricycle racing emerged in France and Britain. In one year alone, 1869–70, there were no less than 159 such races in Europe, mainly in France. Easy for men to ride, these velocipede tricycles were a challenge to adventurous lady riders because of the obtrusive backbone, until a new design using treadle-drive with levers instead of pedals to take power to a cranked axle appeared. From then on, even a voluminous skirt could be worn when riding or racing.

The Rise of the Tricycle

The tricycles produced from 1876 to 1884, of which Starley's Coventry Rotary is the most famous example, are considered first-generation tricycles, and showed a wide variety of inventiveness as the best design was sought. While the two smaller rear wheels concept remained popular, an alternative design appeared in the relative cycling back-water of Ireland. A Dubliner, William Blood, patented a tricycle in 1876 that had a large rear driving wheel with two smaller steering wheels in front mounted on separate forks. This was just one of dozens of tricycle patents registered during the 1870s as the tricycle appeared to threaten the dominance of the bicycle. In 1879, 20 types of tricycles and multi-wheel cycles were being produced in Coventry, England, and by 1884 there were more than 120 different models produced by 20 separate manufacturers. Tricycles were used especially by those who could not ride high-wheelers, such as women, who were confined in the long dresses of the day, and short or unathletic men.

James Starley was as successful with his Coventry Lever Tricycle as he was with his other products.

The market leader, however, was one machine: James Starley's Coventry Lever Tricycle, introduced in November 1876. Starley had used his previously unsuccessful lady's Ariel Ordinary as the starting point for his machine. The Coventry Lever had two small wheels on the right side, which both steered simultaneously. Unusually, two of the three wheels were in line, so reducing the chances of getting stuck in a rut. The significant lateral width between the wheels made for a very stable ride. The large drive wheel was on the left side. The following year, Starley introduced the Coventry Rotary, one of the first rotary chain-drive tricycles. It had a rack and pinion steering system and was another commercial success. Advertisements described it as 'the only machine for the photographer, artist, sportsman, angler or surveyor affording facility for the carriage of photographic apparatus, easel, gun, fishing rod or tripod'.

James Starley continued to explore the possibilities of the tricycle, which led him to revise his original design again by removing the small rear wheel, adding a large wheel and an extra crank. This enabled two riders to sit side by side and each to pedal independently, driving the side wheel nearest to them. By this design Starley had transformed the lever tricycle into the first Sociable. But then came the problem. It proved difficult to steer the thing because the power exerted on the wheels constantly varied, making it difficult to maintain a straight line. Resourceful as ever, Starley soon came up with the solution to

A CLASS FAVOURITE

Ladies cycling side by side on a tricycle made for two. In the 1880s women's cycling was associated with leisure rather than athleticism or practical transportation.

While the tricycle craze began in France, it soon spread to Britain. Between 1881 and 1886 more tricycles were built there than bicycles. Part of this phenomenon can be explained by the British class system, in that as tricycles were more expensive, they were perceived as being more genteel and appropriate for ladies to ride. What was equally important was that the speed differential between the bike and the tricycle had narrowed to just about 3 or 5 kilometres (2 or 3 miles) an hour. To many, it seemed that the tricycle was the way ahead in cycling. The *World of London* magazine wrote; 'There is quite a rage for tricycling this year at Brighton. Owing to the marvellous perfection in steel work, tricycles are now produced, combining great strength with extreme lightness.' As a result of such acclaim, tricycling was to remain popular in Britain long after it fell out of favour in other countries. In contrast, the tricycle was used in the USA primarily by older persons for recreation, shopping and exercise, while in Asia and Africa it became a vehicle for transporting goods or materials.

the problem. He introduced a balance or differential gear into the axle that connected the two driving wheels. Now the power from the two drives could be more evenly distributed as it allowed one wheel to rotate faster than the other when turning round a bend.

Later Tricycle Innovations

As the tricycle craze continued, a second generation of tricycles appeared. The Humber Cripper of 1885, named after the professional racer Robert Cripps, was typical. It had the modern pattern of two rear wheels with a front wheel bisecting their track. The front wheels were usually 46–60 centimetres (18–24 inches) in diameter, while the rear wheels were about 100 centimetres (40 inches). The wheelbase was about 80 centimetres (32 inches), as was the track width, and they weighed about 34 kilograms (75 pounds), although racing models were about 18 kilograms (40 pounds). Finally, a third generation of tricycles appeared around 1892. The Starley Psycho was typical with all three wheels of equal size, in this case, 71 centimetres (28 inches).

The tricycle craze ended around 1900 with the introduction of the safety cycle with its pneumatic tyres, which provided the stability previously only found in a tricycle. Except for having modern bicycle components added, the tricycle has not really evolved in any substantial way since the turn of the nineteenth century.

A more sophisticated tricycle of the 1880s.

© www.sterba-bike.cz

13: Pneumatic Tyres
The Easy Ride

The safety bicycle offered a safer ride than the Ordinary and the cyclist's comfort was improved by the introduction of the diamond-shaped frame, but the wheels remained a serious problem. The very first cycle wheels were made entirely of wood, giving a jarring ride over anything but the smoothest ground. Even the introduction of iron rims did little to improve things. Hope seemed at hand when hard rubber tyres replaced metal tyres, but this radical change in material only made riding slightly more comfortable. True comfort in cycling would not become possible until the coming of the pneumatic tyre in the late 1880s.

Year:
late 1880s

Manufacturer:
Dunlop

Location:
Belfast

Although rubber was available in the early nineteenth century, it was not stable enough to be used successfully in manufacture. For this reason, the 'rubber fever' that had swept the Western world in the early 1830s had ended as suddenly as it had begun. At first everybody had wanted things made of the new waterproof gum from Brazil and factories had sprung up to meet the expected demand. Then, abruptly, the public had become disillusioned with a material that had amazing potential but proved to be completely unstable. It froze bone-hard in winter and melted like glue in summer. Such an unreliable substance would be quite unsuitable for something that needed to be as dependable as a bicycle tyre. What was needed was a technique that could give rubber stability.

The coming of the pneumatic tyre spelled the end of boneshaking.

Charles Goodyear's Discovery

In 1844 Charles Goodyear dropped some India-rubber mixed with sulphur onto a hot stove and accidentally discovered the process for the vulcanisation of rubber. The problem then was getting the financial backing to transform it into a viable industrial process. Two more years passed before Goodyear could find anyone who had faith enough in his discovery to invest money in it. At last, in 1844, by which time he had perfected his process, his first patent was granted. In the subsequent years more than 60 patents were granted to him for the application of his original process to make various products, including bicycle tyres and rubber condoms. Soon after the discovery of vulcanisation, tyres were made out of solid rubber. These tyres were strong, absorbed shocks, resisted cuts and abrasions, and were a vast improvement; however, they were very heavy and did not provide a smooth ride. Attaching them to the rim was also a problem until Thomas B. Jeffery came up with an improved tyre that could be tightened to the bicycle rim with a wire, so making it more secure. Before this, tyres were glued to the rim and often came off unexpectedly.

Goodyear's invention was as important to the progress of the bicycle industry as the invention of pedals had been. He had transformed rubber, making it into a flexible material potentially perfect for bicycle tyres. This was an innovation that would eventually allow the bicycle to escape from the town and take to the country. Yet this was only half the story, for vulcanised rubber still needed a process that would transform it into an inflatable tyre.

Charles Goodyear, who discovered the process for the vulcanisation of rubber.

The Creation of the Inflatable Tyre

The first attempt at making a pneumatic tyre was by Robert Thomson in 1845. Thomson, who had been to America, returned to Britain and was given a workshop by his father where he invented what he called 'aerial wheels'. Thomson fitted his tyres not to a bicycle but to a horse-drawn carriage that he demonstrated in Regent's Park, London, alongside a hard-tyred rival. With its inflatable tyres it proved far easier to pull and although the journalists watching thought it would make the vehicle much slower because the tyres were soft, it proved to be significantly faster. The other obvious benefit to all who were watching was that it was far quieter, with little road noise.

TWO INVENTORS

The credit for the pneumatic tyre must go to two men: John Boyd Dunlop, who developed it in Ireland in 1888, and Robert W. Thomson of England, who had patented it 43 years earlier in 1845. By a strange coincidence, the two men invented the same thing decades apart, although neither one was aware of the other. Yet that is exactly what happened. Thomson, who was researching a full decade before Dunlop, was the true inventor but he had the misfortune of introducing the pneumatic tyre too far ahead of its time. Thomson, who was more confident than Dunlop in the future of the air-inflated tyre, saw his hopes for the pneumatic dashed by an

John Boyd Dunlop. The greatest name in tyres, whose company still lives on.

unresponsive buying public and his invention was soon forgotten. He was unable to establish a commercial market for it in that horse-and-buggy era, and so Thomson's name is little known by the general public and often appears as a mere footnote on the pages of history. Perhaps just as ironic is the fact that Dunlop, who had less faith in the pneumatic tyre as the optimum means of dampening road vibration, saw his invention sweep the world and has since been honoured as one of the world's great benefactors.

The inventor riding in comfort on his invention. John Boyd Dunlop out for a spin on his bike.

In his patent application, Thomson's 'aerial wheels' were described as involving 'the application of elastic bearings round the tyres of wheels of carriages, rendering their motion easier and diminishing the noise they make while in motion'. To make this work, Thomson used a hollow belt of India rubber and gutta percha that was then inflated with air. This, Thomson insisted, would provide a cushion of air between the wheel and the ground or the rail or track on which it ran, at every part of the wheel's revolution. This elastic belt, as Thomson described it, was made of several layers of canvas saturated with a rubber solution, after which the tyre was vulcanised. Leather was used as a protective cover or outer casing, and the tyre was inflated with a 'condenser', known today as a tyre pump. Thomson tested his version of the air-inflated tyre successfully on horse-drawn vehicles but it failed as a commercial proposition.

When Thomson died in 1873 the concept of the air-inflated tyre was temporarily set aside. The real breakthrough came in 1887 with John Dunlop, a Scottish vet living in Belfast. When his son complained of a sore bottom after riding his bicycle to school over cobbled streets, Dunlop's solution was to replace the hard rubber tyres with air-filled pneumatic ones and he noticed that the ride became a lot smoother. This proved not only more comfortable but faster too, as his son began consistently winning cycle races. At a famous cycle race on the Queen's College playing fields in May 1889, Dunlop persuaded the cycle champion Willie Hume to use his new pneumatic tyres. Hume won the race, creating such a demand for the new tyres that the Dunlop Rubber Company was swiftly formed. The invention caught on like wild fire and soon Dunlop's tyre replaced all other forms of tyres in the world.

AIR-FILLED AND AIRTIGHT

The principle of an air-filled tyre was only half the solution to the problem; what was also needed was a tyre with an airtight seal on the rim. The solution to this difficulty had been made possible by Thomas B. Jeffery, a bicycle manufacturer and inventor, who in 1882 had registered the patent for an improved tyre that was held on by a wire fixed to the tyre. The wire could be tightened to the bicycle rim, making it more secure. Before this, bicycle tyres were held to the rim by means of glue; they were not very secure as they usually came off the rim.

The Further Evolution of the Pneumatic Tyre

By 1892 pneumatic tyres were so widely used that cycle manufacturers were obliged to retool their existing models to take the width of the new tyres. One unexpected benefit was that the better ride enabled cyclists to explore parts of the country that had previously been inaccessible. So successful was the pneumatic tyre in racing that tracks themselves had to be improved with higher perimeter banking. Tyre technology continued to improve and in 1896 the American H. J. Doughty produced a steam-heated press for vulcanising bicycle tyres. This made mass production possible, as well as allowing complex patterns to be added to the outer rubber.

'The inflatable tyre is undoubtedly the tyre of the future, throwing open a vast field which the makers of the present day can hardly realise.'

– R. J. Mecredy, Irish racing champion (1896)

Advances were made in Europe, too, with the Michelin brothers in France taking out patents in 1892 for bead-edged tyres that were secured to the wheel rims by rings. Dunlop's patents were also bought by French manufacturers as the rage for cycling swept the country in the 1890s. Yet the final step in the evolution of the pneumatic tyre was to come from America with August Schrader. He was an enterprising German-American immigrant who began dealing in rubber products in lower Manhattan. By 1845, he was supplying fittings and valves for rubber products made by the Goodyear Brothers. Around 1890, he read reports of English cyclists' success using pneumatic tyres and realised the need for a more efficient and effective tyre valve to allow inflation. This was the Schrader valve, an invention that is still in use today. The complete valve consists of a valve stem into which a valve core is threaded. The valve core is a poppet valve assisted by a spring.

Schrader's final contribution to the improvement of cycling was the Schrader tyre valve cap, patented in 1896. A valve cap is essential; if one is not fitted, dirt and water can enter the outside of the valve, potentially jamming it or contaminating the sealing surfaces and causing a leak. Rock salt and other chemical de-icers used in winter are especially damaging for the brass parts in the Schrader valve.

The Schrader tyre valve cap, patented in 1896 and still in use on many bicycles today.

14: The Swift
Clerks on Wheels

By the mid-1890s, increased bicycle production and a competitive market lowered prices. Yet prior to the First World War the bicycle was still not a vehicle of the working classes. Its political importance at the beginning of the twentieth century lies instead predominantly with the middle class. Whatever the social class of the rider, for the first time in history the ability to travel a considerable distance other than on foot or on a horse required no more than access to a bike. Much of this had been made possible by the coming of safety bicycles such as the 'Swift'.

Year:
 1885

Manufacturer:
Sutton

Location:
Coventry

The Swift was the product of the Coventry Sewing Machine Company and James Starley. Together with Josiah Turner, Starley had in 1859 set up a company to import and market sewing machines from America. Ten years later they began to produce bicycles, tricycles and quadricycles to meet the new cycling craze. 'Coventry Machinists', as the company was now called, was to become the second largest cycle maker in Great Britain, and Coventry the city that produced over 70 per cent of British cycles. Significantly, their second model was called the 'Club' in recognition of the sudden popularity of the cycling clubs that were springing up all over Britain.

Even before the arrival of the safety bicycle, the Ordinary had attracted adventurous young men and the occasional woman. Bicycling had become a cult and by 1878 there were many cycling clubs in Britain, France and the USA. The larger clubs often had more than 100 members who would meet regularly

James Starley's Swift was a best-selling version of the British safety bicycle and was exported to all parts of the world.

to plan expeditions and to exchange technical information. One of the most popular was the National Clarion Cycling Club, established in 1895, and by the end of that year it had 80 affiliated clubs. Its objective was to organise 'Cyclists for Mutual Aid, Good Fellowship and the Propagation of the Principles of Socialism, along with the social pleasures of Cycling'.

The years following the First World War saw the bicycle adopted across society and the practice of cycling becoming the means by which vast numbers of 'ordinary' people conducted their 'ordinary' lives.

'Bicycles became general utility vehicles. They crowded the racks outside factories and, at lunchtimes and the ends of shifts, sudden bell-ringing torrents of cloth-capped workers came cycling out of factory gates.'

– J. McGurn (1887)

Many of the club members were ordinary office workers, clerks or shop assistants who met at weekends to go bicycling in the country. Socialists also considered it a morally elevating practice suitable for the working class. Cities at that time were thought to be unnaturally smelly, with 'odours of death, madness and poverty', and cycling afforded escape from these conditions. The socialists pioneered a rhetoric of fresh air and countryside, of escaping the city as a healthy practice.

In the 1890s the safety bike merely increased the volume of this activity, as owning a cycle became possible for an even larger number of people. In one year alone, 150 safety bicycles were sold in the USA, effectively doubling the nation's cycling population. The surge in bike ownership was no less in Britain where bicycles like the Swift were now available at a relatively modest cost and travel became far more democratic and no longer the preserve of the upper classes. The bicycle now became a vehicle associated with middle-class socialist politics. With the increase in flexible and independent mobility it provided, it was an ideal means of spreading the message of socialism to far-flung places. The bicycle contributed to an expansion in the geographical and political horizons of both the middle-class socialist cycling preachers and the working classes who would later embrace cycling.

With these new bicycles came a new social optimism. H. G. Wells wrote: 'When I see an adult on a bicycle, I do not despair for the future of the human race.' His novel *Wheels of Chance* is set during a romantic biking holiday that brings the lovers together. In the novel are many descriptions of contemporary bicycles and how even a relatively lowly draper's clerk could now afford a dated, second-hand machine; and a great many references to the changing social mores of the day, and how women were being liberated by cycling. He also describes the unique pleasures of cycling, saying 'after your first day of cycling, one dream is inevitable. A memory of motion lingers in the muscles of your legs, and round and round they seem to go. You ride through Dreamland on wonderful dream bicycles that change and grow', and he hopes that 'cycling tracks will abound in Utopia'.

15: The Ivel
Riding Tandem

The earliest forms of the tandem bicycle began to appear on the roads at around the same time as the pneumatic tyre first came in to use. But it was not until 1886 that the first practical tandem appeared, based on the design of the safety cycle. This was the 'Ivel', produced by Dan Albone, a prolific inventor and racer at Biggleswade in England. Built on the cross-frame principle it had a diagonal backbone that provided a low riding position, making it suitable for ladies as well as for gentlemen. This made it one of the first omnisex bicycles in history.

Year:

1886

Manufacturer:
Albone

Location:
Biggleswade

T he term 'tandem' came to refer to the seating arrangement (fore to aft, not side by side), not the number of riders. A bike with two riders side by side is called a sociable. Tandems became popular because they allowed a lady and gentleman to share a ride together. Of course, the possibility of men and women sharing a bicycle had interesting implications for courtship and social relationships.

Ladies First?

One question raised by the tandem was whether ladies should ride in the front or rear seat. This was a problem that Albone had perhaps foreseen as he had linked the handlebars of the Ivel together so that the machine could be steered from either seat. Other early tandem models were specifically designed to put

The tandem dilemma.
Should the lady or the
gentleman sit in front?

'After you, madam.'
The etiquette of riding a
tandem with a lady.

the lady in front as an act of courtesy. Among the firms who were pioneers of this type of machine were the Humber, the Singer, the Rudge, the Raleigh, the Whitworth and the Chater Lea. Other manufacturers soon entered the market with tandems placing the lady specifically in the front or rear. Generally, it was believed that the gentleman's place should be in the front where he could steer, brake and, in case of danger, leap from the machine to avert disaster by supporting his lady passenger. Some, however, felt a gentlemen should be in the back seat, as it was rude to turn one's back on a lady. The definitive answer appeared to come from the *CTC Gazette*, which in 1889 announced that, 'ladies, like luggage, are wisely consigned to the rear.'

By placing the lady in front it was thought in those days that she must occupy the place of honour, and the fact that she was likely to receive the first brunt of a collision, not to speak of cold winds, was forgotten. Naturally, the mere male was entrusted with the steering and balancing, and to enable these functions to be controlled from the rear handlebar the two sets of handles had to be connected by a rod on the off-side. This arrangement meant that the front rider had handles to hold but was not expected to do any steering or balancing, nor could she interfere with her partner's control of the machine, or ignore his instructions, as that might cause a spill at a critical moment.

A Bicycle Built for Two

Whatever the arguments about front or rear seats, there is no doubt that tandems like the Ivel became popular because of their use in courting rituals. Prospective suitors could take their girlfriend out for a bike ride without the lady having to exert herself by pedalling too hard. The popularity of the tandem at this time was immortalised by composer Henry Dacre in his comic popular song 'Daisy Bell (Bicycle Built for Two)'.

The early frame designs, which were rather crude, consisted of a strengthened dropped front frame attached to a rear quadrilateral terminating in the usual rear fork. The rear rider's pedal crank axle was connected to the front crank axle by a chain, so that the thrust of each rider's pedals was communicated to the rear road-driven wheel. The frame described above was weakness itself, and much binding of chains and bearings caused the machine to run rather hard.

Early versions of the tandem included a ladies' velocipede that could be connected to a velocipede ridden by a man in front. The lady could then be towed along. Later, Ordinaries and tricycles with basket seats to carry a female passenger were tried, as was a convertible tricycle with a detachable ladies' seat. The most successful attempt was by James Starley in 1878 with his tandem tricycle, the Salvo Sociable. It featured two seats side by side alongside two large driving wheels. The problem was that the two riders pedalled at different rates, making the machine unstable. Starley's solution was a differential gear that evenly distributed the power from the two drives.

By 1897, tandem design had evolved sufficiently that the machines enjoyed a resurgence of popularity. The 'rear-steering' machines were known in America as courting bikes. The man who could afford such a contrivance would be able to ride to the house of the lady of the day and collect her for an outing. Bearing in mind the necessity of a chaperone in conservative society, such adventures would undoubtedly have contributed to changing attitudes in Victorian times.

'Sharing a bed is really nothing compared with sharing a tandem.'

– A. A. Milne (1926)

Yet the tandem had other qualities besides that of a social vehicle that brought the sexes together, the most important of which was speed. While rear-steering and 'lady-back' tandems were the ideal machine for collecting a lady friend from her house, 'double gents' tandems were also used for fast pacing, as a much higher speed could be achieved with two men pedalling. A tandem may weigh less than twice the weight of a one-man cycle, so producing an excellent power to weight ratio. Although they are significantly heavier than traditional one-person bicycles, tandems can provide double or even four times the normal pedalling power. Moreover, this power is produced with minimal frictional loss in the drive train and the

wind resistance is no more than with a conventional bicycle. Going downhill or on the flat, most of the power produced by the single cyclist is used to overcome wind resistance. Yet with a tandem the wind resistance is no greater but the power produced by two riders is doubled, thus enabling fast speeds to be achieved.

Another advance came in 1898 when Mikael Pedersen created his first two-person tandem, as well as a first four-person one. His tandem was modelled on his idiosyncratic Pedersen cycle, the two-seater weighing in at 11 kilograms (24 pounds) and the four-seater at 29 kilograms (64 pounds). Such models encouraged the new sport of tandem racing, which was often faster than single machine racing, leading to frequent accidents and injuries.

It is vitally important, before setting out with a tandem partner, to agree how to stop: the pedals are connected, so both riders must stop and dismount simultaneously to avoid falling over. This co-ordination among the riders provides a much more sociable element to tandem riding. In his autobiography *It's Too Late Now*, published in 1939, the English writer A. A. Milne touched on this when he recorded memories of riding a rear-steering tandem tricycle with his brother Ken when he was eight and Ken was ten:

'We had a tandem tricycle. Ken sat behind, and had the steering, the bell and the brake under his control; I sat in front, and had the accident. Sharing a bed is really nothing compared with sharing a tandem. Bent double against a head-wind or a hill, the one in front feels, with every labouring breath, more and more certain that the one behind is hanging his feet over the handlebars and looking at the scenery; and the one behind (according to Ken) is just as convinced that he is doing all the work himself, and that the one in front is merely going through the motions of an entirely unfounded exhaustion.'

16: Elswick Sports
Ladies in the Saddle

Initially, the bicycle was mainly the preserve of rich men of leisure. The high-wheeler required the rider to sit far above the ground, and was considered inappropriate to both the dress and physical anatomy of women. With the emergence of the safety bicycle in the 1880s, women increasingly began to participate in cycling. Companies like the Elswick Cycle Company were quick to capitalise on this new market with such bicycles as a ladies' version of their Elswick Sports. The growing sales of ladies' bikes helped Elswick Hopper to develop a strong export trade to the whole British Empire and the rest of the world by 1912.

Year:

1912

Manufacturer:
Elswick

Location:
Newcastle Upon Tyne

Bikes like the Elswick brought the more adventurous lady to the road.

The longstanding debate over women and bicycling was fierce, between women striving for social independence and those who viewed that independence as a threat to the morals of Christian society. There was the problem of dress, too. The combination of long heavy skirts and constricting corsets greatly restricted women's mobility. There was also the matter of several layers of petticoats, hat and gloves. In 1851, Mrs Libby Miller visited her cousin Amelia Bloomer in Seneca Falls, New York, wearing a Turkish-inspired fashion of her own invention and caused a local scandal.

Luckily for the moralists, the Ordinary bicycle had prevented women from participating in the sport for nearly 20 years. There was simply no practical way to get around the hoop skirt issue with this design. For the most part, and for many years, women had to stand by idly and watch as the men in their lives experienced the new sensations of bicycling.

With the establishment of the chain-driven rear wheel and reduction gearing, the wheel sizes became smaller, opening up many new possibilities in design. The search for an expanding market inspired the bicycle manufacturers to create a machine that would allow a woman to ride in a skirt and corset without sacrificing her dignity. Times were fast changing and as the famous women's emancipationist Mrs Elizabeth Cady Stanton proclaimed, 'woman is riding to suffrage on a bicycle'. *The Englishwoman's Domestic Magazine* was far more conservative on the prospect of women on bicycles. It questioned whether a true Englishwoman would ever be as at home on a bicycle as her French cousins appeared to be. It wrote: 'Will they really become the rage? If so, are we to go shopping as well as promenading on them?' But cycling now became an attractive proposition for any-one able to afford a machine, and was quickly embraced by affluent women of leisure. In Britain, by 1890 the Cyclists' Touring Club had 60,000 members, of whom over 20,000 were women.

'Mother's out upon her bike, enjoying of the fun, Sister and her beau have gone to take a little run. The housemaid and the cook are both a-riding on their wheels; And Daddy's in the kitchen a-cooking of the meals.'

– Flora Thompson, from the *Lark Rise* trilogy (1939)

Many women at the end of the nineteenth century apparently also cycled in order to challenge Victorian bourgeois morality and the aesthetic tastes and sentiments from the domestic to the public sphere. Their cycling was about feminising, domesticating and civilising public space often perceived as masculine, raucous and rowdy. Women's movement into the public sphere often provoked masculine anxieties, which surfaced in ridicule, labelling and sexist joking.

There were those who remained convinced that cycling threatened not only a woman's moral reputation but her physical and mental health. It was argued that cycling 'heats the blood… destroys feminine symmetry and poise' and is 'a disturber of internal organs'. An American doctor even suggested that, 'in young girls the bones of the pelvis are not able to resist the tension required to ride a bicycle, and so may become more or less distorted in shape, with perhaps, in after life, resulting distress'. It was even suggested that cycling might be sexually stimulating and that the combination of straddling the saddle with the pedalling motion would lead to arousal in the female.

NEW-FOUND FREEDOM

Advertising reproduced a dominant association of the bicycle with new freedoms. Many of the posters that advertised bicycles to women tapped into late-nineteenth-century discourses on women's new freedoms and quest for mobility. Posters at this time sometimes portrayed bicycles and their women riders with wings and in flight, thus emphasising the sensations of freedom and flying that this new mobile technology supposedly produced. For some women, the bicycle clearly was part of a conscious struggle for new political freedoms. Chief among these bicycling women was the so-called 'New Woman', who was politically engaged, physically active beyond the domestic sphere, and searching for new ways to push the developing demands of women. The distinguishing characteristics of the New Woman were her independent spirit and her athletic zeal. The New Woman played sport, wore her skirts above her ankles and loosened her corsets – hence the phrase 'loose woman'.

Riding Out in Style

Some critics were concerned by the risqué clothes of women cyclists, such as the divided skirt, that had become popular. Could such a garment encourage masculine behaviour or, even worse, cause women to become 'inverts' (in other words, lesbians)? So seriously did the mayor of Chattanooga, New York, take this threat that he brought in a law banning the wearing of such bloomers as a 'menace to the peace and good morals of the male residents of the city'. Faced with such hostility, women brave enough to ride their cycles in public considered it a privilege that they were allowed to ride at all.

More militant women refused to be cowed by this masculine prejudice and The Rational Dress Society was founded in England in 1888. This encouraged women to give up their restrictive corsets, weighted skirts and heeled and pointy shoes and to wear practical clothes if they wished. Naturally, this had great appeal for women cyclists but many still kept their skirts to avoid being too closely associated with militant feminists. French women cyclists were less concerned with clothes as a political statement and more as a fashion opportunity. Some had even taken part in indoor cycle races as early as 1868, although the scantily clad 'velocipedestrienne' performing for the men at the music hall was hardly a symbol of female emancipation. *La Vie Parisienne* magazine questioned whether the cycle was really an appropriate conveyance for a lady.

Women cyclists now ventured out from the indoor Paris arenas and began to ride through the streets in the racy new fashions of the day, aware that the cycling costume was considered one of the most chic and modern. As an article of the time put it, 'the safety bicycle fills a much-needed want for women in any station of life, it knows no class distinction, is within reach of all, and rich and poor alike have the opportunity of enjoying this popular and healthful exercise'.

How to look good on the bike: a growing problem for both sexes.

Women Join the Race

Competition, however, was not encouraged in the USA or England, although women did race from as early as the mid-1880s. The reaction of the cycling press was particularly hostile. As late as 1892 *Cycling* magazine in London published an article condemning women racers. Less than a year later, when a 16-year-old named Debbie Reynolds rode 193 kilometres (120 miles) from Brighton to London and back in eight and a half hours while wearing her 'rational dress', the same magazine gave her such a scathing review that she became an instant hero and a martyr for the dress reformers and ultimately for the cause of women's emancipation in general.

Women cyclists were grudgingly tolerated and forbidden from competing with men, and were limited to riding four hours a day. This did not stop 16-year-old Monica Harwood from riding 690 kilometres (429 miles) to win London's first women's six-day race in

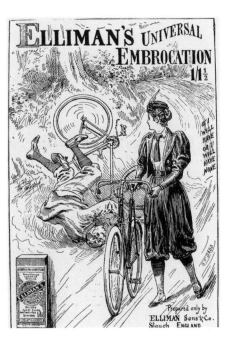

Getting up to speed: the emancipated lady out on her bike.

1895. Across the Atlantic the women's champion Frankie Nelson earned the title of the 'Queen of the Sixes' after winning the New York equivalent in both 1895 and 1896. However, another American woman named Annie Kopchovsky had already became the first woman to ride around the world in 1894. Annie's ride was the result of a wager between two wealthy clubmen of Boston, that no woman could match Thomas Stevens (the first man to cycle around the world a decade before). During the course of Annie's ride she followed the progress of dress reform, starting in skirt and blouse, switching to the bloomer and eventually donning men's trousers for much of the trip. No wonder the novelist John Galsworthy was so impressed by the coming of the bicycle for women:

'The bicycle… has been responsible for more movement in manners and morals than anything since Charles the Second. Under its influence, wholly or in part, have wilted chaperones, long and narrow skirts, tight corsets, hair that would come down, black stockings, thick ankles, large hats, prudery and fear of the dark; under its influence, wholly or in part, have blossomed weekends, strong nerves, strong legs, strong language, knickers, knowledge of make and shape, knowledge of woods and pastures, equality of sex, good digestion and professional occupation – in four words, the emancipation of women.'

'The bicycle… has been responsible for more movement in manners and morals than anything since Charles the Second.'

– John Galsworthy (1930)

17: Lucas Bicycle Lamps
Lighting the Way

When the first two-wheeled cycles appeared on the market, there were no options available for lighting the way along the road other than with lanterns containing candles. These would have provided only limited light and would therefore have been of little benefit to a rider. Later, progress was made when oil lamps came into use, and by the time that the Ordinary became popular in the 1870s, oil lamps were commonly fitted to the front wheel hub of all leading bicycles.

Year: 1880

Manufacturer:
Lucas

Location:
Hockley

The Lucas cycle lamp. Now riders could go out more safely at night.

atters improved again dramatically in 1896 when carbide lamps first appeared. Before the development of a reliable battery-powered bicycle lamp by Konosuke Matsushita in 1923, the problem of seeing and being seen while cycling at night was overcome by these gas-powered lamps. They were fuelled by combining calcium carbide with water. This process produced acetylene gas, the same substance that would later be used to power lamps in the first motor cars.

The problem was that although these lamps were good at providing a bright bicycle light, they needed continuous maintenance. Due to the hassle involved, cyclists welcomed the battery-powered lights that began to appear in the 1890s. They gave a better light, as well as far greater reliability.

Lucas's Bright Idea

The evolution of the bicycle light owed much to men like Edward Salsbury, who claimed to have invented such a lamp in 1876 fuelled by either paraffin or coal oil. A far more famous light maker whose products are still sold around the world and who was the first big name in bicycle lighting was Joseph Lucas. In 1872 he established his company selling household lamps at Hockley near Birmingham. Lucas began producing his own patented oil hub lamp in 1879, followed by a whole range of similar lights that made night-time riding safer and more efficient.

One feature that kept Lucas ahead of the market was his invention of an axle bearing that made it easier for the lamp to remain still while the front wheel was in motion. Lucas lamps became market leaders because they were easy to fit, being made to divide in half so that they could be inserted through the spokes of the front wheel. Once in place the two halves could be clipped together over the hub. Another improvement was the addition of a mechanical or winding wick holder that allowed better wick adjustment and flame control, so saving fuel.

Smaller and more sophisticated: the carbide cycle lamp.

With the arrival of the safety bicycle Lucas developed what was to become their most famous model, the 'Silver King'. Neater and easier to clean than its rivals, the King attached to the front of the handlebars and contained sprung parallel bars that gave shock resistance to the lamp on a bouncy road. The company were keen to supply a developing market and even produced a lamp called the 'Microphote' specifically for lady riders. As well as providing

The electric battery gives a better and more reliable light.

the hardware, Lucas supplied their customers with the fuel to run it and riders were advised to exclusively use the company's own clean-burning oil. This was given the trade name 'Briternwhite'; Lucas also made their own lamp wicks in various sizes to fit their cycle lamps.

LIGHTING AND THE LAW

Lighting regulations in various countries kept pace with the development of bicycle lamps, but not all jurisdictions required use of lights after dark. In Great Britain the law requiring use of rear lights was resisted by cyclists' groups on the grounds that it compromised the rider's obligation to be able to stop well within the distance they can see to be clear.

From Oil Lamps to Dynamos

Lamp technology kept pace with progress and as road conditions improved along with the increased use of pneumatic tyres from about 1891, it was no longer found necessary to manufacture such large, shock-resistant lamps. Slowly, over a period of four years, all cycle lamp manufacturers began to make smaller models so that from 1895 a large range of small oil lamps was being offered to the ever-increasing numbers of enthusiastic cyclists.

Then, in the 1890s, the first battery-powered lamps began to appear. Early battery lamps generally used a lead-acid battery. These steadily evolved until acid batteries used in bicycle lights had been replaced by an improved version of the battery – the self-contained dry cell battery. These auto-dry cells produced more benefits than lead-acid batteries, because they were smaller and were much more reliable.

The next step forward was to be the invention of the dynamo. This mechanism makes use of the energy that is created by the movement of the bicycle. Once they appeared on the market, dynamos sold well. They were much more practical at the time, because the storage density of batteries was very limited and the rider often risked being plunged into the dark when out riding at night. Yet replaceable-cell battery lights had a renaissance with the invention of the alkaline battery with its much greater storage density.

A whole range of lighting components for bicycles has steadily evolved.

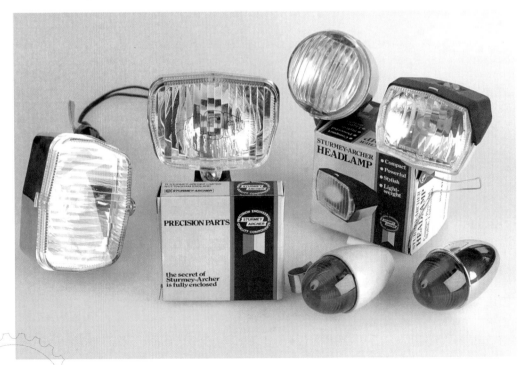

THE patent Dynohub is completely revolutionary in design. It provides electric lighting from a dynamo mounted in the front hub. Little or no effort beyond that normally required to propel bicycle is necessary, and there is no maintenance cost. It consists of the usual cycle hub with the addition of a drum at one end, to which is attached a permanent magnet revolving round an armature fixed to the hub spindle. An air gap between magnet and armature completely eliminates friction and wear, whilst a metal plate covers the front of the dynamo to exclude dirt and moisture.

The headlamp, connected to the Dynohub by twin cable, incorporates 4-point switch and stand-by battery, whilst a tail-lamp may be fitted if required.

FEATURES OF THE 12 VOLT DYNOHUB.

HIGH OUTPUT. This set is of 12 volt 23 amp. rating. The high output of the dynamo is fully utilised in the headlamp which has a duo-parabolic reflector to give both a long penetrating beam and at the same time adequate local illumination. A good light is given at slow walking pace.

VOLTAGE CONTROL. The dynamo generates up to 16 volts (obtained at 30 m.p.h.), and the unique voltage control prevents overload of bulbs and minimises the possibility of fusing.

DIM AND DIP LIGHT. The "dimmed" light is obtained by passing current from dynamo through the pilot bulb instead of main bulb. The position of this bulb also gives a dipped light.

NOISELESS. As there are no high speed moving parts, the Dynohub is absolutely noiseless.

EFFORTLESS. The effort required to generate the light is actually imperceptible. There is only one moving part, and this rotates with the wheel at the wheel's speed of about 160 r.p.m. at 12 m.p.h. as against the 4,000 r.p.m. at 12 m.p.h. of tyre-driven dynamos.

PROTECTED. By its location and its built-in construction, the Dynohub is ideally protected from accidental damage, dirt and water.

NO MAINTENANCE COST. Beyond the occasional replacement of batteries for pilot light, there is no maintenance cost whatever.

NO TYRE WEAR. As the Dynohub is not driven off the tyre, there is no tyre wear occasioned by its use.

LONG LIFE AND FREEDOM FROM TROUBLE. As there are no separate moving parts and no separate bearings, the Dynohub will last as long as the hub itself. It does not need lubricating at any time throughout its life.

Selling bike lamps was a competitive business. Technical details were all-important.

Power source was not the only aspect of cycle lighting that progressed. As moulding techniques for plastics became better, the lens optics of the bicycle lamp could be improved at low cost, so making better use of the light output and providing a more efficiently focused beam.

During the 1980s, the lighting market became more globalised: in Europe the French 'Wonder Lights' and Ever Ready brands gradually disappeared in favour of American, Japanese and German products. Many advances have been made in the bicycle light industry recently. Dynamos have become extremely efficient and high-output halogen lamps, light-emitting diodes and high-intensity discharge lights have added to both the quality and storage capacity of cycle lighting.

As LED lights have gained popularity and fallen in price over the last two decades, high-powered safe bicycle lighting systems have become more and more affordable. Ten years ago, a light system with high, medium and low light settings and a heavy NiMH battery pack would have generated 100 lumens and cost a lot. Today, a modern LED is just a fraction of that cost and weighs half as much, and incorporates a flashing safety setting for day or evening use by commuters.

'Today in the 1890s everything is bicycle.'

– American writer Stephen Crane (1896)

18: Dursley Pedersen
Eccentric Design

One of the most innovative designers of the nineteenth century was Mikael Pedersen, who holds a secure, if eccentric, place in cycling history. Born in Denmark in 1855, Pedersen was a man possessed of a unique mixture of creativity, imagination, ability and drive who, with his grasp of mechanics and technical skills, was able to transform his numerous ideas into practical reality. What was to defeat him, however, was a stubborn and erratic personality that led him into legal and financial disputes that were to deny him the commercial success that his talent deserved.

Year: 1897

Manufacturer:
Pedersen

Location:
Gloucester

P edersen's dream was to create a unique bicycle; to make his dream a reality he moved to Dursley in Gloucestershire, England, in 1893. Granted a patent for his new cycle design the following year, he created a cycle with several revolutionary features, including low-slung 'cow horn' handlebars that Pedersen claimed were for resting the feet! Early examples were made of wood but by 1896 he had perfected a method of jointing metal for which he again acquired a patent. This frame design, combined with a novel hammock-style saddle strung between the front and rear, resulted in a unique concept.

A unique design with a beauty of its own: the iconic Dursley Pedersen.

A UNIQUE DESIGN

A Pedersen bicycle looks like no other because of its unique design. To obtain the maximum amount of lateral rigidity the cycle is made up of a series of triangles. Each triangle is arranged to absorb the principal stresses at its apex. The result is that all tubes in the frame are subjected only to compression stress. The hammock-type saddle is suspended between two pieces of the triangular frame. Pedersen paid as much attention to the finish of his cycles as he did to the mechanical design. Among the accessories he offered to complement the basic machine was a golf and gun bag carrier, and various other bags and supports. The company even offered a Pedersen-designed ankle-length split skirt to protect the modesty of lady riders. Technically, Pedersen was determined to stay ahead of the market by incorporating such innovations as a ball bearing headset and adjustable handlebars.

Needing financial backing, he became involved with Ernest Hooley, one of England's most charismatic financiers and a corporate fraudster. Together they formed the Pedersen Cycle Frame Company.

Confident of success, Pedersen then persuaded other bicycle companies to produce his new design under licence. At the National Cycle Show in 1897, at least six other manufacturers presented their own versions of the Pedersen bicycle alongside the original. Then came the first setback. The cycling press was unimpressed by Pedersen's design and poor reviews led to a minimal number of orders.

Pedersen's response was, with the help of R. A. Lister, to start another company, the Dursley Pedersen Cycle Company, to produce the machine on his own. Realising that success would come with racing performance, Pedersen now built a super-lightweight racing machine. It was made from extremely thin-walled tubing, had 61-centimetre (24-inch) wood rim wheels and all components were drilled to save weight. This bicycle still exists and reportedly weighs less than 5 kilograms (10 pounds)! As this unique bicycle began to win races and set new speed records, the cycling press changed its mind.

Unusually for a cycle designer, Pedersen paid almost as much attention to the seating design as he did to that of the main frame. As a cycling enthusiast he found safety bicycle saddles uncomfortable, so he

The network construction of the saddle afforded perfect ventilation.

© Colin Kirsch, www.OldBike.eu/museum

Pedersen in town. Its distinctive upright shape is instantly recognisable.

designed and made an amazing hammock-style seat, made from 40 metres (130 feet) of woven cord, suspended between the handlebars and rear frame. It was designed to be soft and comfortable for long rides and to follow the movement of the body. It was later advertised as having 'perfect ventilation'. After finding his new seat didn't fit a conventional safety bike frame, Pedersen set about designing a new, complex, triangular frame of thin diameter tubing duplicated for extra strength. This was said to have been inspired by the Whipple-Murphy lattice truss used in railway bridges since 1847.

A saddle as idiosyncratic as the rest of the machine.

Good press reviews now generated customer interest, and sales dramatically increased. At the peak of its success, the company employed over 50 people and was producing more than 30 cycles a week. Pedersen then began to produce a variety of cycles: tandems, tricycles, four-wheelers and even an early folding version. There were now eight different frame sizes on offer, all enamel-coated, including a nickel-plated version and a choice of colours.

Decline of the Dursley Pedersen Cycle Company

Pedersen's troubles returned in 1903 when his ambitious designs overreached his manufacturing ability. His catalogue that year offered a complete three-speed hub gear based on the countershaft principle. Unfortunately, its friction clutch proved a failure and unreliable in use. Headstrong as ever, Pedersen refused to modify the design and sales orders could not be met because of the stock of faulty machines. The result was to force the company into liquidation; it was sold off two years later to Pedersen's financial backer, R. A. Lister.

Although the new owners corrected the faulty clutch design they retained the unpopular egg-shaped hub flanges. Dursley Pedersen bicycles and the Pedersen hub gear continued in production, although Pedersen himself was no longer involved in the production and had been forced to cede his patents to the company, giving up control of his inventions. Sadly, the great promise of the Pedersen cycle had come to an end and production finally stopped in 1917. Only about 8,000 bicycles were thought to have been actually produced. During the First World War bicycle manufacture had fallen, licence fees to Pedersen remained unpaid, and his poor business sense saw him cheated out of payments. Tragically, increasing alcohol misuse, a failed marriage and poor health saw Pedersen reduced to a pauper back in Denmark by 1920.

Victim of war. Pedersen sales plummeted during the First World War.

The Dursley Pedersen bicycle was an expensive, unusual and controversial bicycle but it filled a gap. It was produced at a time when the difficult to ride Ordinary bicycle had given way to the chain-driven smaller-wheeled safety bicycle but before the now-familiar diamond shape had become standard. So original was the concept that the design lived on with other manufacturers. Pedersen switched his attention to designing a three-speed hub for motorcycles, but the hub design was never a commercial success. Finally, in 1978, Jesper Sølling rediscovered the Pedersen design and began building the frames again.

AN INNOVATIVE DESIGNER HONOURED

After more than a century, Pedersen's design continues to be an example of unique craftsmanship in a world of mass-produced convention. Pedersen may have died in poverty in Denmark but his reputation lingered on. In 2003 his remains were brought back to Dursley and over 300 people attended his reburial there – all of them enthusiasts of Pedersen's talents and his unique contribution to the history of cycling.

19: Malvern Star
Traversing Australia

The sport of cycling has held a special place in the Australian nation's heart since the nineteenth century. Following the invention of the velocipede, the first races were held at the Melbourne Cricket Ground (MCG) in 1869, with a number of female competitors taking part. The first high-wheeler was imported to Melbourne in 1875 and the Melbourne Bicycle Club was formed three years later, becoming the centre for cycling in Australia. Early bicycles were all imported from Britain but it was not long before Australian-made bikes were on the market, among which were the successful Austral and Malvern Star.

Year:

1900

Manufacturer:
Finnegan

Location:
Melbourne

The Malvern Star was started by cyclist Tom Finnegan, who set up the business with the prize he earned (240 gold sovereigns) by winning the 1898 Austral Wheel Race. Finnegan specialised in touring and racing bikes, which he called the Malvern Stars. Part of Finnegan's success was due to the endorsement of Don Kirkham, one of the best-known Australian cyclists. Finnegan's brand logo was a six-pointed star, which matched a tattoo on his forearm and soon became familiar with Australian cyclists.

Back in the 1860s, Australian women, as well as men, had been captivated by bicycles. Just a few months after the first velocipede races were held for men at the MCG in 1869, the *Australasian* newspaper reported that a number of females had also participated in cycling contests, held as part of

Malvern Star, ca. 1925.
The best-known cycle on
the Australian continent.

local athletic sports meetings. Soon, the Austral Wheel Race at the MCG became the Melbourne Cup of the cycling fraternity, and large amounts of prize money were offered to contestants at annual meetings from 1886 to 1910. Many members of the Melbourne Cricket Club were horrified when the event began to attract not only professional cyclists from all around the world but also a large number of bookmakers. The race created an atmosphere more akin to that of a racetrack than that of a stately cricket oval. Though the Austral was a summer event, cycling itself was a year-round leisure activity, patronised by a wide cross-section of society.

Record-breaking attempts followed with Alf Edward in 1884 becoming the first person to cycle from Sydney to Melbourne, taking almost nine days to complete the trip. Although some women also took to the Ordinary, and tricycle races were held for women in South Australia in 1885, many held longstanding objections about female involvement in cycling.

By 1895 the safety bicycle was fast approaching the peak of its popularity, as both males and females now realised the benefits that the relatively inexpensive new machine could bring to work, as well as to leisure. In Melbourne especially, the appeal of the bicycle continued unabated. One journal, the *Melbourne Punch*, even suggested traffic was becoming so thick the city would eventually have to put special tracks underground for cyclists. The reason: new bicycles were so fast that cyclists were at risk of killing themselves and others.

Romance on a bike. Cycling together on a Malvern Star in Australia.

A NATION OF CYCLING ENTHUSIASTS

Australians' enthusiasm for cycling was reflected in many outlets. One newspaper report suggested that the bicycle should be part of the 'new' national coat of arms. In a rather striking design, the traditional faunal emblems of kangaroo and emu are depicted standing either side of a pneumatic tyre, while a safety bicycle is silhouetted against a rising sun. The words 'Advance Australia' are inscribed at the foot of the illustration. Other enthusiasts wanted to write songs about the marvellous new machine, including 'My Bicycle', a song written by Joseph Gee in 1896. There were also specialist cycling magazines such as *The Australian Cyclist* that in its first edition, on 7 September 1893, declared its faith in 'the freemasonry of the wheel' and set about promoting all aspects of cycling with almost evangelical zeal.

Detail of the characteristic frame decoration of Australia's most famous cycle – the Malvern Star.

An increasing number of entrepreneurs soon realised there was money to be made from the popularity of the bicycle. It was common for existing businesses, many with no direct connection to cycling (such as booksellers or piano dealers), to become agents for particular brands. One of the first purely Australian brands of cycle was Speedwell, manufactured by Bennett & Wood, a firm established in Sydney by Mr Charles W. Bennett and Mr Charles R. Wood in 1882. Both men were accomplished high-wheeler enthusiasts and racers. They became heavily involved in bicycle racing in the Sydney area prior to opening their own bicycle shop. Initially, they imported and sold machines such as the Rover and Raleigh. Then, as the first safety bicycles became popular, they were one of the first companies in Australia to embrace the new machines and offer them to the public. The business thrived and grew. By the early days of the twentieth century, Bennett and Wood were manufacturing their own bicycles under the name Speedwell, with the Royal Speedwells being the highest-quality bikes built.

Australian Cycle Racing

For the first half of the twentieth century, track racing and one-day endurance events dominated the Australian cycling calendar. Track racing was extremely popular, as thousands of people flocked to the wooden velodromes to witness closely fought races. While the velodromes drew large crowds in an era before radio and television, many long-distance races were also promoted. The Melbourne to Warrnambool, first raced in 1895, remains one of the oldest and longest continuous one-day races in the world. Others to survive include the Goulburn to Sydney and the Grafton to Inverell in New South Wales.

OLYMPIC CHAMPIONS

Australia's female cyclists have contributed greatly to the nation's cycling success. Australian women have raced at six Olympic Games on the road and have twice claimed gold in the road race. The first Olympic Games road cycling gold medal was won by Kathy Watt in Barcelona in 1992; in 2004 at Athens Sara Carrigan again claimed the honour for Australia. Watt was the first Australian to win a medal at the Road Cycling World Championships with her third place in the time trial in 2005 in Colombia.

During the twentieth century the first Australian to ride in the Tour de France was Don Kirkham in 1914; then, 14 years later, Sir Hubert Opperman led a full team of Australians to contest the 1928 Tour. 'Oppy' finished eighteenth and placed third on one of the stages. Over the years more Australians made the journey to race in Europe but it wasn't until 1981 that an Australian wore the leader's yellow jersey in the world's most famous bike race. Phil Anderson, or 'Skippy' as he was known in Europe, would go on to win the best young rider classification and finish tenth overall. Anderson was one of a group of Australians forging a career on foreign shores in a sport that football- and cricket-mad Australians knew little about.

> 'Before you can learn to win a race you have to learn to finish it.'
>
> – Russell Mockridge, Australian cycling champion (1932)

European-style stage racing had more recent beginnings. As part of the Victorian centenary celebrations in the 1930s, a 1,600-kilometre (1,000-mile) road race was organised. Hubert Opperman, who had been riding in Europe, was coaxed back for the event. Oppy had recorded the fastest time in the Melbourne to Warrnambool three times in the 1920s before venturing overseas. These early riders set a precedent that would later be followed by the international success of such Australian cyclists as Phil Anderson, Kathy Watt and Cadel Evans.

Hubert Opperman was one of the first and arguably the greatest of Australian cycle racing champions.

20: La Française Diamant
The First Tour de France

Appropriately, the first ever Tour de France race in 1903 was won by a French bicycle. It was a La Française machine, black with a tricolour head, and ridden by one of the champions of the time, Maurice Garin. The La Française company had been founded in 1890 by Pierre-Victor Besse and Francis Trepier as Société La Française, to manufacture velocipedes and components at 27 rue Saint-Ferdinand in Paris. In that first ever Tour, the company would sponsor eight riders in the race and the first five finishers would all be riding La Française cycles.

Year:
 1903

Manufacturer:
La Française

Location:
Paris

All the bikes used in the first Tour de France were similar in design and, like the La Française Diamant, had steel frames and handlebars, wooden wheel rims and big balloon tyres. Braking was very simple. It worked by the rider pulling a lever attached to a steel rod that pushed a leather pad directly onto the tyre tread. By today's standards the bikes were heavy, weighing 15 kilograms (33 pounds) or more. All the bikes also had just one gear. Well, they did have two, but when the rider wanted to change he had to stop and remove the rear wheel to place the chain on the other sprocket.

Born Out of Scandal

The story of how the Tour de France began is as dramatic as any of the stages in its long history. It was a strange irony that one of the biggest political scandals of the nineteenth century would indirectly bring about one of the greatest modern sporting events. In 1899 the popular cycling magazine *Le Vélo* ran a piece supporting Captain Dreyfus, a French officer later found to be unjustly accused of espionage. Comte Jules-Albert de Dion, an engine manufacturer, strongly believed Dreyfus was guilty; at one time, debates became so heated he hit the French president in the head with a walking stick. The incident resulted in 15 days in prison and a 100-franc fine. Dion was also one of the major advertisers in *Le Vélo* and he now, together with such other manufacturers as Clément and Michelin, withdrew all his advertising from the magazine.

Captain Alfred Dreyfus. The debate over his guilt led indirectly to the creation of the Tour de France.

Dion then went further by starting a rival sports sheet called *L'Auto*. Devoted to sports in general with an emphasis on cycling, it was to be printed on legendary yellow paper, in contrast to the green of *Le Vélo*. The editor was Henri Desgrange, a cycling promoter, former racing champion and winner of the world one-hour record in 1893.

Although *L'Auto* began well with sales of 80,000 copies a day, the competition with *Le Vélo* was so intense its circulation began to decline dangerously. Desperate to boost sales, in November 1902 Desgrange had lunch in a Parisian restaurant with Géo Lefèvre, a writer hired from *Le Vélo* to cover cycling. Lefèvre had a suggestion to boost sales. He is reported to have said to Desgrange. 'Let's organize a race that lasts several days longer than anything else. Like the six-days on the track, but on the road. The big towns will welcome the riders.' 'What you are proposing,' Desgrange replied, 'is nothing less than a Tour de France.' This did not come as a total surprise for, besides track events in 'velodromes', throughout France there were already established long-distance road races, from Paris to Vienna and St Petersburg, and from Paris to Rome.

(Left) The battered remains of a once great bike, a Française Diament.

Poster announcing the start of the first ever Tour de France.

Planning the First Tour de France

The first race in 1903 lasted 19 days and was composed of six stages, from Paris to Lyon, Marseille, Toulouse, Bordeaux, Nantes and then back to Paris. Compared to modern stage races, these first stages were extraordinarily long, averaging over 400 kilometres (250 miles), compared to the 171-kilometre (106-mile) stage average today. Because the stages were so long, all but the first started before dawn: the last stage started at 21.00 the night before. However, the riders were given a generous one- to three-day rest between stages. Unlike the present-day Tour, the route was relatively flat with just a single mountain stage. Of the several lesser cols that were climbed the first was the col des Echarmeaux (712 metres, 2,336 feet), on the opening stage from Paris to Lyon, followed on the Lyon to Marseille stage by the col de la République (1,161 metres, 3,809 feet).

Maurice Garin, battered stage winner in the first Tour de France, and his team.

The course through rural France was a near nightmare. The riders had to cover over 480 kilometres (300 miles) on roads made of hammered stone chips at best or travel along country roads rutted by cart wheels and pitted by the feet of livestock. The weather made it an endurance test. If it was hot, the roads were iron hard and covered with choking dust; if it rained, they became a sea of mud.

The riders rode not in teams but as individuals, having paid the entrance fee of ten francs for the entire race or five francs to compete in a single stage. Sixty cyclists, all professionals or semi-professionals, lined up at the start. Of these, 49 were French, four Belgian, four Swiss, two German, and one Italian. A third of them were commercially sponsored by bicycle manufacturers, while 39 entered without commercial support. Another 24 riders took the opportunity to enter for specific single stages. Already the race was seen as a festive event and a cavalcade of cars, festooned with advertising and throwing free samples to spectators, travelled two hours ahead of the cyclists.

At a time when it was normal for a professional cyclist to hire pacers, who would lead them during the race, Desgrange annoyed many by forbidding it throughout the Tour. Moreover, he hired stewards to keep a close watch on the riders to ensure that none of them took shortcuts. There was no yellow jersey for the stage leaders, who wore a simple green armband, but stage winners were well rewarded, receiving prize money of between 50 francs and 1,500 francs per stage. Overall, the 14 best cyclists in the general classification each received a prize ranging from 3,000 francs for the winner to 25 francs for 14th place. The remaining seven cyclists to finish in the general classification each received 95 francs, 5 francs for each of the 19 days that the race had taken, provided that they had not won more than 200 francs in prize money and did not have an average speed of less than 20 km/h (12 mph) on any stage.

Final triumph. Maurice Garin enters Paris to win a historic victory in the greatest road race in the world.

Unlike the modern race, any rider who dropped out could rejoin the race at the start of the next stage, although he would no longer count in the general classification. So Hippolyte Aucouturier, who gave up during the first stage, was able to return to the race and even won the second and third stages. Again, Charles Laeser, winner of the fourth stage, had not even completed the third. There were to be two or three days allowed between stages. These were not only needed for the top men to recover, but for the stragglers to finish. The last man on the first stage was on the road for ten hours short of two days!

All agreed that it would be a tough race. There were 78 men who signed up for the whole Tour, although a few extra riders had arranged to ride in a single stage that was local to them. The field consisted of a mixture of established racing stars and those willing just to take a chance. A few of the riders raced under a pseudonym because the professional riders were considered a rough breed of mercenary. Other riders came from well-known families and did not want their real names to be known. The one that stands

out most on the starting list was a Belgian who had entered himself simply as 'Samson'.

To keep a close check on the competitors, Lefevre had decided to follow the entire race himself using both train and bicycle through its 2,414-kilometre (1,500-mile) course round France. To save costs he would act as the official timekeeper, as well as writing daily reports for *L'Auto-Velo*.

Memories of the Tour de France. The rider Aucouturier, climbing the Ballon d'Alsace, changes the front wheel of his bicycle.

A Race to Remember

At 3 p.m. on 1 July 1903, 60 entrants came up to the starting line outside a café called Au Reveil Matin in Montgeron, which is now part of Paris but was then a small satellite town. The café is still there, on the Rue Jean-Jaurès, and a plaque outside it records the first Tour. The pre-race favourites had been Maurice Garin, known as the 'Little Chimney-Sweep', and Hippolyte Aucouturier, and it was Garin who dominated the race from the start setting off at a speed of 35 km/h (22 mph). Having left Paris mid-afternoon the riders were still peddling hard as night fell and Garin said later that he did not expect to finish until 8 a.m. the next day. During the night, Garin's main rival Aucouturier developed painful stomach cramps, and was unable to finish the stage.

> 'Two hours before they pass all find excuses to be at the turn of the road, to view their faces... with haggard lines under their eyes.'
>
> – New York World (1903)

It was during this first stage that the first ever breach of the Tour rules occurred. Jean Fischer, who had won the Paris–Tours race two years earlier, was seen to be illegally using a car as his pacemaker. Meanwhile, Garin kept his lead throughout the night and was the first to cross the line in Lyon at around 9 a.m. the following morning.

Although now excluded from the general classification, Aucouturier rejoined the race for the second stage and won the sprint. He continued to do well, winning the third stage, and looked to win the fourth as well until he was seen using the slipstream of a car, and was removed from the race. So the stage winner was a Swiss, Charles Laeser, making him the first non-French winner of a stage of the Tour de France.

By the fifth stage, Garin was still in the overall lead, with his nearest rival, Emile Georget, almost two hours behind. What little chance Georget still had finally disappeared when he had the misfortune of getting two flat tyres and then fell asleep with exhaustion at the side of the road, leaving Garin to win the stage and extend his already formidable lead.

CHEATING FROM THE START

Cheating was so common in the 1904 event that Henri Desgrange declared that he would never run the race again. Not only was Garin, the overall winner, disqualified for taking the train over significant stretches of the course, but so were the next three cyclists who placed, along with the winner of every single stage of the course. Of the 27 cyclists who actually finished the 1904 race, 12 were disqualified and given bans ranging from one year to life. The race's eventual official winner, 19-year-old Henri Cornet, was not determined until four months after the event. These events were a curious prelude to the big doping scandals to come with Lance Armstrong in the mid-1990s.

In the early days of the Tour, riders would often stop for a glass of wine along the way.

Garin started the final stage from Nantes to the Velodrome in Paris with an almost three-hour lead and nonchalantly requested the other leading riders to do the sensible thing and let him ride to victory as a mere formality. Fernand Augereau, however, refused to agree, causing Lucien Pothier to hurl his bike at him, knocking Augereau to the ground. The other riders then ignored the mayhem and set together to the finish. Garin easily won the sprint and entered the Velodrome to be crowned the overall winner of the first Tour de France.

Garin's winning lead over the other riders was 2 hours, 59 minutes and 31 seconds, and remains the greatest ever margin of victory in the Tour. Of the 60 competitors from France, Belgium, Germany and Switzerland who had started the race, only 21 finished the gruelling course. The last competitor finished two days later. The early races were notorious for mayhem. Riders strewed broken glass and nails in the road to cause punctures behind them, competitors were given drinks that made them sick, many got surreptitious tows from cars or motorbikes, and some were held up and delayed by hired thugs. The excitement was intense and *L'Auto*'s circulation more than doubled. *Le Vélo* went bankrupt.

21: Sturmey-Archer
Freedom of the Gear

Leonardo da Vinci is credited with developing the idea of the chain and cog in the fifteenth century. However, it would take nearly 400 years for the idea to become a practical reality of bicycle design. An effective chain drive needs to transmit power efficiently from the rider's legs to the rear wheel. It also must be designed so that pedalling resistance is within a comfortable range for the cyclist. This would have been impossible in the days of wood construction; only with the development of stronger materials and other technological and engineering advances did this become possible.

Year:
1902

Manufacturer:
Sturmey-Archer

Location:
Nottingham

Conquering the gradient. The first hub gear systems overcame the problem of the single gear and were to revolutionise the efficiency of cycling.

By the 1880s, the chain drive was commonplace but a chain drive alone without a gear system is only effective on the flat or going downhill. When dealing with head winds, climbing hills or even pushing off from a standing start, the rider has to stand on his pedals and strain while pedalling at a very low rate. The benefit of gears is that they allow the rider to pedal at a comfortable and efficient rate whether cycling uphill or downhill and also dealing with a head or a tail wind.

The Arrival of the Gear System

Before the invention of the gear, the system on the old high-wheelers was that the pedals were attached directly to the wheel. One turn of the pedals equated to one turn of the wheel. The arrival of a gear system would allow the cyclist to change that ratio. When dealing with steep hills, the rider could now choose a gear that let him or her turn the pedals many times to turn the wheel just once. In contrast, on flat terrain or going downhill, the rider could choose a gear that turned the wheel many times for each turn of the pedals. This was a major advance in cycling technology.

However, variable gear ratios certainly did not find much acceptance among the racing fraternity. Tyres and punctures were trouble enough in road racing, without having to unravel all those sprockets, settings and chain. Track racing, which was the most keenly followed sport, employed single ratio fixed-wheel transmissions. In long-distance events, the usual set-up would be a single 18-tooth sprocket, combined with a 46- or 47-tooth chain ring. However, for a hilly event, dismounting to walk up gradients was not unknown and was not the disgrace it is today. Nevertheless, when confronted with a major alpine climb, it was the most experienced rider who bothered to make sure that he had fitted a suitable ratio. Some riders fitted double freewheels, and much skill was required to choose the exact moment to leap from the bicycle and slip the chain from one sprocket to the next.

Other riders would fit a double freewheel on both sides of their rear wheel, and even more skill was required to dismount, loosen the wing nuts (the day's equivalent of the quick-release), reverse the wheel and be back into the race again with the least time lost. With such a set-up, riders had a choice of four ratios, albeit hardly available at the push of a lever.

> 'Freewheels. Only for those who wish to loiter about... in the grease among traffic.'
>
> – Joseph Pennell, American artist (1912)

The Birth of Sturmey-Archer

One of the greatest advances in this new gearing technology was to result from the commercial success of an English bicycle manufacturer. The Raleigh Bicycle Company, located in Nottingham, was purchased by Frank Bowden, a prosperous lawyer, in 1888. Raleigh was to become the largest cycle manufacturer in the country with Bowden constantly improving his designs and manufacturing techniques. Then, in 1902, Bowden, who was already committed to finding a more efficient gearing system for his machines, was approached by Henry Sturmey and James Archer with a design originally conceived by a poor Irishman, William Reilly. Bowden hired them both and the Sturmey-Archer brand was born.

Sturmey-Archer was soon the biggest world name in hub gearing, and for many years held sway over almost identical products put out by competitors. Major British cycle manufacturers, such as Hercules, BSA and Brampton, made their own hub gears, but all finally gave this up with the onset of the

Sturmey-Archer was the first big name in bicycle gear systems. Their hub gear was to dominate the market for decades.

Founders of the world-beating Sturmey-Archer company. They made one of the most important contributions to the progress of cycling.

Henry Sturmey	Frank Bowden	James Archer
1857–1930	1848–1921	1854–1920

Second World War, while Sturmey-Archer became part of the Raleigh Industries group and maintained its position of prominence. The original 1902 Sturmey-Archer three-speed hub was based on Reilly's design of a fixed-gear three-speed mechanism. The trouble was that although the rider was able to shift gears easily, he could not coast. Within a year the problem had been rectified so that it was now possible to coast along in all three speeds. By 1913 Sturmey-Archer had achieved market dominance, producing 100,000 units a year, and was an integral part of the British cycle industry, with worldwide exports. By 1952, production exceeded 2 million units a year. The Sturmey-Archer three-speed gear had become a vital part of the British affordable bicycle that was exported and used throughout the world.

The whole Sturmey-Archer range was impressive too, with two-, three-, four- and five-speed hubs being made. Close, wide and medium ratios, as well as fixed and freewheel varieties, represented, even by today's standards, a wide choice. Indeed, its comprehensive range had a bewildering list of models designated by groups of initials such as ASC, AM, FM, FC, FW and AW. Eventually, a three-sprocket block was introduced to replace the single sprocket. Fitting this to a three-speed hub gave the rider a choice of nine ratios. One snag with this arrangement was that the purist could not always get the exact selection he or she wanted – something that can usually be done with derailleur gears.

An early Sturmey-Archer gear change lever.

Although Bowden was a brilliant businessman who had built a bicycle manufacturing empire, he became less interested in innovation and more concerned with holding down costs. For this reason Raleigh, the parent company, barely allowed Sturmey-Archer to survive. Raleigh wanted nothing more than basic over-geared three-speed hubs, so the creative skills of Sturmey-Archer were sacrificed to the priority of cutting costs on a minuscule budget. Yet Sturmey-Archer gears remained user-friendly and required virtually no maintenance. From among the competing systems Sturmey-Archer maintained its popularity, although its design rarely changed and parts were always available. The most desirable feature of the Sturmey-Archer gear was always ease of shifting. Instead of shifting while steering with one hand the rider just flicked a trigger on the handlebars.

In the 1920s the limitations of the three-speed hub became more apparent, particularly for racing machines. The double-pivot derailleur gears such as Simplex began to eat into the Sturmey-Archer market, forcing them to produce a single epicyclic three-speed hub with wide, medium and close ratios. Trigger controls were improved and were now mounted on the handlebars rather than the top tube. The company had also seen the potential of dynamo lighting and in 1937 it produced the six-volt Dynohub that proved particularly useful during the Second World War.

None of this prevented the Sturmey-Archer reputation being gradually eroded as Suntour and Shimano began making derailleurs so reliable they hardly ever required repairing. Power shifters, bar-cons and self-adjusting front derailleurs began closing in on the superior simplicity of Sturmey-Archer gears. The quality of Taiwanese production had also improved; when Sturmey-Archer finally faced financial collapse in 2000 it was SunRace, a Taiwanese company, that came to the rescue, and bought the company assets more or less intact. The stock and manufacturing equipment were moved to Taiwan and SunRace resumed production of existing Sturmey-Archer hubs as well as introducing some new designs.

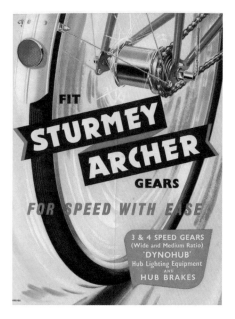

As part of the Raleigh Industries Group, Sturmey-Archer had the financial backing to fund ambitious advertising campaigns.

A WORLD RECORD

In 1939 Tommy Godwin set the world record for the longest distance ridden in a year by riding 120,805 kilometres (75,065 miles). In order to do so, he had to average 330 kilometres (205 miles) every day for the entire year. He rode the equivalent of three times around the Earth's circumference. To top it off, he did all of his riding on a more than 14-kilogram (30-pound) Raleigh with a four-speed Sturmey-Archer hub. Raleigh and Sturmey-Archer were Godwin's sponsors. When he finished his record-setting year, he spent several weeks learning how to walk again before heading off to fight in the Second World War.

22: Labor Tour de France
Torsion Resistant

The racing credentials for the Labor cycle company came from its experience in making cycles for Louis Darragon, the world and French national champion in 1906 and 1907. Darragon had the unusual distinction of being one of the few professional racers actually killed while competing. In April 1918 he died in the Vélodrome d'Hiver in Paris after crashing at full speed. His pedal had broken because of poor-quality materials being used in wartime. The tragedy, as dramatic as it was, had little effect on Labor's sales and the company continued to be the leading producer of fast racing cycles.

Year:
1922

Manufacturer:
Labor

Location:
France

What made Labor different was its willingness to try something new. The company set out to try to improve on the basic diamond-shaped bicycle frame that had by 1910 become standard throughout Europe. After experimenting with many alternatives it came up with a radical new frame design that was incorporated into what the company called its new 'Tour de France' model. What was so different about the new design was that instead of supporting the wheel on both sides, the new machine used a single side attachment for both front and rear wheels.

This gave the machine a singularly odd appearance, but it had one significant if theoretical advantage over a conventional machine: the tyres could be changed without having to remove a wheel. Although this may have seemed an attractive idea on the drawing board, it proved a disadvantage on the road. Labor discovered that whenever the unfortunate rider had a puncture or needed to change a tyre, he had to lift up and manoeuvre the whole machine around first.

The Labor had a distinctive frame design.

The Labor Tour de France certainly looked different to other bikes. Apart from the forks, the most distinctive feature was the frame. It featured a curved tube below the cross bar at the top that looked in shape like a curved bridge. Also, instead of a slotted rear dropout, it used a bottom bracket to tension the chain. In order to compensate for any supposed loss of rigidity, Labor added an additional stay to the centre of the seat tube. In spite of this additional tubing, at 13 kilograms (26.6 pounds) the Labor weighed no more than contemporary bikes.

The Labor was the bike of choice of several leading French racers, including Louis Darragon.

What inhibited Labor sales was not the bicycle's radical looks, but its high price – for it cost 40 francs more than Labor's conventional model, which sold for 300 francs. What it did achieve was to create for Labor a reputation for producing the most torsion-resistant of bicycles. This was reinforced by a particularly imaginative advertising campaign that ran for some years in French magazines and featured a school room full of monkeys who were seen working hard on designing Labor cycles.

Although sales were never spectacular, the Labor 'Tour de France' did prove itself on the French racing circuit with Paul Deman as rider in 1920 and Albert Dejonghe in 1922 winning the Paris–Roubaix classic. Deman also won the Paris–Bordeaux race in 1922 and Bou–Azza, the first ever Tour of Morocco. The torsion resistant Labor did particularly well in these races as the route comprised many cobblestone and other rough sections.

Although the Labor company was bought by Alcyon in the early 1920s, the concept of the single-blade fork was to be revived in the 1990s when Cannondale in the USA incorporated it into their mountain bike design.

THE IVER JOHNSON

The Labor design was a typical example of innovative French bike design. However, it was not unique at the time for it had been foreshadowed in the USA by the Iver Johnson Truss-Bridge bicycle of 1902. This was built on similar principles to the Labor and had an almost identical look.

The American champion Major Taylor had even raced on an Iver Johnson truss-frame in France from the turn of the century, which led many to think that Labor had most likely copied the American design. Nor was Iver Johnson alone, for a number of other American companies had used a similar torsion-resistant design.

23: The Automoto
Early Tour Racers

Ottavio Bottecchia was the first Italian to win the Tour de France in 1924, riding a French bicycle. Supposedly, for most of the route he sang: 'I have seen the most beautiful eyes in the world but never as beautiful eyes as yours.' A year earlier, also riding an Automoto, he had finished second, and in 1923 the Tour had been won by his great rival Henri Pélissier on a similar machine. This confirmed Automoto as the leading racing brand at the time. The company was established in 1901 at Saint-Étienne, which had become the centre of the French cycle industry. Automoto would be first choice for many Tour riders during the 1920s.

Year:
1924

Manufacturer:
Automoto

Location:
Saint-Étienne

After his historic win in the 2012 Tour de France, Bradley Wiggins said that his next ambition was to emulate his hero Bottecchia and next time wear the leader's yellow jersey from start to finish. Bottecchia was a colourful character, typical of the early days of the Tour. In the First World War he had been a sharpshooting specialist in the Austrian army and his skill was rewarded when he was presented with his first bicycle – but one with a machine gun attached to its handlebars. Captured by the Italians, he escaped from a prison camp and survived the rest of the war. He then decided that his future lay in cycle racing and determined to become the very best.

Bottecchia's choice. The Automoto proved to be an Italian classic and one of the most successful racers of the time.

An Italian Cycling Legend

Bottecchia certainly became the first of the great mountain climbers. One of his rivals, Nicholas Frantz, said, 'it would be dangerous to follow Bottecchia on a climb. It would be suicide. His pace is so high, so relentless, it would suffocate another rider.'

He led the 1923 Tour from Cherbourg after the second stage and wore the yellow jersey of leader as far as Nice. Such was the reaction in Italy that the *Gazetta dello Sport* asked for one lira from each of its readers to reward him, with Mussolini being the first to subscribe. After Nice, however, Bottecchia was forced to pass the yellow jersey to the French champion Henri Pélissier, who won in Paris with the prediction, 'Next year Bottecchia will succeed me.'

Pélissier's predictions of a Bottecchia win proved correct, for in 1924 the Italian became the overall winner. Although Bottecchia was a hero to many, he offended some Italian fascists by taking off the yellow leader's jersey during the stage nearest to the Italian border. That day he wore his team jersey, one of several in the peloton and therefore less conspicuous. None of the surviving newspaper reports of the period can explain Bottecchia's decision. One theory was that he was afraid of being mobbed and delayed. Others suggested that he wanted to avoid Mussolini's Black Shirts for he had already received death threats and his tyres were slashed.

Automoto combined fine engineering with a particularly Italian attention to detail.

'It would be dangerous to follow Bottecchia on a climb. It would be suicide. His pace is so high, so relentless, it would suffocate another rider.'

– Nicholas Frantz (1924)

Henri Pélissier, who revealed the temptations of drugs and alcohol experienced by Tour riders long before the present-day scandals.

EARLY TEMPTATIONS

Henri Pélissier boasted to a journalist that Tour de France riders had 'cocaine to go in our eyes, chloroform for our gums, and do you want to see the pills? We keep going on dynamite. In the evenings we dance around our rooms instead of sleeping.' While not all competitors relied on 'dynamite' it had already become common practice for Tour cyclists to drink alcohol during the race – a situation that would continue until the 1960s, when the French authorities finally passed a law forbidding the use of stimulants in sport.

Bottechia crossing the Alps on his way to a famous victory in Paris.

The following year Bottecchia, again riding for the Automoto team, won the first stage of the Tour and then added two more on the way to the Pyrenees. This year he had a new challenger, the Belgian Adelin Benoît, who was riding for Thomann-Dunlop. Both riders exchanged the lead all the way to Bayonne, before Benoît took what appeared to be a commanding lead. The reply from the Automoto team was immediate; with his teammate Lucien Buysse, Bottecchia closed the gap. From that moment at Perpignan on, they were untroubled by the competitors. Bottecchia won the final stage into Paris with Buysse protecting his rear. By this self-sacrificing support Buysse became the first domestique (a team rider's assistant) in Tour history.

A Mysterious Demise

'The unpleasant hand of destiny fell on his shoulders. It was as though the misery of his origins had caught up with him. Dark thoughts and a presentiment of the future haunted him.'

– Bernard Chambaz (1928)

This would be Bottecchia's last Tour win. In 1926 he retired from the Tour in the Pyrenees 'weeping like a child' during a thunderstorm on a stage that those who were there described as apocalyptic because of the cold and the violence of the wind. He was never the same man again. As the writer Bernard Chambaz said of Bottecchia: 'The unpleasant hand of destiny fell on his shoulders. It was as though the misery of his origins had caught up with him. Dark thoughts and a presentiment of the future haunted him. He no longer had the heart to train. He feared that he'd been "cut down by a bad illness". He coughed and he ached in his back and his bronchial tubes. The following winter, he lost his younger brother, knocked down by a car.'

Nevertheless, Bottecchia seemed determined to make a comeback and was preparing for a return to the race the next year. After going out for a training ride near his home town on 3 June 1927, his injured body was found beside a road. His skull was cracked and several other bones were broken. Yet, his bicycle lay some distance away, completely undamaged. Some hours later he died. Was it an accident or assassination? The accident theory is supported by the accounts of witnesses and a medical examination that also referred to several fractures. The inquiry into his death was quickly closed. The accident theory suited everybody from the Mussolini regime to the rider's family, who collected a large insurance payout.

The only events that appear certain are that, that morning, Bottecchia rose at dawn and then rode to his friend Alfonso Piccini's house to go training together as on other days. When Piccini decided not to go, Bottecchia went on alone. Everyone seemed to have a different opinion; the priest who gave him the last rites is said to have attributed the death to fascists unhappy about Bottecchia's more liberal opinions. But Bottecchia was a barely literate racing

Distinctive design features were used throughout the Automoto.

cyclist at the end of his career, not a politician or celebrity who could sway opinion. Furthermore, Mussolini had been first to contribute to the *Gazzetta dello Sport* benefit fund.

The mystery continued. An Italian dying from stab wounds on the New York waterfront later claimed that he had done it on the orders of a named Mafia godfather, although nobody of the name was ever found. Some suggested a fight, but that would have left visible wounds. Much later, a farmer in Pordenone on his deathbed gave another explanation. He said, 'I saw a man eating my grapes. He'd pushed through the vines and damaged them. I threw a rock to scare him, but it hit him. I ran to him and realised who it was. God forgive me!' The farmer said that he dragged the body off the farm and onto the roadside. If that was true, how did the body end up 55 kilometres (35 miles) away? The final riddle is what Bottecchia was doing in a vineyard in June when grapes don't ripen until late summer.

24: Vialle Vélastic
Pre-Mountain Bike

From the early days of cycling, riders had thought of a bike that would be light and flexible enough to ride across country. Clearly this would have been impossible in the era of the high-wheeler or in the early days of the safety bike. Then, as technology improved and frames became lighter, the possibility gradually became a reality. An early example of riding bicycles off-road was when road-racing cyclists who used standard machines began cyclo-cross as a means of keeping fit during the winter. Cyclo-cross eventually became a sport in its own right in the 1940s, with the first world championship being held in 1950.

Year:
1925

Manufacturer:
Vialle

Location:
France

Many of the ideas that later paved the way for more specialised off-road machines in America such as the Breezer Beamer were in fact introduced as early as 1925. The most interesting of these bikes was the Vélastic from the Vialle brothers and their Etablissements Industriels des Cycles Èlastiques of France. It was claimed in newspaper advertisements that this could make cycling as comfortable as sitting in an armchair. It was even supposed to be possible to ride down a kerb without noticing the drop – an

THE EARLY DAYS OF CYCLO-CROSS

The sport began in the early 1900s, when amateur riders would race each other to the next town. They were allowed to take shortcuts through farmers' fields, jump over fences or cross ditches. It is believed that riders used this early form of cyclo-cross to stay in shape during the winter months when there was no road racing. Riding off-road in these difficult conditions increased the intensity at which the cyclists were riding, thereby improving their ability to handle their bikes when riding back on the road. Daniel Gousseau is credited with organising the first French national championship in 1902.

essential prerequisite for any cycle that might be used across country.

What made the Vélastic so unusual for its time was its unusual construction, for a considerable portion of the frame is formed by a leaf spring. Another radical feature is the absence of a seat tube, as the rider sits on the end of the spring. This makes it a very flexible machine, although the strength of the rest of the frame is designed to maximise torsional strength.

Adjusting the seat is also an unusual process as the rider, if a tall person, simply pulls the leaf spring a little further out of the frame. This in turn makes for an even softer suspension. In the same way, smaller, lighter people do the reverse adjustment, producing a slightly harder, tighter suspension. Today a manufacturer would offer springs of differing hardness to cater to the varying weights of riders. The Vélastic was certainly a bicycle that was ahead of its time in several ways. The choice of the name 'Vélastic' is just as ingenious as the bicycle itself, as it beautifully summarises the machine's attributes in a single, onomatopoeic word.

Ernest Strobino.
One of the early stars of cyclo-cross.

The eccentric frame design of the Vialle Vélastic (left) was to make it a collector's favourite in later years.

'The ideas that paved the way for the Breezer Beamer were introduced in Vialle Vélastic as early as 1925.'

– Michael Embacher, *Cyclopedia* (2011)

25: The Velocar
The Recumbent Racer

Although recumbent bicycles have become more popular in recent years, they are still a minority interest. At one time they were thought to offer a new form of comfortable cycling to the mainstream public. Interest in the recumbent began in 1896 when a M Challand exhibited in Geneva an innovative bike that had a horizontal cranking system to allow greater thrust on the pedals. Challand's bike also had a very low seat that allowed for easier mounting and improved stability. This bike became known as the 'Challand Recumbent' and was the first of its type.

Year:

1933

Manufacturer:
Mochet

Location:
Puteaux

The problem that stopped Challand's bike being a commercial success was that it weighed about three times as much as its rider! A similar machine to the Challand later appeared in London, where it was described as being, 'as comfortable as a rocking chair and with remarkable mechanical ingenuity'. The machine in question was fitted with an anti-vibrating easy-chair-like saddle that also, 'affords wonderful relief to a tired back and which proves a luxury when coasting down long hills'. The problem was the belief prevalent at the time that a recumbent was a slow bike; it was assumed that a comfortable bike could not be a fast bike.

The 1945 Mochet Velocar.
Early recumbents often
had a strange hybrid
appearance.

Mochet's Velocar

In the early twentieth century, the recumbent still retained the interest of designers; some thought it might play an important role in the future of the bicycle. Much of this optimism came from the innovative vision of one man, Charles Mochet. Shortly before the First World War at Puteaux in France, Mochet had built small, lightweight, motor-powered cars, but with limited success. He then applied his basic concept to a pedal-driven four-wheeled vehicle that proved surprisingly fast – so fast, in fact, that it began to be used as a pace vehicle in bicycle races. The only problem was that it had a tendency to tip over at high speed.

'There is room in this world for many, many, many different kinds of bicycle.'

– Gardner Martin, designer (1960)

Mochet then had the bright idea to improve the stability. He divided his Velocar in half to make a two-wheeled version, with 50-centimetre (20-inch) wheels, a wheelbase of 146 centimetres (57 inches) and a bottom bracket that was about 12 centimetres (5 inches) above the adjustable seat. Mochet now set out to prove that his recumbent bike was faster than the conventional cycle and ideal for touring. To show its racing credentials, Mochet sought a proven rider with a good track record. His first choice was the well-known and highly successful Henri Lemoine. The comfort and ease of steering of the Velocar impressed Lemoine but, scared of ridicule, he could not be persuaded to ride it in a contest. Mochet then approached Francis Faure, brother of the famous cyclist Benoît Faure, who had a less impressive track record. Francis was a decidedly lesser rider than either Lemoine or his brother Benoît, but after thoroughly testing the machine Faure agreed to race it.

As the field lined up for the first race, Faure was the subject of ridicule. He was asked if he was so tired that he needed a lie down and why did he not sit up and ride like a man. However, the laughing soon stopped as Faure set off at speed and left the entire disgruntled field behind. From that moment, taking advantage of the Velocar's clear aerodynamic superiority, Faure went on to defeat every first-class track cyclist in Europe. The following year Faure proved unbeatable in 5,000-metre (5,700-yard) distance events. Even when racing against top riders, who would take turns pacing each other, Faure still won. As well as success on the track, Velocars had begun to win road races, with Paul Morand triumphing in the Paris–Limoges race in 1933.

The sensational progress continued, with Faure setting various new short-course world records, while other cyclists on recumbents were easily beating their rivals in road races. The Mochet team then decided to attack the cycling 'ultimate': the one-hour record. Mochet was unsure whether or not a new record by the Velocar would be acknowledged by the UCI (International Cycling Union), and put that question to them in October 1932. The UCI confirmed that as the Velocar had no add-on aerodynamic components there would be no reason to invalidate a new record set by the Velocar.

A New World Record?

On 7 July 1933, Francis Faure rode 45.055 kilometres (27.9 miles) in one hour at a Paris velodrome, so smashing the almost 20-year-old record set by Oscar Egg. The Velocar's success caught the public imagination, but soon questions began to be asked about the Velocar. Was it a true cycle or something else and would Faure's records be confirmed? An answer was now imperative as on 29 August 1933, at Saint Trond, Maurice Richard, on an upright bicycle, had also beaten Oscar Egg's one-hour record, having ridden 44.077 kilometres (27.4 miles) in one hour. Which of these, the recumbent's or the upright's, was the true new record? Equally important, would the recumbent be legitimised as a legal bicycle and free to ride in UCI-governed competitions? Or would, as many now wished, the Velocar be banned forever from the sport?

At the crucial meeting of the UCI that would decide the issue, an amateur rider demonstrated the Velocar to the committee by pedalling it around the conference room. The delegates were divided. The English UCI representative was in favour of the Velocar and thought it could be the bicycle of the future, but the Italian, Bertholini, did not think the recumbent should be classed as a bicycle at all. What concerned many delegates was that a second-class cyclist like Francis Faure was now setting world-class records and even presuming to take the holy grail of cycling, the one-hour record.

When it came to the vote, the UCI approved the Maurice Richard record before issuing a new definition of what constituted a sport bicycle. Such a machine, it decreed, must have a bottom bracket located 24–30 centimetres (9 1/2–11 4/5 inches) above the ground; the front of the saddle could only be 12 centimetres (4 3/4 inches) behind the bottom bracket, and the distance from the bottom bracket to the axle of the front wheel had to be 58–75 centimetres (22 4/5–29 1/2 inches).

Francis Faure at a Paris velodrome in March 1934, travelling at speed on his Velocar.

According to these rules, a recumbent was not a proper bicycle after all despite having two wheels, a chain, handlebars, a seat and human propulsion. This ruling would take effect on 1 April 1934. Many thought that the decision set back the acceptance of a safer and more aerodynamically efficient bicycle by 50 years. The formation of the IHPVA and other organisations dedicated to racing and promoting human-powered vehicles, regardless of their recumbent or upright configuration, is largely responsible for undoing that damage, as the present renaissance of recumbent bicycles so clearly demonstrates.

A new attempt on the record was made in 1933 by Marcel Berthet on a hybrid machine. This was an upright bicycle but with a streamlined fairing more likely to be seen on a recumbent. Berthet was determined to be the first cyclist to break the 50-kilometres-in-one-hour (31-mph) barrier, which he did on 18 November 1933. His record was placed in a special category created by the UCI for 'sport bicycles'.

To placate the vociferous recumbent lobby, a new category called 'Records Set By Human-Powered Vehicles (HPVs) without Special Aerodynamic Features' was created by the UCI. It was in this class that in 1938 Francis Faure and Georges Mochet decided to try to better the record of Marcel Berthet. Faure also determined to be the first cyclist to ride more than 50 kilometres (30 miles) in one hour without aerodynamic components.

So, on the eve of the Second World War, Francis Faure became the first cyclist to travel over 50 kilometres (31 miles) in less than one hour without a pace vehicle. The first timed lap took place with Faure's head exposed and no bottom fairing. Faure achieved 48 kilometres per hour (29.8 miles per hour). He was also able to complete a lap in five minutes – 20 seconds faster than a cyclist on a normal racing bicycle.

This lap speed would not be sufficient to beat the one-hour record, so the Velocar was modified. In the next run the vehicle would have a smaller opening for Faure's head. His average speed rose to 49.7 km/h (30.9 mph), saving an additional 10 seconds per lap. Then a bottom fairing was added for the third attempt. Francis Faure was now able to shave an additional 18 seconds off his lap time. The fourth run took place with the track having been polished. This time Francis Faure beat the 55-km/h (34-mph) mark, requiring only four minutes and 20 seconds for each 4,000-metre (4,375-yard) lap. It was decided to make a determined attempt at the one-hour record with this configuration. It was to be aborted, however, because the wind in his eyes caused Faure to lose control of the vehicle. A fifth attempt was made using a Triplex fairing to enclose Faure's head. It worked fabulously. On 5 March 1939, on the Vincennes Municipal Cycling Track, Faure became the first cyclist to travel 50 kilometres (31 miles) in less than one hour without a pace vehicle. The press went wild, both in Europe and the USA, with pictures of Francis Faure, Georges Mochet and the Velocar appearing in all the bicycling journals.

26: The Hercules
Women Racers

Marguerite Wilson, a great British cycle-racing star of the inter-war years, was arguably the greatest female rider of all time. Wilson, from Bournemouth, started as an amateur in 1935 aged 17. Riding a Hercules she bagged all 16 records in the Women's Road Record Association list. In 1938 she broke three records; the next year she turned professional and went on to break 11 more. The pinnacle of her achievement was to complete the Land's End to John O'Groats marathon in 2 days and 22 hours and 52 minutes. Only the coming of the Second World War brought an end to the racing career of this remarkable woman.

Year:

Manufacturer:
Hercules

Location:
Birmingham

The Hercules, Wilson's cycle of choice, came from a company that was Britain's most successful exporter of cycles. The Hercules Cycle and Motor Cycle Company was founded in September 1910 in Birmingham by two brothers, Edmund and Harry Crane. They chose the name Hercules because of its associations of durability and robustness. The business prospered; by 1928 Hercules was producing one in five of all British cycles exported, and by 1935 no less than 40 per cent of all Britain's total output. The success of Hercules, in contrast to the poor performance of other Birmingham-based manufacturers, was attributed to a number of factors, including both the strong brand name and a highly efficient production line.

Hercules was a great British cycle brand of the early twentieth century and was at its peak in the 1930s.

© Colin Kirsch, www.OldBike.eu/museum

Women in the Saddle

Marguerite Wilson on her Hercules was a true champion, but women had raced cycles long before professional racers like her had appeared. The problem they faced was male disapproval. From the time of the first appearance of the bicycle, men had been suspicious of a lady in the saddle. Not only might these females compete against the men but their appearance in a race was thought to be immodest and more appropriate to the music hall than the race track. In France, watching the curious sight of women on bicycles became a popular pastime for men, particularly in the city of Bordeaux. At first the women appeared not to be able to manage their machines properly, making the spectacle all the more amusing and sometimes salacious as they fell off. Some lady riders soon became adept at the high-wheeler and the cash prices offered by the promoters increased in value as the competition grew hotter.

Marguerite Wilson riding in typical determined fashion.

HERCULEAN SALES FIGURES

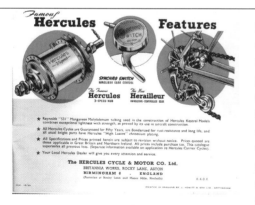

Hercules supplied a great deal more than just a basic machine.

By 1923, Hercules were producing all the components used on their bicycles, apart from the inner tubes and tyres. Their factory used mass-production methods to turn out more than 1,000 cycles a day, with each taking less than ten minutes to assemble. By the time that Marguerite Wilson was reaching the peak of her career in 1933, well over half the bikes produced were being sold abroad. This earned the country £6 million overseas and letters of congratulation from both the King and Prince of Wales. By the end of the 1930s, Hercules had produced well over 6 million bicycles and could claim to be the biggest manufacturer of cycles anywhere in the world.

A colour engraving of a velocipede race in Bordeaux, 1868. Fashion was as important to ladies' races as the matter of who won.

More outlandish contests featuring women on bikes soon appeared. A certain Parisian, Ernestine Bernard, offered a new kind of spectacle when she arrived in Toronto in 1879 and raced against a horse in a three-mile race. What shocked the audience, according to one spectator, were the 'scant garments' that she was wearing, although he thought them 'appropriate for the occasion'. When two other women riders from the Paris Hippodrome performed in London in 1869, a surprised diarist recorded approvingly 'there was nothing indecent in their performance or in the girls' behaviour if you once grant that a woman may, like a man, wear breeches and sit astride in public'.

In the 1890s as attitudes changed, women realised there was a need for practical or 'rational' dress. For cycling, this meant specific cycling costumes characterised by shorter or divided skirts or Turkish trouser-style bloomers. The effect of this more appropriate dress was that women found it easier to pedal their bikes and go faster and often to race against each other, and, if the opportunity occurred, even against a man! This male obsession with female dress for cyclists continued into the twentieth century, affecting even the riders themselves. In 1928 an English lady rider told the *Cycling Touring Club Gazette* that in warm weather she had discarded her skirt and 'ridden through the countryside in a petticoat. I felt cool and refreshed and did not care a jot what anyone thought.'

There were changes in attitudes to other aspects of women cyclists, too. Many doctors no longer thought cycling a health risk to women and instead endorsed it as a healthy exercise for young females. Free at last, many women discovered a natural talent for the bike riding and especially for endurance cycling. By the early 1880s, some women had begun competing against each other in athletic and endurance events such as track cycling in velodromes and even taking part in

Hercules promoted their machines as being available for the whole family.

18- and 24-hour races both in Europe and North America. Some female athletes even dared to compete against the men. Their achievements were covered in newspapers such as *The New York Times*, which reported the story of 24-year-old Jane Yatman, who rode 1,120 kilometres (700 miles) in 81 hours, 5 minutes. Her last 40 kilometres (25 miles) were described as 'torture' for she rode through a drenching rainstorm. Other ladies were content to avoid such challenging experiences and contented themselves with using the bicycle to explore the countryside in a more leisurely manner.

AN EMPOWERING PASTIME

Women's involvement in cycling as a sport was seen as a big step forward by female emancipationists. In the USA, Elizabeth Cady Stanton, a leader in the women's movement, wrote in an 1895 article for the *American Wheelman*, that 'the bicycle will inspire women with more courage, self-respect, self-reliance…'

It was a prophetic statement as women were leaving their homes alone to socialise and cycle on country roads and in parks and becoming more involved in public life. This was a valuable contribution to the campaign for more young women to gain their freedoms together with a feeling of empowerment.

American ladies took to the bicycle as enthusiastically as their European cousins.

Early Women Champions

As more women racers took to the road, their ability in competition became more apparent, particularly in the USA. As early as 1879 Lizzie Balmer had raced 29.7 kilometres (18.5 miles) in two hours at a display in San Francisco. Two years later, Elsa von Blumen of New York rode 1,600 kilometres (1,000 miles) in a six-day marathon in Pittsburgh. The following year in Boston, Louise Armaindo, albeit within a generous head start, almost beat the male American champion John Prince in a 80-kilometre (50-mile) race.

Gradually, the numbers of women joining cycling associations increased, as did their participation in touring and racing. This trend was helped by the availability of lighter bicycles and the fashion for less cumbersome clothing. In Britain in 1925 a Mrs Du Heave was the only female rider in the Reading Wheelers 12-hour race, yet she came in third. This success inspired the foundation of the Rosslyn Ladies Cycling Club, where she again triumphed, winning their 12-hour event with a distance of 330 kilometres (205 miles). Women like Mrs Du Heave eventually came together in 1934 to found the Women's Road Record Association to document the best performances of women riders. The first champion of this small group was Lilian Dredge, who, riding a Claude Butler, broke six records including the women's Land's End to John O'Groats.

The success of these early female racers and particularly that of Marguerite Wilson had inspired women riders throughout the world, yet it was not until the Los Angeles Olympics of 1984 that a women's road race was included. American champions at the time included Sue Novara-Reber, who won seven consecutive world championships. She was followed by Connie

Some ladies took up the cycling challenge with enthusiasm. One even matched herself against a racehorse... and won.

Beryl Burton was a British and world champion racer in the 1960s, pictured here (centre) after winning the 1967 Cycling World Cup in Heerlen.

Paraskevin-Young, Beth Heiden, Connie Carpenter-Phinney and Rebecca Twigg. In Europe, Maria Canins of Italy and Jeannie Longo of France were dominant. Between 1985 and 1995 Longo won three women's Tour de France and five world championships, together with setting a woman's one-hour record of just over 45 kilometres (28 miles).

For the British there was Eileen Sheridan, who was also a Hercules rider and broke a large number of records riding for Hercules between 1952 and 1954. However, it was Beryl Burton who finally took the place of the great Marguerite Wilson in the 1970s. In the course of a career that spanned five decades, the fiercely competitive Yorkshirewoman won seven world titles, two road race championships and five track pursuit titles. She also won 96 national titles, 12 road race championships, 13 pursuit titles and 71 time-trial titles. A maverick and a loner, Burton supervised her own training, only rode in the races she wanted to and had little contact with the sport's governing bodies. What was most satisfying to her fellow women cyclists was that she regularly beat the men that she was competing against.

In 1967, she overtook and beat Mike McNamara in an Otley CC 12-hour time trial on her way to setting a women's record of 446.19 kilometres (277.25 miles). This achievement is all the more significant given that McNamara's distance of 445.02 kilometres (276.52 miles) in the same event was itself a new men's record. The next year, in 1968, she set a women's 160-kilometre (100-mile) record in a time of 3 hours and 55 minutes. It was the fourth fastest ride over that distance in Britain by any rider of the time. Such feats in another, more popular, sport would have earned Burton worldwide recognition. Folklore about Burton was endless; one story claimed that as she overtook McNamara, she nonchalantly offered him one of her liquorice allsorts!

'Beryl Burton is the greatest British sportsperson you've probably never heard of.'

– Maxine Peake, actress (2012)

27: Bartell Special
Six-Day Racers

Six-day cycle racing had its origins in Britain in the nineteenth century before its popularity spread to the rest of Europe and the USA. In the early days, an individual competed on the track alone and the winner would be the rider who completed the most laps. The format was then changed to a two-man team, with one man racing while the other rested. What made it such a gruelling sport was that it originally took place over a 24-hour period. Later, a six-day race comprised six nights of racing with the riders competing from 6 p.m. to 2 a.m. – still a massive endurance test, nevertheless.

Year:
1935

Manufacturer:
Bartell

Location:
USA

In a six-day race, the overall winners would, naturally, be the team that completed the most laps in the full time period. Where the teams ended level on laps, the team with the most points gained from intermediate competitions would be the winner. One of the stars of six-day racing in the late 1920s and early 1930s was the Czechoslovakia-born Frank Bartell, riding his own Bartell Special. A professional track racer, in 1935 Bartell set the human-powered land speed record, covering a mile at an average speed of 129.5 kilometres (80.5 miles) per hour. Bartell went on to produce his own hand-built machines, but never developed it into a volume business.

Bartell's 1926 Appelhans bike. The Bartell Special was one of the finest track bikes of the inter-war years.

Spectator appeal came from these intermediate competitions and usually included a mixture of time trials, motor-paced sections and sprint and elimination races. In the main race or 'Madison', named after Madison Square Garden where the two-man format began, a rider from each team would be on the track at the same time, taking it in turns to race and then 'hand-slinging' their teammate back into the action.

Frank Bartell on the machine that he largely designed himself.

The precursor to a British six-day cycle race was an individual time trial held at the Agricultural Hall in Islington, London, in 1878. A professional rider called David Stanton offered a bet that he could cover 1,600 kilometres (1,000 miles) in six successive days by riding 18 hours a day. A Mr Davis put up £100 and the stake was held by the *Sporting Life* newspaper. Stanton started at 6 a.m. on 25 February and won the bet in 73 hours, riding on a high-wheeled machine at an average speed of 22 km/h (13.5 mph). So popular was the event that another was held the following year in the same hall. It was hoped to attract a big crowd of 20,000 a day. The local newspaper, the *Islington Gazette*, was happy to promote the event, reporting that, 'A bicycle contest was commenced at the Agricultural Hall, on Monday last, for which £150 is offered in prizes for a six days' competition.' The race started at 6 a.m. with only four of the 12 individual entrants on the track. As in the earlier race, riders could join in when they chose and sleep as they wished. The winner was a Bill Cann from Sheffield, who led from start to finish of the 1,705 kilometres (1,060 miles) covered.

A TEST OF ENDURANCE

The amount of cycling stamina needed for six-day racing is enormous, even when contrasted with the Tour de France. In the modern Tour the competitors cover about 3,540 kilometres (2,200 miles) in 20 or more days. In a typical indoor six-day cycle race of the past, each team would ride 4,500 kilometres (2,800 miles) in less than a week. This display of endurance attracted many spectators in the first part of the twentieth century in Europe and the USA.

A Gladiatorial Sport

While six-day racing gained popularity in Europe, it was to find its true home in the USA around 1890. The American stars became so proficient that they were often invited to compete in Europe. This was the age of dance marathons and flagpole sitting, when spectacle was all-important. Six-day cycle racing offered that and more, with men competing against each other in a contest of athletic endurance. There were problems with the riders' stamina, for in a single day, a cyclist would ride for as many hours as his body and mind would allow. Sometimes the exhaustion caused such delirium that *The New York Times* felt obliged to declare: 'An athletic contest in which the participants "go queer" in their heads, and strain their powers until their faces become hideous with the tortures that rack them, is not sport, it is brutality.'

Six-day racing was becoming a gladiatorial sport. While early races required cyclists to ride for 18 hours a day, the circus-like competition soon degenerated into a non-stop 144-hour fiasco. Cyclists were pushed well beyond the point of exhaustion, while bands played alongside and spectators gambled on the results. The crowd in the grandstands showed a morbid fascination, hoping to see one of the riders collapse and crash to the ground. The *Brooklyn Daily Eagle* was disgusted that: 'The wear and tear upon their nerves and their muscles, and the loss of sleep make them peevish and fretful. If their desires are not met with on the moment, they break forth with a stream of abuse. Nothing pleases them. These outbreaks do not trouble the trainers with experience, for they understand the condition the men are in.' The condition included riders suffering delusions and hallucinations before they wobbled and fell.

When Teddy Hale won a race in 1896, he finished looking 'like a ghost, his face as white as a corpse, his eyes no longer visible because they'd retreated into his skull'. These sadistic spectacles disgusted many people and such was the outcry against the dangers of a solo six-day race that in 1898 both New

SETTING THE PACE

Pacing by a car or motorbike was a feature of six-day racing. The motorised vehicle took away the effects of the head wind, allowing the bike to reach far higher speeds. Later it fell out of favour as kit was thought to compromise the simplicity of the sport, a contest of endurance between riders, as well as hiding the cyclist from the spectators.

The reason why riders were prepared to endure the suffering was simply because they were well paid, particularly when crowd numbers increased as the riders' condition deteriorated. Promoters in New York paid Teddy Hale the huge sum of $5,000 when he won in 1896. By the 1930s the sport had reached its peak of popularity in Europe and, as in the USA, was a great money earner for the promoters. In 1935, the German six-day specialist Walter Sawall had become so wealthy that he owned several villas as well as a private plane. Sawall was one of the richest professional sportsmen of his day.

Six-day racing was a gruelling business, with riders having to fight against accumulated fatigue.

York and Chicago introduced laws forbidding cyclists from racing for more than 12 hours a day. In order to get round these laws, promoters paired up riders into two-man teams, at least one of whom was required to be on the track at all times while the other man rested or took refreshments by the side of the track. This new 'Madison' racing style caught on across the country and gave six-day racing an air of legitimacy. This new style of six-day racing then appeared in Europe, with the first race with two-man teams taking place outdoors at Toulouse in France in 1906.

Six-day races continued to do well in Germany until the Nazis came to power and banned the sport, although it continued in Belgium and France. After the war, six-day racing began again in Europe. The first in Germany for 17 years was held in 1950 and the following year it returned to Wembley in London. Races continued throughout the night, as they had in the USA, but the costs of keeping stadiums open in a time of austerity proved too much. It was abandoned altogether when racing made a brief reappearance at Earls Court in 1967. The following year at Wembley a new organiser, Ron Webb, scheduled just afternoon and evening racing with a break between each session. Other organisers were not impressed and insisted Webb simply call his race a 'six' rather than a true 'six-day' event. Yet one by one, all Europe's promoters were forced to follow suit and today there are now no old-style 24-hour races left, the last having being held in Madrid in 1968.

28: Schulz's Funiculo
Early Mountain Climber

The French have enjoyed a long affair with the bicycle since the early nineteenth century. Cycling became not only the national sport in France, but also a national passion. This was most apparent in the 1930s when there was a significant reaction against the flood of increasingly mass-produced cycles on the market. Among cyclists there was a renewed interest in designing and producing more hand-built machines for both touring and track racing. An attempt to meet this demand came from Jacques Schulz, of Colombes near Paris, one of the most inventive designers of the time.

Year:
1935

Manufacturer:
Schulz

Location:
France

J acques Schulz set out to produce his own version of a 'flexible' cycle, which he called the Funiculo. It was designed so that it could be used in all environments, from track to road or even field.

In producing the Funiculo, Schulz was following the pattern of his fellow French *constructeurs*, who built not only their custom-made frames but also many of their own components, such as brakes, stems, fitments, hubs and gear changers. What Schulz set out to change was the fact that many of the contemporary so-called touring bikes were basically racing frames with some touring parts bolted on almost as an afterthought. He felt that his task was to produce a proper French long-distance amateur bicycle that was conceived as a functional whole. Each of the necessary features would be carefully thought out and incorporated into the frame design itself. The result would be a beautifully designed, elegant and innovative piece of engineering.

The Funiculo was an attempt to combine multi-functions in one machine.

Schulz was not alone in his ambition. Many other French cycles of the 1930s featured such advanced ideas as internal brake cables and lighting cables, braze-ons for shift levers and front derailleurs, cartridge bottom bracket bearings, cantilever brakes, oval chain rings, and quick-release mechanisms for hubs and brakes. Many of these components were made out of lightweight aluminium. The result was not only a good-looking machine but a light one, too. Many of these bikes weighed 11–14 kilograms (24–30 pounds) and that included all the equipment needed for a long-distance tourer with its panniers and lights. Such a light bicycle is comparable in weight to some of the best bikes made today.

Climbing with Ease

By the end of 1935, Jacques Schulz had produced both a dramatic-looking new standard bicycle and a tandem version. Recognition by the cycling press was not slow in coming. In 1937 a French cycling magazine described the Funiculo as having *l'armature souple*, a flexible frame that was visibly the most radical aspect of the machine. Yet the novel gear system on the Funiculo was perhaps its most attractive feature. It was able to cope with sprockets featuring up to 40 teeth, meaning that the bike with its single chain ring at the front was able to climb mountains easily. In this respect, the Funiculo can be seen as the true precursor of the mountain bike that would be developed in the USA after the Second World War.

Schulz's ingenuity can be seen throughout the bike. The Funiculo's front brake was particularly innovative and proved a highly effective solution to an old problem. The brake system was of an unusual design, with the rear brake activated through two cables running in parallel inside the frame as in other French designs of the time. The arms, however, were not pivoted in the traditional sense. Smaller non-mechanical details also displayed touches of Schulz's creative design sense. For instance, the cover in front of the seat tube was used for stowing the bicycle pump.

> 'There's not a moment where you don't think about being president – unless you're riding mountain bikes as hard as you possibly can.'
>
> – George W. Bush (2013)

Not everything turned out to be a total success. For all its customised special features, the Funiculo was poorly shod, coming equipped with only the standard tyres of the time. These could be easily punctured by glass splinters or nails. For such an extraordinary high-end bike, it is astonishing that ordinary road detritus could be allowed to pose a threat. For this reason its performance across country or as a mountain bike would have been very limited.

The Funiculo may have been a commercial disappointment, but looks alone made it a very distinctive machine much sought after by later collectors. Today there are just three Schulz bicycles still known to exist in Europe and only one of them can still be ridden.

29: Köthke
Track Tandem

In the early days of cycling, it was soon established that although a bike could be fast, a tandem could be faster and a tandem track racer even faster still. Before their decline in popularity after the Second World War, tandem racers continued to be made in Europe. One of the most respected was made by the German company owned by Fritz Köthke in Cologne. His frames were used by amateurs and professionals alike.

Year: 1928

Manufacturer:
Köthke

Location:
Cologne

Modern racing tandems such as this Matrix incorporate all the technical advances made in bicycle design.

U nlike his rivals, Fritz Köthke was more of a merchant than a frame builder, shipping all the parts he needed for his lightweights mainly from Britain and the United States. His focus on using only the highest-quality components and materials ensured that his lightweight racing tandems were highly sought after.

The high-speed capability of machines like the Köthke made tandem racing a particularly exciting and spectacular sport to watch. The downside was that with the tremendous speed and power of the tandem came the risk of devastating accidents. Many a tandem sprint team ended up in hospital; public disapproval led to the sport's disappearance from the Olympic Games and, later, from America's velodrome schedules. Eventually, the tandem sprint became almost entirely an exhibition piece and was confined to the slower speed events and to the Paralympics.

In recent years tandem racing has become a popular event at the Paralympics, where it first appeared at Seoul in 1988. One of its strengths is that it pairs the riders together for mutual support. The blind or visually impaired cyclist rides behind while the unimpaired rider acts as the sighted 'pilot' in the front. This allows the rear rider to really concentrate on maximising his cycling performance. At the London 2012 Paralympics Anthony Kappes and Craig MacLean won gold in an all-British tandem sprint final.

Cyclists Jiri Chyba and sightless Marek Mofla riding a Duratec track tandem. Tandem racing is one of the most popular of all Olympic (and Paralympic) cycling sports.

Yet between the 1920s and 1950s the tandem enjoyed great popularity. Off the track the tandem became a popular machine for both touring and road racing. It was made even more attractive as lighter and stronger tandems came onto the market. As an Olympic sport it remained on the schedules from 1906 to 1972. Typical of the excitement that tandem racing could generate was the final of the 1928 Olympics in Amsterdam. The Dutch pair faced the British favourites, who led the race until the final corner, when the Dutch overtook them to win the gold.

Breaking Records

As with the single bicycle, the ultimate tandem test was the one-hour record. In 1936, Maurice Richard of France and his partner, riding a Delange racing tandem, became the first pair to push the record beyond 45 kilometres (28 miles) with a new record of 48.668 kilometres (30.241 miles) in the hour. Cycles Delange, which sponsored the attempt, was a Paris-based company specialising in high-end cycles and with a catalogue that claimed that 56 world records had been broken using their machines.

The following year the record fell to an English duo, Ernie Mills and Bill Paul, who had set the British 12-hour record on a tandem in 1934 and re-established it in 1936 with a 'world's best performance'. Riding at the same stadium in Italy as Richard, the Velodromo Comunale Vigorelli, they set a new world tandem hour record of 49.991 kilometres (31.06 miles). This record was to stand until September 2000 when at Manchester Velodrome it was beaten by Simon Keeton and Jon Rickard of Rutland Cycling Club.

30: Derailleurs
Racing Gears

Throughout the nineteenth century, cyclists longed for an efficient gearing system that would allow them to maximise speed whatever the gradient. Before derailleurs came into use, racing cycles had double-sided rear hubs with up to two cogs on each side. Changing gears meant the rider had to dismount, loosen the wing nuts that held the rear wheel, turn the wheel around to use a different sized cog, remount the chain, and then tighten the nuts again. As with tyre changes on modern Formula One cars, choosing the right time to change was a critical part of racing tactics. A better solution was needed.

Year:

1938

Manufacturer:
Simplex

Location:
Paris

Campagnolo. One of the three most important gear systems in the history of cycling.

To overcome this problem, various derailleur systems were designed and built, some using steel rods to move the chain from one gear to another. These early derailleurs had their jockey wheel mounted on a bracket brazed to the chain stay. Among them was one designed by the cycling journalist Paul de Vivie, who in 1905 invented a two-speed rear derailleur that he used for riding in the Alps.

Early Gear Changers

A passionate advocate of cycling, de Vivie rode his first high-wheeler at the age of 28, and soon sold his silk business to start a bike shop. He also founded the magazine *Le Cycliste* in 1887, where he wrote under the nom de plume 'Velocio', touting the joys and benefits of cycling. A tireless inventor, he was convinced that geared bikes, then an oddity, were the future of cycling. Though existing gear-changers were awkward and unreliable, Velocio was undeterred.

He spent much time inventing various gearing schemes. Through his efforts in both engineering and publicity, the derailleur was ultimately perfected, and a relatively dependable version was produced by Tulli.

The disadvantage of these early derailleurs was that the jockey wheel had to be sufficiently far forward to clear the largest sprocket. Therefore, it was a long distance from the small sprockets, so that changes between the high gears were slow and required considerable overshoot.

The great names among French derailleurs are Simplex and Huret, rivals with similar products. From 1938 to 1954 they had few competitors from other rear-mounted derailleurs until the Italian company Campagnolo set standards in design and quality that were difficult to match. Eventually, both Huret and Simplex abandoned their regular designs for Campagnolo's parallelogram innovation, the principle of which is still current today.

Simplex and Hurer were the leading French gear manufacturers from the 1930s.

Before the coming of multiple chain wheels, the single jockey rear mechanism design was very popular. These were snappy in action and coped perfectly with close ratios; moreover, they were less fiddly when removing the rear wheel for a fast tyre change. However, multiple chain wheels demanded an additional means of taking up the chain slack and this introduced the double-jockey mechanism. It came with the Simplex Tour de France and a similar design by Huret. The Simplex and Huret front mechanisms were simple and highly effective. Unlike today's mechanisms, which are operated by a convenient lever mounted on the frame down tube or on the handlebar, these early changers were operated directly by the rider dropping his arm to just above the chain wheel, where an operating rod shifted the gear from one chain wheel to the next.

A PROBLEM FOR DERAILLEURS

Progress in the development of derailleur gears was not helped when they were banned from the Tour de France between 1919 and 1937. During those years, derailleurs were not generally allowed in road races because they required freewheeling. Mixing riders with fixed and freewheels produced problems on the turns; fixed-gear riders were limited by pedal scrape on the turns, while freewheeled riders were not. However, there was also a series of special races for derailleur-equipped bicycles, typically hill climbs, that were sponsored, at least in part, by the derailleur manufacturers.

Return to the Tour. The parallelogram derailleur. This system offered a new efficiency in gearing.

Another more viable system had appeared in 1928 with the introduction of the Super Champion gear from a company founded by the champion cyclist Oscar Egg, and the Vittoria Margherita gear. These derailleurs employed chain-stay-mounted 'paddles' and single-lever chain tensioners mounted near or on the down tube. Both these systems, together with the rod-operated Campagnolo Cambio Corsa, were eventually superseded by parallelogram derailleurs. A welcome boost to development came in 1937 when derailleurs were again allowed back into the Tour de France. However, they did not become common road-racing equipment until 1938 when Simplex introduced a cable-shifted derailleur. This was the next generation of derailleurs, with a jockey wheel that moved both in and out to change gear, and forwards and backwards to follow the change, in sprocket sizes.

A MORE SOPHISTICATED SIMPLEX

The Simplex used a cage very like those often used today, where the cage pivot is behind and below the shaft for the jockey wheel. The problem with this design was that the bushing was really too short for its required diameter and stroke; if dirt entered the sliding fit, the shifting became difficult. The big advantage that the Simplex had over its rivals was a second chain-tensioning spring and pivot at the upper end of the main arm. This spring-loaded pivot ensured that the upper pulley remained close to the sprockets, irrespective of sprocket size. The close coupling of pulley and sprocket ensured crisp gear changes.

The Campagnolo Derailleur

Another leading name in the evolution of derailleurs was Campagnolo of Vicenza, in Italy. As a young racing cyclist, Tullio Campagnolo had been crossing the Croce d'Aune pass in the 1927 Gran Premio della Vittoria race. Needing to remove his rear wheel to change gears he found the large wing nuts so frozen that his cold hands could not budge them. This was the standard road-racing gearing system until 1938. It comprised the double-sided hub, usually known as the 'fixed and free'. That is, the hub was threaded for a freewheel on one side and a fixed gear on the other. The cogs were chosen so that the cyclist had a relatively high fixed gear for the flatter parts of the course and a relatively low free-wheel for the climbs and descents. For some events that did not involve such steep descents, the riders preferred a double fixed wheel, fixed on each side. The cyclist dismounted, as Campagnolo had done, loosened the wing nuts that held the rear wheel, turned the wheel around, remounted the chain, and tightened the nuts again. The nuts were also used, probably more frequently, when changing flats.

'Something must change in the rear.'

– Tullio Campagnolo (1940)

That day Campagnolo may have lost the race but he vowed to make sure that gear technology would change. So he went back to his workshop and in 1930 introduced the first quick-release hub, answering the challenge he had made to himself three years earlier. Then, in 1940, he invented the dual-rod Cambio Corsa shifter. This consisted of two levers and rods, attached to the right-side seat stay. One of the levers actuated the quick release on the rear wheel; the other operated a fork-like device that moved the chain from side to side. There were no jockey pulleys or other take-up mechanisms on the chain.

Staying ahead. Campagnolo Cambio Shifter of the 1940s.

The rear dropouts were horizontal and somewhat longer than they are today, since 'slack' in the chain was taken up by allowing the wheel to move backwards and forwards. There then followed the Roubaix shifter, which combined the quick release and chain mover into a single lever. The shifting was archaic by today's standards, but it was widely used in the professional peloton for at least a decade, until the introduction of Campagolo's Gran Sport derailleur in 1951.

Following the Second World War, the Campagnolo derailleur became standard for racers, used by such great names as Fausto Coppi and Gino Bartali. These Campagnolo cable-operated, parallelogram systems are still used on today's bicycles. Campagnolo offered more – a complete drivetrain group set that included the derailleurs, shifters, hub, cassette and chain. Along with the parallelogram rear derailleur, Campagnolo invented the parallelogram front derailleur. The combination proved unconquerable. For decades, most racing bicycles and all bicycles where price was no object were always Campagnolo. Before that, the typical front derailleur was just a fork on a pivot that extended forwards from the seat tube, with its upper arm extending up to a handle. The rider reached between his knees and flipped the fork over.

Tullio Campagnolo's emergence as the definitive component manu-facturer was due in large part to the man himself, and to his concept of linking the producer and the end user. Foreshadowing the R&D of today's companies, Tullio began following the races personally, listening to the suggestions of the riders and modifying the products to meet their needs.

A Shift in the Right Direction

In 1949 another advance was made in derailleur history when the modern parallelogram movement replaced the sliding bushing. This was later modified by Suntour, who 15 years later, in 1964, improved the design with the 'slant-parallelogram' version – the slant allowing the jockey wheel to stay a roughly equal distance from the sprockets regardless of their size and much improving gear changing. The problem was that it was often necessary to change gears 'approximately' and then make a small adjustment to correct, which slowed down the whole gear-changing process. Also, it limited the number of gears it was possible to have, since the adjustment between the gears needed was quite broad. This system continued for about 20 years. It worked very well but had one drawback – changing gears depended on moving a lever that changed the tension in the cable and thus pulled ('derailed') the chain to the appropriate socket.

Once the patents expired, the other manufacturers adopted this design, at least for their better derailleurs. Before the 1990s many manufacturers also made derailleurs, including Simplex, Huret, Galli, Mavic, Gipiemme, Zeus, Suntour and Shimano. However, the successful introduction and promotion of indexed shifting by Shimano in 1985 required a compatible system of shift levers, derailleur, cogset, chain rings, chain, shift cable and shift housing. This need for compatibility increased the use of group sets made by one company, and was one of the factors that drove the other manufacturers out of the market. Today Campagnolo and Shimano are the two main manufacturers of derailleurs, with Campagnolo making only road cycling derailleurs and Shimano making both road and off-road. American manufacturer SRAM has been an important third, specialising in derailleurs for mountain bikes, and in 2006 they introduced a drivetrain system for road bicycles.

The latest development in the technology is the use of electronic gear changes, with the significant advantage of providing very exact gear changes and a reduction in the amount of cables required. In spite of all these advances in gearing, there are still many cyclists who prefer to use a single fixed gear on their bike, with no option to change gears regardless of terrain. This, they argue, aids training and provides a more authentic cycling experience.

More complexity. As time passed, gear systems gained ever more cogs.

31: Baines VS 37
A 1930s Classic

The Baines VS 37 was a classic British racing bicycle of the 1930s, designed by Reg and Willie Baines. The number 37 refers to the size of the wheelbase in inches. Nicknamed the Whirlwind and later the Flying Gate, it was one of the iconic machines of its era. The Baines brothers were not too keen on the moniker that was applied to their short-wheelbase frame design, but the public seemed to like it and it stuck. Such was the attraction of the Baines that later models became highly desirable items for those who collected historic bicycles.

Year:

Manufacturer:
Baines

Location:
Eccleshill

This was an era of relative prosperity for makers like Baines, for in the years following the First World War the bicycle was adopted across British society and the practice of cycling become normal. Cycling became the means by which vast numbers of ordinary people took to the roads and escaped from the towns and cities at weekends.

The Baines family, who became part of the post-war cycle boom, had a long history in the cycle trade before Willie and his brother took over the business in 1924. While leafing through an old bicycle design book one day, Reg came across the details of a bike with a very steep seat tube and short chain stays. This, he was convinced, was relevant to the contemporary debate on how to make a frame that would help a bike go faster. Correspondence in cycling

Baines VS 37.
Sturdy British classic
of the 1930s.

The Bayliss Wylie hub. A key feature of the Baines bicycle.

magazines argued that shorter chain stays would produce a frame that was more efficient because the bottom bracket flexed less. Baines began work on such a design; instead of the conventional curved seat pin, he thought it neater to continue the top tube beyond the seat tube and then mount the seat pin on the end in a short dummy seat tube supported by an extra pair of seat stays.

The new frame design for the VS 37 first appeared in *Cycling* in November 1936, just before the company went into low-run production. There was a positive response from cyclists and, as demand grew, the Baines brothers were able to open two more manufacturing units. The frame design was complicated and required a great deal of precision in production. The lugs were hand-cut and the frame demanded correct mitring and clean brazing. Special bottom bracket shells and top seat tube lugs were cast by Vaughans in Birmingham to accommodate the vertical seat tube.

FLYING TO SUCCESS

By 1938 there were three Flying Gate models: the original VS 37, the V38 and an International TT model. This later model was created after Jack Fancourt won the 1937 Isle of Man TT mass-start race on a Flying Gate frame. The International TT model used the same frame design as the VS 37 but with a longer 100-centimetre (39 ½-inch) wheelbase more suitable for road racing and derailleur gears. This model was raced with many successes by Jack Fancourt and Jack Holmes at mass-start races at Brooklands and Donnington in 1938 and 1939 and at the 1938 World Championships in Valkenburg.

The Second World War brought things to a halt, but once it was over frame production restarted at Baines. It was now largely confined to one model, the Whirlwind. This was a customised machine built with a wheelbase and frame design tailored to the rider's wishes. In the post-war years it was not possible to get the special bottom bracket shells and special seat tube lugs cast, so when supplies ran out fillet brazing was used instead.

The Flying Gate Revisited

Although Baines stopped production in 1953, the Flying Gate design was resurrected in the late 1970s by another Englishman, Trevor Jarvis, who acquired the rights to the design. Jarvis's love affair with the Flying Gate Bicycle began when he renovated one and found that the bike seemed to go like the wind. The difference between this bicycle and others he had ridden, he said, was quite remarkable. Jarvis was a design engineer and keen cyclist who had his own small engineering company in Burton-on-Trent. As a cyclist, he wanted to start building bicycle frames alongside his engineering operation, but realised that with many long-established businesses in the industry, he would have to come up with something exceptional if T. J. Cycles were to become a recognised brand.

This time, however, the bike was simply called the Flying Gates. Quite a number were produced in the late 1970s and early 1980s at T. J. Cycles in Burton-on-Trent. Some of these were intended for time trialling; others were made for touring. In 1984, Jarvis moved production to Tenbury Wells, where production continues to this day in small quantities. Many of Trevor's frames feature very fancy hand-cut lugwork and some feature wheelbases as short as 89 centimetres (35 inches).

There were many distinctive touches in the Baines, not least the decorative style of the gear-change lever. It gave an almost personal and hand-built touch to the machine.

Baines was only one of a number of very capable bike manufacturers operating in 1930s Britain. Another was F. W. Evans; he was not himself a frame-builder but rather a man of ideas and a bike-shop proprietor. He was editor of *Cycling* magazine for a couple of years in the very early 1920s before setting up his first bike shop in 1922 in London. One of the features of the new Baines design was the double fixed hub with two fixed sprockets – one on either side of the wheel, which was turned around to give two different ratios. The problem was that this was always a slightly fiddly job as the chain tension had to be got just right. Another contemporary of Baines was William Rathbone 'Rath' Pashley, who founded Pashley and Barber in Birmingham. He declared in a confident sales message that they were 'manufacturers of every type of cycle' and that 'Birmingham produces the finest cycles, these are Birmingham's best'.

Pashley Guv'nor.
A British machine that challenged the supremacy of the Baines.

What the Flying Gate design had to offer from the very beginning was that, apart from its use in racing, the frame was ideally suited for touring because of its rigid construction and firm ride. The machine could handle heavy loads and climb hills exceptionally well due to the frame's rigidity. Yet the frame was always very responsive because the wheelbase was shorter, due to the vertical tube allowing the rear wheel to move closer to the bottom bracket, shortening the drive and making the bicycle more positive. A vertical tube takes the sideward thrust from the cranks far better than a sloping seat tube.

Another advantage of the Flying Gate design is that the small-diameter struts from the rear dropouts to the vertical tube hold it absolutely firm, so eliminating the whip between the head and the seat when the bicycle is loaded up for touring. These struts add very little additional weight because the tube is smaller in diameter than a conventional seat tube. The clever part is that the top tube can be made to any length without altering the geometry of the frame. This means it is almost infinitely variable to suit cyclists of all heights and is especially advantageous on tandem frames.

32: Bianchi
The Great Fausto Coppi

One of the sporting heroes who helped restore the Italian nation's battered self-esteem after the Second World War was the great cyclist Fausto Coppi on his favourite racing machine, the Bianchi, painted in the Bianchi colour of turquoise green. Coppi's cycle was said to be always as immaculately turned out as one of its rider's own suits. Apart from their distinctive racing colour, Bianchi are true legends of the road bike world. One of Italy's oldest cycle companies, they were established in 1885 in Via Nirone in Milan.

Year: 1952

Manufacturer:
Bianchi

Location:
Milan

E doardo Bianchi's first big idea, conceived over a century ago, was to reduce the diameter of the front wheel of his bike and balance the gap of the motion with the addition of a chain, and then to lower it down to the height of the pedals.

This was the start of Bianchi's version of a safety cycle. He followed it with another machine, reducing the wheel diameter further and giving it front and rear wheels almost of the same size. With production on stream, Bianchi gained his first international sporting success in 1899, when Tomaselli won the Grand Prix de la Ville de Paris. By the time that Fausto Coppi was old enough to ride a racing bike, Bianchi was the most important name in Italian sport.

The Making of a Legend

Fausto himself was born on 15 September 1919 to a poor farming family and left home to work for a butcher some 20 kilometres (12 miles) away. Even at this early age his extraordinary talent was already on display. As he rode to work every day on a bicycle, he pedalled so fast that he sprinted past many serious amateur riders on the road. One of the first to recognise his potential as a rider was masseur and former cycling team manager Biagio Cavanna. Under Cavanna's tutelage, Coppi made rapid progress, turning professional in 1940 and riding for the Legnano team, and then claiming his first victory in the Giro d'Italia at just 20 years old. In 1942 he set a world hour record of 45.798 kilometres (28.458 miles) that stood for 14 years until it was broken by Jacques Anquetil in 1956.

Coppi joined the Italian army when the war began and found that the officers were very lenient to him in the hope that he would keep in training on his bike. In March 1943 he was sent to North Africa, where he was taken prisoner by the British Army. Kept in a prison camp, he was given odd jobs to do and by chance met a British cyclist, who was astonished to find the great Fausto Coppi cutting his hair. Having seen him in cycling magazines the British soldier knew exactly who his famous hairdresser was. When the war ended Coppi returned to cycling and joined Bianchi's team, with which he would always be associated. Although Coppi was a great athlete, he was fragile physically. He possessed a massive rib cage and an exceptional heart but had a delicate skeleton that contrasted with his well-developed thighs. His brittle bones were the result of malnutrition as a boy. During his racing career he suffered more than 20 serious bone fractures including to the collar bone, pelvis, femur and a displaced vertebrae.

Perhaps this physical frailty made him a pioneer of more rigorous training methods. As well as these physical routines, he preferred a radical diet that ignored the traditional cyclist's breakfast of steak. Coppi suffered from digestive problems and a sensitive stomach, making him prone to pick up any illness that was going round. For this reason he preferred to eat small amounts often. He would avoid protein and preferred carbohydrates.

Everything in Coppi's life was as meticulously planned as his diet. Racing tactics were carefully examined and his back-up team thoroughly briefed. Each race was treated with military efficiency; key points would be identified in every stage and the right place chosen at which he would attack his rivals. His equipment was always in perfect condition.

Straight from the race. Fausto Coppi's weather-beaten Bianchi.

A Champion in a Great Era

Fausto Coppi's big adventure with Bianchi started in 1940, with his first victory at the Giro d'Italia. His second triumph occurred in 1942, when he took the world one-hour record. Then, two years after the war ended, Coppi became world champion in the pursuit race and also gained his second Giro d'Italia. Those who watched him race to victory were convinced that much of his success was due to his smooth pedalling style, which has been described as being near 'perfect'. He was certainly a mixture of contradictions and his early attack in the 1949 Giro d'Italia showed what a maverick he could be. Such an early move with 190 kilometres (118 miles) still to go may have seemed crazy at the time, but his success fully justified his self-belief, unbelievable stamina and unique racing instinct.

That stamina was to make Coppi a champion during one of cycling's great eras. His record is extraordinary, with five victories in the Giro d'Italia and his first Tour de France win in 1949. On that occasion, everybody assumed that he was already out of the contest, having crashed badly during the Saint Malò stage, which earned him a huge delay penalty. Instead of giving up, he managed to gain one hour over the Frenchman Marinelli, the race leader. He also caught up with Bartali, who finished second. Coppi was to win the Tour de France again in 1952, dominating the competition.

At the time there were two Italian cycling heroes, Fausto Coppi and Gino Bartali, and both were followed closely by the Italian media. Bartali was the incumbent Italian champion when Coppi first came on the scene and they were to share a rivalry for nearly 15 years. Bartali was the conservative, religious one who was venerated in the rural south of Italy, while Coppi was the more worldly one, obsessed with the latest training methods, and hero of the industrial north. The two referred to each other as 'that one' and 'the other one', and battled through the Giro d'Italia, Tour de France and numerous one-day classics in an epic struggle for athletic superiority and the hearts of Italy.

MILAN–SAN REMO, 1946

One of Coppi's greatest victories was in the 1946 Milan–San Remo race. He attacked with nine other riders just 5 kilometres (3 miles) into the 292-kilometre (181-mile) race. On the climb up the Turchino mountain, Coppi dropped the nine riders; he went on to win by 14 minutes over the second placed rider and by 18.30 over Gino Bartali and the rest of the peloton. Coppi's victories in the 1950 Paris–Roubaix and 1953 World Championship Road Race capped off a brilliant career. From 1957 his career declined, although he was still attracting big appearance money due to past achievements. By 1952 Coppi had virtually no rivals who could touch him when he was in his best form. He won the Tour by a staggering 28 minutes and was totally untouchable not only in the mountains but also in the time trials.

Their racing lives became entwined in 7 January 1940 when Eberardo Pavesi, head of the Legnano team, took on Coppi to ride for Bartali. Coppi, who was meant to be the assistant, won the Giro and Bartali, the star, had to follow on behind with the rest of the team. In the 1948 world championship in the Netherlands, both climbed off their bikes rather than help each other after an incident. This provoked condemnation from the Italian cycling association, which claimed that both men had forgotten to honour the Italian prestige they represented as they were concerned only with personal rivalry. Both were suspended for three months. It appeared that a thaw in the relationship might have set in when they shared a bottle on the Col d'Izoard in the 1952 Tour, but the two fell out over who had offered it.

Fausto Coppi's greatest losses, however, were in his private life, with the tragic death of his younger brother Serse in 1951, followed by scandal surrounding an adulterous affair. His own premature death from malaria at the age of 40 was strangely appropriate for a man who had tempted fate and been dogged by scandal.

It may be foolish to compare riders from different eras, but cycling writer Bill McGann upholds that if Fausto Coppi were not the greatest rider of all time, then he was second only to Eddy Merckx. Coppi won it all: the world hour record, the world championships, the grands tours, classics as well as time trials. The French cycling journalist Pierre Chany says that between 1946 and 1954, once Coppi had broken away from the peloton, the peloton would never see him again. Merckx, he said, won by driving himself to the limit in an act of pure will – but Fausto Coppi won simply with elegance.

33: BSA Paratrooper
Bikes in War

The history of the use of bicycles in war could form a book in itself. Perhaps the best-known example is that of the BSA Airborne Bicycle during the Second World War invasion of Europe. The only British troop-carrying glider available then was the Hotspur, with limited space. As a result, the BSA (Birmingham Small Arms) company developed a bicycle that could be folded in half, so a paratrooper could jump out of an aircraft with it. Once landed, he could then unfold it and use it as a conventional bicycle. Production of this bicycle was given immediate priority and enough were ready by the time of all the major landings such as D-Day and Arnhem.

Year: 1944

Manufacturer:
BSA

Location:
Birmingham

For over a century, military planners had been intrigued by the bicycle and its potential use in war. Obviously the bicycle could carry more equipment and travel far longer than a walking soldier. The problem was to determine exactly how they could be used. In the age of solid rims and hard tyres, such use would be limited, but in the 1890s with the arrival of pneumatic tyres a new potential appeared possible. With this new mobility, bicyclists appeared capable of taking over the role of the horse-mounted dragoon on the battlefield and working as scouts and messengers.

So enthusiastic were military planners at the end of the nineteenth century that some armies in Europe and the USA formed bicycle units, or cycle detachments. This provoked other armies throughout the Western world to begin testing the bicycle's potential in war. Such questions as whether it would make a viable gun platform were asked. Experiments were carried out with side-mounted rifles that could be fired from the handlebars as well as sidecar-mounted machine guns. None of these attempts proved particularly successful and attention turned to providing a form of mobile bicycle cavalry.

One of the first experiments in this deployment was by the British, who used cyclists as scouts during field manoeuvres in the annual British Army Easter exercises of 1885. This proved successful, so in 1885 a number of units of the British Rifle Volunteer Corps established cyclist sections, equipped with high-wheelers and used primarily for patrolling the English coastline. These experiments must have pleased some military commanders for, in 1888, the 26th Middlesex (Cyclist) Volunteer Rifle Corps was formed. It remained the only cyclists' battalion until Lord Haldane's reforms created the Territorial Forces in 1908. British plans became even more ambitious, and in 1890 the army carried out unsuccessful trials on an eight-wheeled, eight-man, pedalled contraption, so demanding on the physique of its crew that it was dubbed 'the Hernia Horror'.

During the Second Anglo–Boer War of 1899–02, cyclists were used extensively both by the Boers for scouting and by British and Empire forces as despatch riders and for patrolling exposed railway lines. There was even a documented incident, at Hammanskraal in the Transvaal, in which 11 New Zealand cyclists chased and arrested ten Boer horsemen. The Boers had their successes as well. Commandant Danie Theron raised the bicycle-mounted 'Theron se Verkenningskorps', or Theron Reconnaissance Corps, described by the British Commander-in-Chief, Field-Marshal Lord Roberts as 'the hardest thorn in the flesh of the British advance'. The experiences of the Boer War must have proved to the British that the bicycle had its place in war, for in 1908, five British infantry battalions converted to cyclists' battalions, while three new battalions were formed. During the next eight years a further five 'wheelmen' or cyclists' battalions were raised.

The French were experimenting with the military bicycle, too. In 1892, Armand Peugeot, long before he became a leading car manufacturer, produced the first dedicated folding bicycle for the French Army. Equally successful was the Italian Edoardo Bianchi's 1905 military bicycle for alpine use, in many ways a forerunner of today's mountain bikes. Given the political climate of the times, it was no surprise that the Austrians and the Germans were also examining the use of the military bicycle.

Soon the Americans followed suit with various units being issued with cycles. One of the first was the First Signal Corps of the Connecticut National Guard, which in 1891 was officially the first USA military unit to have a bicycle section. They proved that a cyclist on his own could deliver a message faster than an entire flag signaller team. Other units then began to issue bicycles to their messengers and relay riders following their lead.

Cycle at war. The famous BSA paratrooper of the Second World War.

The Bicycle in the World Wars

It seemed, at first, that the bicycle would play a significant role in the First World War. After mobilisation, cyclists' battalions were employed either in home defence, acting as a cadre from which troops were sent to France, or they were split up into divisional companies and used in reconnaissance roles. The war began as a mobile conflict and both sides used a large number of bikes to help troops get to the front lines quickly. As the action became bogged down and degenerated into grim trench warfare, there was no room or need for two-wheel machines. Behind the front, cycles were occasionally used as transport for snipers but mainly by scouts and dispatch riders. As with everything about that war, the scale of the deployment was enormous. Britain put more than 100,000 soldiers onto cycles, mainly the BSA Bicycle Mark IV, but that number was far exceeded by the other combatants. The French deployed 125,000 bike-mounted troops and the Germans, 150,000.

A generation later, the outbreak of the Second World War offered the bicycle another opportunity to show what it could do in an armed conflict. As the Germans rapidly advanced across Europe they put their bicycles to good use. Behind the many tanks that spearheaded the invasion of Belgium and France came thousands of bikes. These were used by the German Army to transport infantry behind the thousands of tanks, lorries and even horse-drawn wagons. There was another unforeseen use for the bicycle, this time on the home front. Because of wartime shortages of petrol throughout the Second World War, many nations used the bicycle to save on fuel. This was particularly true in Great Britain during the Blitz, and even in the fuel-rich USA petrol was rationed and the bike provided a low-cost transport alternative. But it was in its role as a vehicle for battlefield communications that the bicycle was to play its most important role in the two world wars.

AT WAR IN EUROPE

In German-occupied Europe it was the resistance groups that made the best use of the cycle. The Polish in particular had invested in them, with each Polish Infantry Division having a squadron of mounted scouts, cavalry and messengers. The Finns deployed cycle troops extensively throughout both their wars against Soviet Russia in the late 1930s. Bicycle units spearheaded their advances in 1941. When the snow fell, the troops put down their cycles and transferred to skis. Sweden, too, had begun using the cycle for military purposes, the 27th Gotlandic Infantry Regiment having replaced its horse cavalry with bicycle-mounted troops as early as 1901. By 1942 Sweden had six bicycle infantry regiments and even as late as the 1980s there were still special bicycle rifle battalions in the army.

French soldiers on bikes riding to take up position on the Western Front during the Second World War.

The British Army also made extensive use of bicycles during the war, but more as short-distance communication vehicles carrying messages between units. Their presence in the D-Day invasion could prove as much a hindrance as an asset. Private Walter Scott of the Royal Army Medical Corps later recalled a bad experience during the Normandy landings: 'I had to get my bike up to my unit's meeting place on the promenade. The bike proved horribly awkward. Eventually it packed up altogether and fell over, blocking the progress of the tank which was disembarking behind me.'

It was in the Far East that the use of the bicycle was most significant, foreshadowing the role it would later play in the Vietnam War. When Japan invaded China in 1937, some 50,000 bicycle-mounted troops were used. Even more telling was the Japanese use of bikes in the conquest of Malaya and Singapore in 1941. Bicycles provided quiet and flexible transport for thousands of Japanese troops, as well as making few demands on the national war machine. Yet it was not Japanese-made bicycles that were used but local Malaya ones. With ship space limited for the invasion, orders were given to leave bicycles behind. Instead, knowing that bicycles were plentiful in Malaya, the Japanese high command ordered their troops to systematically take them from local civilians and retailers as soon as they landed. With their confiscated bicycles, Japanese troops were able to move faster than the withdrawing Allied Forces, often successfully cutting off their retreat. The speed of the Japanese advancing from the rear, usually along plantation roads, jungle paths and over improvised bridges, caught the Allied defenders by surprise. The only counter-tactic devised by Australian troops was to cut off the cycle troops from their accompanying motorised forces by blowing up bridges after they passed.

Armaments Delivered by Bike

There is no doubt that the most successful makes of bicycle ever used in war were the modest French-made Peugeot and Czech-built Favorit machines used by the Vietnamese, for these were the low-tech means that would help a peasant army triumph over the advanced military hardware of two Western nations. On 7 May 1954, the beleaguered French bastion at Dien Bien Phu fell to the Viet Minh forces. For the six months prior to their triumph, Viet Minh had been able to bring up a massive stockpile of food and ammunition that would guarantee their victory. The Vietnamese used 600 Russian-made M trucks, as well as sampans, ponies and some 200,000 porters carrying spine-breaking loads. However, the heart of their logistical network was 60,000 cycle-mounted men and women who pedalled the loads in the largest military bicycle-transport feat in history.

With their large carrying capacity, bicycles made a highly effective means of transport on Vietnam's narrow jungle roads and tracks. Averaging 40 kilometres (25 miles) a day, the cyclists used narrow trails that were seldom straight for more than 4 yards (a few metres) and were studded by stumps, roots and snags. 'Our bicycles had first to be turned into pack bikes, with the crossbar capable of carrying 200 kilograms [440 pounds] or more,' said Ding Van Ty, one of the bicycle brigade leaders. 'We had to strengthen every part then camouflaged everything with leaves and moving at night.' He described how the seat was removed and a metal, wood or bamboo rack was tied in place over the rear wheel to make a frame from which bags or boxes were suspended. Then other freight was tied on with ropes or strips of inner tubes. Sometimes the cycle frame and the front forks were reinforced with metal,

Vietnam. The greatest triumph of the bicycle as a logistics machine in modern warfare.

wood or bamboo struts. A wooden bamboo pole was lashed to the handlebars, protruding far enough out so that the porters could steer the bicycle when fully loaded. Often a second pole was inserted into the seat tube so that the bike could be pushed along or held back when going downhill.

Such a simple modified two-wheeler could carry up to 270 kilograms (600 pounds) compared to the 35–45-kilogram (80–100-pound) load of a foot porter. The record for the largest single bicycle load at Dien Bien Phu was an astonishing 328 kilograms (724 pounds), while one of the Favorits was claimed to have hauled a total of 100 tons throughout the campaign in 1961–62. There was, of course, a price to pay, and although French and later USA airpower was unable to stop the flow of supplies along the Ho Chi Minh Trail, the terrain itself took its toll on the Viet Minh and later North Vietnamese porters. The 72 military cemeteries that now line the route are testimony to the dangers and hardships that the porters suffered. Between 10 and 20 per cent of the total number are estimated to have perished from disease, exhaustion and even wild animal attacks – far more than were killed by bombs or bullets.

In the 1960s, the USA repeated the mistakes of the French and were surprised by the effective use of the bicycle. Such was the American disbelief that a Senate committee was formed to investigate why the USA was making little progress in the war. The eminent journalist Harrison Salisbury, who had just returned from Hanoi, told the committee how bicycles enabled the Viet Cong and regular North Vietnamese Army to resupply their forces even under the most adverse conditions. Salisbury concluded: 'I literally believe that without bikes they'd have to get out of the war.' An astonished Senator Fulbright then asked him, 'Why, then, don't we concentrate on bombing their bicycles instead of the bridges?', a remark that caused great amusement.

As the Americans increased their bombing to little effect, the North Vietnamese Army continued its war of attrition under General Giap. To supply his forces in the field Giap relied on the bicycle, with hundreds of thousands of them on the move every day. The Vietnamese had even devised another role for the bicycle: as a primitive ambulance to carry the wounded away from the battlefield. A local Peugeot subsidiary produced a model specially for that purpose, containing surgical and medical kits and two headlights, with detachable extension cables for lighting a small field hospital. Two bicycles lashed together with long bamboo poles could also carry up to two stretchers.

Giap's bicycle army was now formidable in number and known as the 559th Transport Group. It comprised 50,000 troops and 100,000 labourers, with two battalions of some 2,000 cyclists supplementing the work of the truck convoys by moving supplies to inaccessible areas along the Ho Chi Minh Trail. In this way, Giap could counter USA mobility and military superiority and exert enough pressure to force the USA finally to quit the war.

34: Moulton Standard Mark 1
Folding Bikes

Perhaps the most successful design for a modern folding bicycle came in the late 1950s when Dr Alex Moulton, an English engineer, unveiled his Moulton Standard. Moulton had taken a fresh look at cycle design from the ordinary consumer's point of view. His first conclusion was that the traditional diamond-shaped frame of the conventional bicycle made it inconvenient to mount and difficult to adjust for both the size and the sex of the rider. Moreover, Moulton thought the conventional bicycle uncomfortable to ride because it lacked wide, low-pressure tyres and the large wheels made it hard to store.

Year:
1960

Manufacturer:
Moulton

Location:
London

L ooked at objectively, Moulton had a point – the ordinary bike was totally unsuited to the modern commuting patterns of large cities and could not even be fitted into the boot of the average car.

Early Prototypes

It is another Englishman, William Grout, who is often given credit for inventing the first folding bike almost a century before Moulton in 1878. From most accounts, his bicycle had a folding front wheel and a frame that could be disassembled rather than folded up. This excluded it from being classed as a true folding bicycle. Another hybrid was the first Faun Folding Cycle produced in England in 1896. While it was not the first folding bike, the bike's novelty was that it featured folding handlebars that integrated a brake mechanism. This innovation was invented by William Crowe, who was issued a patent for it on 18 March 1899.

Alex Moulton's little machine that started a cycling revolution in the 1960s.

The idea of a folding bicycle had begun to obsess Europe, too. A French military officer, Henry Gérard, filed a patent for a fully documented folding bicycle. Having gained his patent, Gérard was approached by the industrialist Charles Morel. In October 1894 Charles Morel and Lieutenant Gérard entered into an agreement to manufacture and market a folding bike. Morel would finance the project and oversee the manufacture, while Gérard would promote it to the French Army. Production began in April 1895 and was an immediate success; orders flooded in swiftly, quickly exceeding production capacity. This machine was probably the first folding bike manufactured in relatively large volume. The scheme looked so promising that Morel and Gérard opened a retail store in Paris specifically to sell the folding bike to the public. Gérard meanwhile had persuaded the French military to take on and test 25 of the new machines. Word of this new military 'invention' spread fast and both the Romanian and Russian armies began placing orders as well. To celebrate his success, Lieutenant Gérard was then put in charge of a new regiment of folding bike equipped soldiers and promoted to the rank of captain.

As always in the evolution of the bicycle, the Americans were not far behind. One of the first, if not the first, credibly documented in the USA was by the inventor Emmit G. Latta, who in September 1887 filed a patent for such a machine. An excerpt from his patent application reads: 'The object of this invention is to provide a machine that is safe, strong, and serviceable, and more easily steered than the machines now in use, and also to construct the machine in such a manner that the same can be folded when not required for use, so as to require little storage-room and facilitate its transportation.' Latta sold this patent on to the Pope Manufacturing Company, which was buying up dozens of bicycle-related patents at the time. Using the Columbia brand name Pope sold many bikes, but it is not known whether the Latta folding bike was ever marketed by the company.

Folding bikes had a variety of uses, from commuting to shopping.

Early folding bikes involved ingenious and complicated mechanisms.

Another early documented American folding bike was by Michael B. Ryan, who filed his patent in December 1893. Ryan claimed that the purpose of his machine was 'to produce a bicycle, so constructed that it can be easily folded and thus take up less space in length when not in use or when transported or stored'. Once his patent was granted, Ryan became involved with the Dwyer Folding Bicycle Company that was located near his home town of Danbury, Connecticut. Many believe that the Dwyer Folding Bicycle was probably designed by Michael B. Ryan himself, although not openly attributed to him. The evidence for this is that on 13 October 1896, Ryan filed a patent for a folding bicycle that was an improvement on his earlier design and bears an almost exact likeness to the new Dwyer bike. The Dwyer sales brochure also mentions that the Dwyer bikes are fitted with the 'Ryan Adjustable Handle-bars', of which Michael B. Ryan was found to hold the patent.

By now the folding bike was appearing in many countries, mainly in an attempt to attract the military market. Among the companies taking a keen interest in them in the 1890s were Styria in Austria; Dursley-Pedersen in England; Seidel & Naumann in Germany; Fongers, and Burgers in Holland; and Peugeot in France. The most widely known military folding bicycle manufacturer, however, was the English company BSA, or Birmingham Small Arms. Later, the company would produce folding bikes by the thousands for use in both the First and Second World War.

THE BICYCLE OF THE FUTURE

When the Moulton came onto the market, many welcomed it as the most radical advance in cycle design since the arrival of the safety cycle in the 1880s. The press were ecstatic, calling it 'the bicycle of the future' and it appeared constantly in the press and on British television. Sales took off as the Moulton became an icon of the Swinging Sixties and the Moulton sold around the world in its thousands. Many celebrities were delighted to be seen on one. The design expert Reyner Banham praised Moulton's ingenuity and the actress Eleanor Bron wrote a book about her travels around France on her Moulton. So fashionable did the bike become that its riders began to proudly refer to themselves as 'the Moultoneers'.

An Urban Bike for the Twentieth Century

Later in the twentieth century, the market for folding bikes transformed. The interest in it as a military machine had long faded, but the great social changes and above all the increased urbanisation of cities throughout the world offered a new and booming market. This was the market into which Dr Alex Moulton introduced his revolutionary new Moulton bicycle.

Every aspect of the machine had been fundamentally re-examined. Moulton had replaced the traditional diamond frame with a novel F-frame, or Lazy F, that lacked a top tube, making it easier to mount – particularly for those with physical limitations or when wearing bulky clothing. Moulton was also convinced that small wheels with high-pressure tyres would be far more suitable, offering less rolling resistance and a far greater acceleration potential. With this conviction in mind he then approached the Dunlop tyre company and worked with them to develop a range of more suitable high-pressure tyres. Equally important was the need to devise a new form of suspension for both wheels that would add comfort to the ride. This would be the most radical element of the whole design and was to prove 30 years ahead of its time.

Although the sole designer, Moulton had never intended to manufacture the bicycle himself and had shown the prototypes to the Raleigh company in

In the 1960s in London a folding bike became a fashionable and smart accessory.

One of the biggest sellers of the folding bike as the British market matured in the early 1970s was the Bickerton Portable. Designed by Harry Bickerton, it had a lightweight aluminium frame and folded away so that it could be transported with relative ease. The Bickerton Portable was in production from 1971 until 1991, selling approximately 150,000 machines in that time. Then, in 1982, Dr David Hon, a physicist, began production of the first of the Dahon folding bikes. Both Brompton and Dahon are still among the most popular folding bike brands today, with Dahon going on to become the world's largest folding bike manufacturer with an estimated 60 percent market share.

1962. To his surprise, Raleigh declined to take up the offer but later admitted that they had been foolish not to. So Alex Moulton set about manufacturing the bicycle himself, initially at a new factory at Bradford-on-Avon and later outsourcing it to the BMC factory at Kirkby.

Having missed such an excellent marketing opportunity, Raleigh were now forced to enter the market with their version of a folding cycle. The result, launched in 1965, was the RSW16, a machine that was superficially similar to the Moulton but without its innovative suspension. Instead it had wide, low-pressure 'balloon' tyres that attempted to compensate for the lack of suspension but proved slow and cumbersome. Yet Raleigh, the largest manufacturer of bicycles in the world, had the marketing power that Moulton lacked and they ensured that the RSW would become a success in spite of its problems.

Smart and fast. A Moulton breaks the London–Cardiff speed record.

Eventually, Alex Moulton could not compete commercially and in 1967 he sold his business to Raleigh in what he called a 'distress sale'. Production now moved to the Raleigh factory in Nottingham with Moulton retained as a consultant. A maverick character, Moulton often had his advice ignored. When the Moulton Midi was launched without a front suspension and the frames began to crack, it was because Raleigh had overridden Moulton's warning. They were forced to retrofit a special strengthening plate.

Raleigh now consolidated the Moulton range, reducing the number of models and options. In 1970, Raleigh launched the Moulton Mk III alongside its own RSW Mk III, and the Raleigh Chopper. The Chopper became a huge success, and the

Moulton was dropped altogether. Determined to make a comeback, Alex Moulton then decided to buy back his patents from Raleigh. He produced a new design based on the original bike, but designed to attract the top end of the market. This was the AM series that combined low weight with extra rigidity. This was followed in 1998 by the New Series Moulton with its Flexitor front suspension and a triangular rear suspension. Moulton also added slimmer-diameter frame tubes that reduced weight while improving appearance.

'The 50th anniversary of the Moulton bike – what an occasion, what an anniversary, what an icon. Synonymous with the Mini, the mini-skirt – the mini bike.'

– Lord Foster (2012)

Apart from their use in both world wars there was little public interest in the folding bike in the early twentieth century until the 1970s. Following the Moulton's success, dozens of manufacturers in many countries began producing folding bikes. So keen was the public on the small-wheeled machines that this decade became known as the 'Golden Age of the folding bike'. As business prospered, a flood of cheap Eastern European so-called 'U-frame' folding bikes came onto the market, many sold by mail order, at department stores or service stations.

Moulton bikes were as smart as they were efficient, coming in a variety of eye-catching colours.

Cross-braced frame

Small wheels

35: Peugeot PX-10
Death and the Mountain

Tommy Simpson was the first truly famous English road race professional, long before Bradley Wiggins. After a successful amateur career that included winning an Olympic bronze in the 1956 team pursuit and a silver in the individual pursuit in the 1958 Commonwealth Games, in 1960 he decided to dedicate himself to a career as a professional cyclist and relocated to Europe. His chosen machine was a Carlton, said to be resprayed in the colours of whatever sponsor he was contracted to. When he finally joined the Peugeot team he rode one of their standard-issue white PX-10s with its black Nervex Pro lugs.

Year:
1967

Manufacturer:
Peugeot

Location:
France

Peugeot had been sponsoring Tour winners since Louis Trousselier in 1905 and had remained active in the Tour and other European cycle races ever since. At the time Tommy Simpson was using their machine, Peugeot had become the most successful factory team of all time in the Tour de France, winning the race a record ten times. Yet like some other large European bicycle manufacturers, Peugeot was not above purchasing hand-crafted team racing bicycles, made by small independent craftsmen, and then having them painted and outfitted to resemble standard Peugeot factory production models.

The Peugeot PX-10. Peugeot were as big a name in cycle racing as they were in motor manufacture.

The winding and arduous
route to the summit of
Mont Ventoux.

The Long Road to Mont Ventoux

Riding in France, Tommy Simpson continued his successful career and built himself a reputation as a courageous rider who never gave up trying. As with most of his competitors, success in the Tour became the ultimate challenge. In 1962 Simpson became the first ever British rider to win a stage and wear the yellow jersey, although he held it for just a single day. He was a good rider on the flat and a brave descender, but what held him back in those days was his limitations as a climber. Many thought him more suited to the one-day classics rather than the major tours of the European circuit.

Yet in only one season did he fail to win at least one of the classic races and in 1965 he became world champion and was voted British TV Sports Personality of the year. Still his obsession with the Tour de France continued. Before 1967 he had ridden in five Tours de France, two of which he had been forced to retire from through injury. This made the 1967 Tour all the more important to him. This time he was determined not to quit and to produce a good result. Those who saw him before the start of the race commented that he seemed a changed man, far more intense and moody as he faced the biggest test of his career.

As always, the Tour loomed as the centrepiece of Simpson's season. This year it would follow a clockwise direction across northern France before dropping south through the Vosges and Alps. As the organisers' plans were announced, Simpson was taken aback to find out that they had decided to revert to the old formula of national teams. All through the season riders competed for their trade team sponsors; in Simpson's case, Peugeot. Now the

Lugwork detail on the Peugeot team bike.

riders were supposed to abandon those commitments and race for their respective countries. A small group of English professionals with almost no Continental experience would be his only teammates for the big challenge. He knew he would be on his own. Nevertheless, he made the best of it, devising his game plan to ride cautiously on the flat and save himself for the mountains where he knew that large time gaps would make all the difference.

The season had started well with an excellent win in the Paris–Nice race, where he rode with his promising young Peugeot teammate, Eddy Merckx. Even then, warning signs had begun to appear. During the Vuelta, the Tour of Spain, he won two stages but had to be forcibly dragged from his bike by the Peugeot manager, Gaston Plaud, who became alarmed when Simpson, ten minutes in the lead, began zigzagging out of control on the ascent of Port d'Envalira in the Pyrenees. Plaud later wrote that: 'The face I saw was of a very tired man. His features were drawn and he was very white. I knew he was not good in the heat and I said he should not go up Ventoux because he was not healthy enough.' Simpson was at the end of his tether. Plaud's account tallies with that of Simpson's British colleague, Vin Denson, who had himself advised Simpson to retire three days earlier after a difficult Alpine stage during which Simpson had to cope with a serious gastric upset. There is no doubt that he was significantly weakened and dehydrated when he came to the start of the Mont Ventoux stage.

The long approach slope up to the base of the mountain served to shred the field and leave the top riders clustered at the front. As expected, Tommy Simpson was the only member of the British team still in this leading group.

The temperature on the road that afternoon in Provence was a staggeringly hot 54°C and, now beyond sweating, Simpson's heartbeat had climbed to well over 200 pulses a minute. Rationed like most of the riders to just four small bottles of water he was becoming seriously dehydrated but at least he still held seventh place in the overall race. As the field approached the bottom of the mountain Simpson was one of many riders who rode into a cafe and desperately grabbed any drink they could find. Simpson was said to have helped himself to Coke with brandy to ease his sore stomach. Such a mixture would have reacted badly with the amphetamines that he had taken. Although certainly in trouble at this stage, Simpson's condition was not yet critical. Yet critical it soon became as he started up the 21-kilometre (13-mile) climb towards the summit of Mont Ventoux. In spite of his physical problems he had been riding well throughout the day, although one of his teammates thought he was taking more drinks than usual.

After 11 kilometres (7 miles) of a gruelling climb, Simpson began to slip back to a group of chasers about a minute behind the leaders. In that group was Lucien Aimar, the 1966 Tour winner, who remembered how unhappy Simpson was to be stuck so far behind and how he kept trying to bridge the gap back up to the leaders. But no matter how hard he tried, Simpson just could not maintain the tempo necessary to move up.

For the sake of his health he should have retired at this stage but it would have been the third consecutive time that he would have given up, and Simpson was no quitter. Furthermore, his professional career was at a critical stage and leaving the race would have sent out all the wrong messages. Because he had always ridden on the edge his colleagues had almost become used to seeing him suffering for his sport. For this reason, when some of his British colleagues rode past his collapsed body on that fateful day they assumed this was just such another occasion and were not seriously alarmed.

Simpson on the eighth stage of the Tour just days before his tragic death in 1967.

Although he had been dropped by one of the leading groups, towards the top of the climb he was still well up in the broken field and trying to regain contact with a group 180 metres (200 yards) ahead. With the gradients ranging from 8 to 14 percent, the situation became critical. As the peleton exited the forest at Chalet Reynard it passed into the dry lunar landscape that characterises the approach to the summit. At this point, just over 2 kilometres (1.2 miles) from the top and struggling through the white shale landscape, Simpson fell for the first time. Another 460 agonising metres (500 yards) on he fell again and was very probably dead before he hit the ground – heart failure brought on by heat exhaustion. Dr Pierre Dumas, the doctor who travelled with the tour, examined him and immediately ordered his transfer by police helicopter to the nearest hospital. He was given artificial respiration and then flown by ambulance helicopter to Avignon hospital.

Brake lever detail of Simpson's team Peugeot.

Soon after 6.30 p.m. that evening the press at Carpentras were told that Tommy Simpson had died. His was the first known death in the Tour's history and it shocked both the cycling and the general public. The next day an autopsy was performed to shed more light on why a seemingly fit young athlete had died. Had he just been unlucky or had he behaved recklessly in continuing in the race? The post mortem found both amphetamines and alcohol in his blood, while police discovered amphetamine tablets in the pocket of his jersey and in a team support car. The news shocked many in the cycling community. The official cause of death was given as a heart attack brought on by a combination of heat and dehydration, albeit exacerbated by amphetamines and alcohol.

PUT ME BACK ON MY BIKE

One the most haunting images of the Tour de France is that of the British cyclist Tommy Simpson in his white jersey riding to his death near the 1,830-metre (6,000-foot) summit of Mont Ventoux in Provence. In the haunting pictures taken from a press motorbike he is nearing the end. His skin is ghastly pale, as white as his jersey, with sunken cheeks and desperate, staring eyes. As he approaches the last section of the climb he zigzags to and fro across the road. Just 3 kilometres (2 miles) before the summit, on the 13th stage of the race from Marseilles to Carpentras, he collapsed for the first time. 'Put me back on my bike,' he told the crowd in what were to be his memorable last words. At this point a UPI photographer took a shot of Simpson and wired it off with the caption that Simpson had died. When asked later how he could have said that of a man still on his bike the photographer replied, 'I saw it when he passed; death was in his face.'

The Advent of Drug-Testing

As a result of the tragedy a new and darker era in cycling began. Greg LeMond, the three-time Tour winner, later said: 'Because of Tom Simpson's death, dope tests were introduced. I believe many more cyclists would have otherwise died.' Before Simpson's death, cyclists were never regularly tested for the use of performance-enhancing drugs such as amphetamines. Now it all changed and mandatory drug-testing came into force. The new rules required cyclists to submit themselves to regular drug tests. How rigorous and effective these were was later doubted, as the careers of those such as Lance Armstrong were to prove.

At the time, the very subject of drug use was almost taboo. Many people involved in cycling admitted that there was a problem, but few would speak about it openly. One who did was the Irish rider Paul Kimmage, who admitted, 'I have used amphetamines on three occasions and I wouldn't have believed the difference it made until I tried it. It was astonishing really.' Having noticed such a difference when using the drugs, Kimmage could fully understand how they could lead someone to push themselves beyond their limits. 'People talk about the dangers of Formula One and climbing Everest but the numbers would bear no comparison to those who are killed each year as professional cyclists,' said Kimmage. Others have suggested that part of the problem is the financial backing that modern cycling needs. As teams rely on commercial sponsorship they have to show results in order to survive.

It is a different environment to that of national teams – competition for that elusive sponsorship deal is fierce. There is little doubt that Simpson was a cyclist who pushed himself to the limits to keep winning to ensure the continuation of his own sponsorship.

Memorial to one of the greatest tragedies in Tour de France history.

As a reminder of the price that must sometimes be paid to succeed in sport there is today a simple granite memorial to Simpson near the spot where he died close to the summit of Mont Ventoux. It was paid for by British cyclists and is now in their care. Riders, particularly Tommy Simpson's fellow countrymen, who pass it frequently leave small tributes in his memory such as drinking bottles or their own cycling caps.

36: Ugo De Rosa
Eddy Merckx

In 1974 Eddy Merckx was 29 years old and almost a veteran, having enjoyed a spectacular career in racing. His one last ambition was to crown all his past achievements by taking the 'Triple Crown' of cycle racing – the Giro d'Italia, the Tour de France and the World Championship in one season. No one had ever managed to do that before. When he set off for Montreal in Canada to successfully complete the last leg of his historic treble, he was riding a bike built by Ugo De Rosa, although labelled 'Eddy Merckx'.

Year:

1974

Manufacturer:
De Rosa

Location:
Milan

The year began well, with Merckx winning both the Giro and the Tour of Switzerland in the spring. The culmination came in the most arduous of them all, the Tour de France. Beaten in the time trials near the start of the race, he recovered brilliantly to win the two hardest stages in the Alps and rode into Paris as the winner. This was his fifth overall win in the race, a feat only ever equalled by Jacques Anquetil.

Famous bike, famous rider. Eddy Merckx's iconic Ugo De Rosa.

A Partnership

As always with Merckx, the bike he rode that year had been meticulously prepared to his exact specifications by a mechanic that he trusted implicitly. Ugo De Rosa, along with Ernesto Colnago, was then regarded as one of the most exclusive of manufacturers – with their distinctive heart-shaped logo they were the Ferrari of racing cycle frames that gave performance combined with an excellent ride quality.

De Rosa had begun making racing cycles in the early 1950s, but his big break came in 1958 when he was chosen by the famous cyclist Raphaël Géminiani as the maker of the new machine that Géminiani would use in the forthcoming Giro d'Italia. This launched De Rosa as a designer of quality machines and his bikes steadily became a favourite of top Italian riders during the 1960s. More recognition came when De Rosa was chosen by the Faema team, followed by others such as the Tbac and Max Majer teams.

Final confirmation that De Rosa had arrived on the scene came in 1969 when Ugo De Rosa was approached by the ex-champion Gianni Motta, who had been impressed by the quality of the De Rosa design and manufacture. Motta made an offer and De Rosa accepted, becoming the bicycle supplier to the Motta team as well. It was at this time that De Rosa built his first frame for Eddy Merckx, who was already a rising star on the international racing circuit. However, it was not until 1973 that the relationship between De Rosa and Merckx became a formality and De Rosa was appointed the official frame builder and mechanic for the Molteni team that Merckx captained. Bike and rider went on to find fame together.

The Greatest Cyclist of All Time?

Born at the end of the Second World War in 1945, Merckx's racing career lasted for 13 seasons, and for ten of them he totally dominated world cycling like no one before or since. Like every other successful rider, he began as an amateur. After winning the Amateur World Championship Road Race in 1964, Merckx turned professional the following year. His first major victory came in the Milan–San Remo at the age of just 20. By coincidence, his last major victory was to be in the same race, ten years later.

Eddy Merckx, the 'Cannibal'. Arguably the greatest rider of his generation.

In spite of his powerful riding, Eddy Merckx's health was always questionable and this makes his many successes all the more remarkable. For much of

After winning 'The Triple' Eddy Merckx had, to many cycling enthusiasts, proved himself to be simply the greatest rider of all time. He was one of the most determined racers ever to sit on a bike, and his fans nicknamed him 'The Cannibal' because of his insatiable appetite to win whatever the conditions. His racing career was indeed spectacular, with Merckx winning almost every important race during his career, some many times.

his career he appears to have been suffering from a serious heart condition later diagnosed as non-obstructive hypertrophic cardiomyopathy. This was revealed during the 1968 Giro d'Italia when Enrico Peracino, team doctor at Merckx's Faema squad, invited Italy's leading cardiologist, professor Giancarlo Lavezzaro, to examine both Merckx and another rider, Vittorio Adorni. This was mainly to demonstrate a new state-of-the-art electrocardiogram at a sponsor's dinner following stage three of the race, rather than to investigate a specific problem. So it was by chance that when Lavezzaro, expecting to see nothing sinister, checked the results and was shocked to see that the data indicated Eddy Merckx was right in the middle of a full heart attack. Although looking a little tired after a hard day's riding, Merckx appeared to be perfectly all right. Astonished by this contradiction, Lavezzaro asked Merckx to repeat the cardiogram test again the following morning. The result was exactly the same again and appeared to confirm a clear case of non-obstructive hypertrophic cardiomyopathy.

The news presented both Merckx's team and Dr Lavezzaro with a dilemma. Should they tell this healthy-looking 24-year-old rider what they had discovered or even pull him from the race? When they did tell him the news Merckx said that in the past his cardiograms had often produced odd results and anyway, he had no intention of dropping out of the race. Dr Lavezzaro

Ugo De Rosa, a combination of beautiful details to embellish a beautiful machine.

went back to Turin convinced that Merckx would collapse sometime during the last fortnight of the race. Recalling the incident in a later book, Lavezzaro wrote: 'Today Merckx wouldn't be allowed to race. At the time we could see that he had a problem but couldn't make a precise diagnosis without doing a cardiac catheterisation, which obviously wasn't practical at the Giro. We just knew that he was at risk.' Lavezzaro went on to say that today all professional cyclists have to pass a regulatory cardiogram test before they can get their licence and anyone with a result like Merckx's would certainly not be allowed to race.

Health issues aside, Eddy Merckx was not immune from injury or accident. The most serious incident came in 1969 when he took part in a paced exhibition race towards the end of the season. In such races cyclists each follow their own motorcycle pacer around an oval track. On this particular day, a pacer and cyclist fell in front of Merckx, forcing him and his own pacer to fall as well. Merckx's pacer was killed instantly and Merckx was knocked unconscious and left bleeding heavily from a head wound. He suffered serious concussion and required stitches to close the gaping wound. The real damage from the crash was that Merckx had cracked one of his vertebrae and twisted his pelvis. The result of these injuries was that from then on riding a climb was always painful for him. Although he still went on to have numerous successes, many suspected that if it weren't for the accident, he could have won even more.

Other injuries followed, but Merckx carried on regardless. Then, during the 1975 Tour de France while riding a climb in the Puy-de-Dôme, a French spectator viciously punched Merckx in the stomach. A few days later, Merckx crashed and fractured his cheek bone, but still did not abandon the race. In the end, he lost the Tour to Bernard Thevenet by just under three minutes. But the accumulation of injuries was beginning to take its toll; after winning his last Grand Tour in 1974 and his last major classic in the spring of 1976, Eddy Merckx, at the age of 32, finally retired.

In his native Belgium Merckx had become a national hero and a station was named after him on Line 5 of the western branch of the Brussels Metro. Merckx gave his winning De Rosa bike of 1974 to the Pope and it finally found a place of honour in the Chapel of the Madonna del Ghisallo in Rome, a church that is, appropriately, dedicated to bicycle racing.

AN IMPRESSIVE TRACK RECORD

At the height of his career between 1969 and 1975, Merckx won an astounding 35 per cent of all the races that he entered. He won the Tour de France five times, the Giro d'Italia five times and the Vuelta a Espana once, for a total of 11 Grand Tour victories. His record in other classics is equally impressive, with a total of 19 victories in the Milan–San Remo, Tour of Flanders, Paris–Roubaix, Liege–Bastogne–Liege and Tour of Lombardy.

His record in the Tour de France was just as spectacular, with Merckx being the only rider to win every classification, overall, mountains and points jerseys in a single year in both the Tour de France in 1969 and at the Giro d'Italia in 1968. Add to that a record 34 Tour de France stage wins, including six stages in 1969 and 1972, and eight stages in 1970 and 1974, and it is easy to see why he gained the reputation as the finest cyclist of his age.

37: Breezer Series 1
Mountain Bikes

The most important development in cycling since the 1970s has been the arrival of the mountain bike. Series such as the Breezer range have in recent years become just as popular in urban areas as they were in the country. Off-road cycling has a long history stretching back to the time of the 'Buffalo Soldiers'. These experimental units of the USA infantry were issued with customised bicycles that allowed them to carry their gear when patrolling rough terrain. In August 1896, a group from one of these units rode from Missoula, Montana, to Yellowstone in order to test their cycles in mountainous terrain.

Year:
1977

Manufacturer:
Breeze

Location:
California

In Europe, road racers in the early 1900s had begun using cross-country riding as a way to train and keep warm during the winter off-season. Gradually, this practice became formalised and clubs would hold races over mixed terrain courses often referred to as the 'rough stuff'. The growing fascination with cycle tourism that developed after the First World War in Europe certainly encouraged this trend. Riding the rough stuff later became a feature of the British Cycle Tourist Competition that was inaugurated in 1952. Its aim was to explore the most attractive parts of the countryside by bike, no matter how rough the terrain.

The American Breezer helped create the entirely new sport of mountain biking.

Even the traditional British Empire was prepared to experiment with the humble bicycle. A prominent champion of the off-road bike at that time was the British statesman Winston Churchill, who in 1908 suggested it should be used by African explorers. They were ideal, he thought, for negotiating jungle paths, rough terrain and steep hills. On such machines men could average 11 kilometres (7 miles) an hour. He was even more delighted when on a visit to Uganda he found that 'nearly all the officers I met already possessed and used bicycles and even native chiefs are beginning to acquire them'.

By the 1950s there was even a club in Britain called the Rough Stuff Fellowship that specialised in mixed terrain and off-road touring. In many ways it was the European precursor of what would happen in Marin County, California, 20 years later. Its members were committed to getting away from the urban roads and exploring the rural tracks and byways. So strong did the movement become that the Rough Stuff Fellowship is still active today. Nor was Britain the only European country following the trend. The French also had the urge to cycle off-road and some of the more intrepid founded the Velo Cross Club Parisien of France. In the early 1950s, some 20 of its young riders from the suburbs of Paris developed a sport that proved remarkably similar to present-day mountain biking. These riders customised their traditional touring machines such as the French 650-B bike to be tough enough to race over the cross-country courses created by motorcyclists.

Early American Multi-Terrain Bikes

There had been developments in the USA too in the early 1930s. Bicycle sales had declined sharply due to the Great Depression, so Schwinn tested the new leisure market with its Beach Cruiser. Although not a mountain bike proper, it was a heavy single-speed bike with balloon tyres that could handle a variety of mixed terrains, including moderately loose flat sandy beaches. Paper boys and couriers quickly took to the Schwinn, since it could handle gravel paths with ease. However, as heavy single-speed bikes they were not as successful when climbing or when used on hilly terrain.

Long before Joe Breeze and the other Californians turned them into a phenomenon, more primitive mountain bikes such as the Schwinn had attracted interest in the USA. One of the first pioneers to make one was John Finley Scott. In 1953 he had built his 'Woodsie Bike' using a Schwinn World diamond frame, balloon tyres, flat handlebars, derailleur gears, and cantilever brakes. With hindsight Schwinn missed a golden opportunity to develop the first real mountain bike. They were well placed to exploit the coming market, but the company thought all-terrain bikes would be a short-lived phenomenon.

Another attempt at a customised mountain bike came in the early 1970s, when a group of young cyclists, known as the Cupertino Riders or the Morrow Dirt Club from Cupertino, California, 120 kilometres (75 miles) south of Marin, added thumb-shift-operated derailleurs and motorcycle lever-operated drum brakes to their bikes. With these additions they hoped to be able to ride the South Bay Hills with ease. One of the enthusiasts was Joe Breeze, a name that will always be associated with the mountain bike. He built the first modern, purpose-built machine in Mill Valley, California, in 1977.

'These bikes were different, it's like you've got ballet and you've football... they can both be great.'

– Joe Breeze (2010)

But the story began a few years earlier in 1973, when Breeze went searching through the bike shops of Santa Cruz for an old bike that he could use for rough riding. The best he could find was a 1941 Schwinn Beach Cruiser with fat tyres for just $5. Up to then, mountain bikes would be made up from a collection of used parts from other old bikes like the Schwinn. These cobbled-together bikes were generally known as 'klunkers' and were used to ride the mountain trails of California. One of the most popular routes was given the name 'The Repack' because just one descent so overheated the hub brake that they had to be cleaned out and repacked.

The problem in these early days was that the available bikes were not up to the riders' capabilities; even the best of them, like the Schwinn with its balloon tyres and derailleur gears, were just not good enough. Joe Breeze quickly discovered the limitations of his $5 bike while riding rocky trails of nearby Mt. Tamalpais with friends. In the meantime, he joined his new friends Charlie Kelly, Gary Fisher and Tom Ritchey in organising a series of races over

The Schwinn. Customised by many young Californians into early versions of the mountain bike.

the 4.8-kilometre- (3-mile-) long Cascade Fire Trail near Fairfax. This new sport proved wildly popular, with riders from all over San Francisco joining in. Starting at different intervals they all set out on their klunkers to break the 4.7-kilometre (2.9-mile) dirt track record, with its vertical drop of over 480 metres (1,600 feet).

The reason that these customised bikes had such a performance advantage over anything that had gone off-road before was the wheel size. This was the uniquely American 66 x 5 centimetre (26 x 2 1/8 inch) standard, introduced by Frank W. Schwinn in 1933. It had the advantage of holding a large volume of air and left a correspondingly large footprint with tyres that rolled well on dirt and gripped well in the corners. The first few Repack races required the use of a pick-up truck to carry all the bikes back up the hill after every run.

The Mountain Bike is Born

The innovation that transformed these bikes from mere klunkers into mountain bikes was the adoption of technology that had started appearing on bikes that were being imported from Europe. Multiple chain rings and long-arm derailleurs allowed the riders to pedal back up the mountain, and cantilever brakes with motorcycle levers greatly improved braking performance. Before long, bespoke frames were being designed and built and lighter components added. A phenomenon had been born that was set to change the world of cycling profoundly and forever.

The most all-American of bikes, the Schwinn remained a national best-seller.

Yet something even more radical was required if the new sport were to survive – a proper, made-for-purpose mountain bike. Joe Breeze, with the help of his friends, set out to design one. The result was the first all-American mountain bike frame, the Breezer Series I. Nine of these original machines were built, the first of which has been put on display at the Smithsonian Institution in Washington, D.C. As he worked on the creation of his prototype in 1977, welding the frames using cro-moly steel aircraft tubing and building up the bikes with brand-new parts, Breeze took orders for eight more. Without knowing it at the time, Joe Breeze had become the leading designer and proponent of a sport that would get more people in the Western world onto bikes than at any time since the 1890s.

Two years later, in 1979, Fisher, Kelley and Tom Ritchey set up Fisher Mountain Bikes, the first full company dedicated solely to making off-road bikes. From then on, mountain bike design became ever more sophisticated, with Specialized of Morgan Hill bringing its Stumpjumper to the market in 1981. Realising the commercial potential of this new market, Japanese parts makers such as Shimano and Araya rushed to produce dedicated parts for the new machines. These included high-range derailleurs and wide wheel rims to match the new fat tyres. Then, with 3 million mountain bikes already sold, Paul Turner produced an important innovation – the first mountain bike with a full suspension system provided by front and rear hydraulic shock absorbers, marketed as RockShox.

What the Californian riders did in the 1970s was to unify all these historic attempts at producing a serious off-road bike and create a machine for the current age. So successful were their attempts that the mountain bike craze spread throughout the world. In California, mountain bike riders even became

a nuisance as they were accused of interfering with traditional hikers by blocking mountain paths and crowding wooded valleys. Complaints that parkland was being invaded by crazy people on cycles led to the formation of the International Mountain Bicycling Association that brought in regulations that made the relationships between riders and walkers more agreeable.

Much has changed in the technology over the past 40 odd years. Back in the 1970s, mountain bikes had steel frames and forks; today, steel frames have all but disappeared from the middle and upper end of the market. Steel has been replaced by aluminium, titanium and, increasingly, carbon-fibre composite. Gears have changed too and instead of five sprockets on the back wheel there are now up to ten. More ergonomically designed index shifters have appeared, able to be operable while keeping the rider's hands firmly on the handlebars while braking at the same time. Short-arm cantilever brakes have disappeared and have been replaced by more powerful linear-pull brakes or even by hydraulic discs.

A MOUNTAIN BIKE FOR ALL OCCASIONS

The biggest transformation of all is the sheer variety of bikes now available compared to the time when the mountain bike was simply a mountain bike. Now there is a spectrum of specialist suppliers providing dedicated machines for all forms of mountain biking, including free-ride, fully rigid single-speed, 4X, all-mountain or back country, hard-core hard-tail, dirt jump or fully loaded expedition mountain bikes. There's more, too: trail bikes, mud bikes and even snow bikes.

Modern mountain bikes can go almost anywhere. They are fully equipped to meet the challenges of every sort of terrain on even the highest mountain tracks.

Nothing has changed more than the suspension, which has transformed the comfort of the ride. This has given lightweight XC bikes at least 80-millimetre (3 1/5-inch) travel on forks, while some downhill and free-ride bikes provide over 300-millimetre (11 4/5-inch) travel on the rear. Other sophistications have crept in, including platform valving, high- and low-speed compression and rebound damping, pivot location, floating shocks, actuators, lock-out, oil viscosity and axle paths.

A City Cycle

The mountain bike did not stay confined to the countryside. Increasingly, it has proved the ideal machine for the modern city too. It makes an ideal hybrid that could have been specially designed for commuting over short or long distances in urban areas. The urban mountain bike has, typically, derailleur gearing, 700c wheels with fairly light 28-millimetre (1 1/8-inch) tyres, a carrier rack, full fenders, and a frame with suitable mounting points for attachment of various load-carrying baskets or even of a briefcase. It often has an enclosed chain guard to allow a rider to pedal the bike wearing trousers without getting them entangled in the chain. A well-equipped commuter bike typically features front and rear lights for use in the early morning or late evening.

So it is not surprising that in most large cities today, mountain bikes are seen everywhere, their upright position making them more visible to cars. The rider also has good visibility and the handlebar set-up makes the bike more manoeuvrable in tight situations. Moreover, the powerful discs on a mountain bike give far more power than those on a road machine. It is also far easier to ride up kerbs and bounce through potholes as well as to get on and off. Also, mountain bike tyres seem to be a lot more resistant to punctures from all the debris that now accumulates on urban roads. The one big drawback? Mountain bikes always seem to be more popular with bike thieves!

38: The Haro
The BMX Craze

California in the 1970s saw the birth of another cycling craze alongside that of the mountain bike – BMX riding. This new casual sport allowed young people to demonstrate to each other just how clever they could be on a bike. Originally inspired by the well-established sport of motocross, BMX had the one great virtue of being accessible to everyone. Some of the BMX venues were as impromptu as they were legendary. They ranged from the concrete Escondido reservoir channels in San Diego to the Carlsbad Skatepark. Some kids on bikes were even seen riding around empty swimming pools.

Year: 1982

Manufacturer:
Haro

Location:
California

A s with mountain biking, there was at first no specific bike designed for the purpose. Enthusiasts had to customise a stunt machine out of what was already available. Yet again it was Schwinn that came closest to what was needed, and one model in particular, the Sting-Ray, was introduced in 1963. This machine had one great advantage: it was smaller in size than existing models, allowing children to emulate their favourite motocross riders.

The Father of Freestyle
The most influential of all those associated with BMX in the early days was Bob Haro, a Californian teenager who was to develop the sport and create a legacy that is still evident in almost every bike shop in the USA. Born in 1958 in the town of Pasadena, California, Robert Haro was initially drawn to motocross as a teenager and proved good enough to win a number of trophies on the local race circuit. Haro later wrote of his early career: 'I did pretty good, but I just never did have enough money to be

BMX bikes like the Haro brought a completely new look to the traditional machine.

real good.... I was like the full maniac of motorcycles. I was racing all the time. That's all I did. The reason I got started in BMX is that I ran out of money.' Due to the high cost of racing and the upkeep and repair of his Honda motorcycle, Bob switched sports and started riding his brother Scott's BMX bike until it was a near wreck. His father then strongly urged him to do the decent thing and buy the bike from his brother, which he did, 'and I owned my first BMX Bike'.

Discovering an unusual talent for biking, Haro was soon established as a leading BMX rider and travelled around the USA demonstrating advanced tricks on his bike. This was to earn him the title 'The Father of Freestyle'. Then, in the summer of 1981, Haro and Bob Morales made a thorough three-month tour of the country to promote the BMX Freestyle sport. While on the road Haro and Morales discussed the idea of designing a BMX bike with a dedicated frame and fork combination that would be made specifically for Freestyle riding. This ideal BMX would be designed, made and marketed exclusively as a Haro product and the frameset made by the Torker company.

BMX evolved from little more than a child's toy into a sophisticated all-terrain machine with an enormous following in the USA and throughout the world.

These first Haro machines would be sold in a kit that included the frame and fork only available in chrome. Some of the features, including a coaster brake bracket integrated into the rear dropout, were completely new and had never been seen before on a bike. Haro, Morales and Eddie Fiola began testing the prototype frame in the skate parks south of Los Angeles. Then in the summer of 1982, the finalised design went into full production at the Torker factory at Fullerton, California. It was to be one of the defining moments in

ON ANY GIVEN SUNDAY

The BMX story really began in 1970 when Scott Breithaupt, who is often credited with founding the sport, organised the first BMX bike race in southern California. The name BMX came from a documentary film entitled *On Any Given Sunday* that was shot locally in California and featured kids riding their bikes on local dirt tracks. The production caught the imagination of any kid that saw it and gave the world a new sport and the name of the

new sport, Bicycle Motocross. This was quickly shortened to the more handy acronym BMX. What helped to promote the youthful image of BMX was that everyone connected with it seemed little more than a kid themselves. Even the entrepreneurs of the new sport who staged events on local rented sites such as Gary Turner, Jim Melton, John Johnson and Scott Breithaupt, appeared to be youngsters.

Freestyle BMX history. The original Haro Freestyle model in 1983 met the rising popularity in BMX freestyle. The bike was designed to handle all conditions thrown its way and was an instant success. It wasn't much different to other BMX bikes on the market at the time, just more heavy-duty to handle additional stress. Riding the wave of popular demand, the Haro company now began producing other BMX Freestyle models, the Master and the Sport. The company grew rapidly throughout the 1980s by expanding its product line and establishing national and international distribution.

A Worldwide Craze

As custom bikes continued to grow in popularity and designs evolved, riders were better able to test the limits of their skills on new and more flexible machines. This trend continued into the 1980s and BMX riding became far more than just kids simply racing along tracks to see who would come first. Equipped with more versatile bikes, the young riders now began to attempt more complicated manoeuvres and perform skateboard-style tricks. From this the freestyle division of BMX was born. The old days of customised and technically inadequate machines was over as the new specialised machines became universally available.

Having conquered America, BMX biking now began to conquer the world. Now an established phenomenon, BMX eventually reached as far as Australia. The sport was given a huge boost in 1982 with Steven Spielberg's blockbusting film *E.T.* The film featured classic chase scenes between the BMX riders and the 'feds' that excited kids wherever it was shown. The result was that virtually every kid in the early 1980s either had, or wanted to have, a BMX bike. A worldwide craze had begun and local authorities came under great pressure to set up race tracks where kids could practise their BMX stunts. At the peak of the BMX phenomenon, the moderate-sized British city of Leicester had no less than six BMX tracks.

Even those without a proper BMX were putting their existing bikes through hell by trying to pull off that perfect wheelie, pogo, bunny hop, curb endo or other manoeuvre. Out in the streets they were building makeshift

GT BICYCLES

Almost as well-known as Haro in the evolution of BMX was Gary Turner, who also began experimenting with different materials and welding techniques, in order to produce bikes that could withstand the punishment of dirt tracks and jumps.

In 1975 he formed a partnership with Richard Long to begin making and selling top-quality BMX machines. The operation grew and in 1979 they formed a new company called GT Bicycles that promoted itself by sponsoring some of the best riders in the country.

ramps and every cul-de-sac or alley appeared about to get one. Kids came hurtling in all directions as they attempted the latest BMX moves. Pulling off any number of these street skills became every rider's rite of passage. It was even better if it could be done on a shiny new chromed-out BMX bike with fixed gears and mag wheels.

What had become obvious was the need for some kind of regulatory body to oversee the new sport. By 1977, pockets of loosely organised BMX races already dotted the nation

Stunt riding the BMX led to the evolution of many tricks that could be safely performed only by the young.

from coast to coast but there was no central authority. This came with the setting up of the American Bicycle Association. From now on this body would regulate the sport and encourage its expansion on a national level. A second move in the same direction came in April 1981 when the International BMX Federation was founded. More recognition came the following year when the first world BMX championships were held. From its simple origins in California, BMX biking had evolved to become a unique sport in its own right and an interesting new branch of traditional cycling with a particular appeal for the young.

Since January 1993, BMX has been fully integrated into the International Cycling Union (UCI). The sport was to play a major role in the X-Games on ESPN and to eventually become an Olympic sport in its own right. BMX Cycling made its debut at the Beijing Olympics in 2008 as the most recent discipline to have been added to the Olympic programme. In the face of fierce competition, the first BMX Olympic gold medals were won by Latvia's Maris Strombergs and France's Anne-Caroline Chausson.

Today there are three forms of BMX racing that are internationally recognised: racing, freestyle and jumping. Each discipline has its own specially designed type of bike. Racing BMX designs are obviously made to achieve the maximum speed and so require lightweight frames and specialised tyres. In contrast, freestyle bikes must be sturdy, with thick frames and ground-gripping tyres for stunt riding and best performance in skate-park locations. The third type, jump bikes, also need strong, sturdy frames, coupled with durable suspension systems and knobbly tyres. They are designed to handle jumps comfortably, whether on a circuit or in the backyard. Yet the old tradition of customising continues and many riders tailor machines to their own requirements from the vast array of components now available.

39: Lotus 108
Super Bike

There is no doubt that all the major technical advances in the history of cycling have been created by people with a vision and the ability to transform an innovative idea into a reality. Such a man was the British designer Mike Burrows, who in 1987 produced a revolutionary concept for a racing cycle that would transform the sport and begin a controversy that would rage for years.

Year: 1992

Manufacturer:
Lotus

Location:
Norfolk

During the previous century, racing cycle speeds had consistently increased as wheel technology, gearing and frame construction had improved. Yet before Burrows few had realised that no matter how good the components of a bicycle, it was the problem of streamlining that would ultimately define racing performance. Burrows's genius was to produce the solution to the problem that almost 90 per cent of a cyclist's energy was consumed in merely attempting to overcome air resistance. Reduce that resistance and the rider's speed must inevitably increase.

Although destined to produce the most radical racing design of his day, Burrows was not the first to appreciate the problem of air resistance. Throughout the 1980s other designers had come to a similar conclusion and had sought to create an ultra-lightweight racing cycle using a one-piece metal shell that would offer improved rider support while minimising drag. Frame builders, still committed to the traditional metal tubing, began experimenting with new frame configurations and tube shapes. Some experimented with the forward-sloping top tube that became possible when smaller, 650c front wheels were introduced. Others explored using steeper seat angles that would pitch the rider further forward and pointing down, so allowing the use of lower and more dynamic handlebars. Their efforts were helped by the latest developments in wheel design that included the first appearance of disc wheels. Handlebar design had also improved, time-trial racers now having their conventional drop bars replaced with new upturned bullhorn bars. While all these innovations helped improve the general streamlining effect, they failed to deal with the central problem − the weight of the frame.

A Revolutionary Frame

Working alone, Mike Burrows decided to tackle the problem by experimenting with the new materials that had emerged from space-age technology and seeing how they could be applied to traditional cycle design. His eventual solution was to produce a one-piece, monocoque cycle frame made entirely from a new carbon-fibre composite. Carbon, being a versatile material of incredible strength, could be moulded into just about any shape and its spectacular strength to weight ratio made it the potential replacement for aluminium in aircraft construction.

Burrows found that carbon fibre was almost perfect for a racing cycle frame. Light but incredibly strong, the finished prototype of Burrows's machine promised to be a world-beater. When the excited inventor presented his design to leading British cycling manufacturers in 1987, he was amazed at their reaction. None of them seemed impressed and although the British Cycling Federation did show interest, they pointed out that monocoque frames were banned under current UCI (International Cycling Union) regulations.

There the project might have ended, had not the UCI unexpectedly revoked their monocoque ban three years later, removing at a stroke the main objection to the revolutionary bicycle. By chance, Mike Burrows lived in Norfolk, England, near to the headquarters of Lotus Racing Car works; a friend who worked for the company offered to take the prototype to Lotus and test it in their wind tunnel. The results were so exciting that Lotus, with their

The revolutionary Lotus 110 (far left). Nothing would ever be quite the same again.

knowledge of and aptitude in using carbon-fibre techniques in Grand Prix racing cars, became eager to become involved in the birth of what promised to be a new super bike.

Twelve months later, after much testing and fine-tuning, the Lotus Super bike emerged from the Lotus factory at Hethel. Radically different in looks from anything that had gone before, it was to prove equally radical in performance. What Burrows and Lotus had produced was a sleek, black, feather-light cantilevered machine, based on a super-light carbon-fibre monocoque frame with a monoblade fork featuring an aerofoil cross-section. Every detail had been carefully refined, such as its unaligned wheels, with one disc and one tri-spoke both on the same side. Even the handlebars looked futuristic, long enough to allow the rider to sit hunched forwards with arms extended and fingers interlocked. The Lotus 110 had changed the very idea of how a bicycle should look and what it was capable of. Above it all, it offered the least wind resistance in performance to any racing cycle yet produced.

Confirmation that the Lotus could perform as well as it looked came when British cyclist Chris Boardman agreed to compete on it. From the start machine and rider seemed made for each other. Boardman was able to match the Lotus's advanced design with his own ability to achieve the almost perfect time-trialling position to complete the near-perfect aerodynamic package.

World Champion

Riding the new Lotus 110, Boardman took to the track for the Barcelona Olympics of 1992. It was the Lotus's first public appearance and Boardman promptly broke the world record, advancing to the quarter-final with a time of 4 minutes, 27.397 seconds. The following evening, he smashed his own day-old mark, defeating Denmark's Jan Petersen in 4 minutes, 24.496 seconds, winning the Olympic gold medal and setting a world record for the 4,000-metre (4,375-yard) individual pursuit. In pursuit cycling, both participants start the race at opposite sides of the 250-metre (274-yard) track, with the winner riding the allotted distance in the fastest time. Sometimes one rider is so dominant that he overtakes his opponent before the race ends. Boardman on his Lotus did exactly that, outclassing the reigning world champion with a lap to spare and winning Britain's first track-cycling gold medal since Thomas Lance and Harry Ryan's victory on a tandem in Antwerp 72 years previously.

Boardman then went on to victory in the Tour de France Prologue on the same machine but using a road version that did away with the down tube and seat stays. In their place was an oversized top tube connected to a large seat

'These are areas we wouldn't have examined because we were blinkered by thoughts of what I was supposed to look like while riding a bike. It came from bringing people into the process who weren't cyclists [. . .] It was just a wholly different set of thinking which revolutionised the sport.'

– Chris Boardman (2000)

pillar and oversized chain stays. In another innovative feature, the Lotus used Mavic's revolutionary Zap electronic gear-shifting system.

The success of Boardman and the Lotus was to demonstrate the uneasy relationship that exists between sport and new technology. By 1996, expensive racers like the Lotus, costing tens of thousands of pounds, had come to dominate the Olympic sport. In response to complaints from amateur riders and manufacturers alike, the UCI decided to intervene again. The result was a new ban on super bikes, the Lotus included. It was judged to have broken the rules not only because it was made of carbon fibre, but also because it dramatically altered the rider's position from what was considered normal.

Many thought these rules senseless because in almost every Olympic sport the equipment used has been transformed by technology and design. In any case, no one could deny the supremacy, albeit temporary, of the Lotus and the brilliant combination of Mike Brewer's radical design and the Lotus Company's skill in carbon-fibre technology.

As a postscript to the technological adventure and the controversy there is the story of what happened to the actual bikes. Fifteen Type 108s were built, including one prototype in 1991, as well as three frames for use in the Olympic Games. A further eight replicas were offered for sale at £15,000 each. Of the 15, at least two are on display, one at the Lotus Factory at Hethel, and Boardman's hour record bike at the Museum of Liverpool.

Chris Boardman, who would ride to victory on the Lotus in the 1992 Olympic Games.

40: Colnago
Great Time Trialler

One evening in October 1994, the Swiss cyclist Tony Rominger mounted his Colnago bicycle in the semi-deserted Bordeaux velodrome and set out to break the world one-hour record. The standing record of 53 kilometres (33 miles) had only been set in the previous month at this same venue by Rominger's great Tour de France rival, Miguel Indurain. More famous for his climbing ability than his power on the flat, Rominger had little experience of velodrome track riding. His one asset was a machine carefully prepared by Ernesto Colnago based on his road time-trial bike.

Year: 1994

Manufacturer:
Colnago

Location:
Cambiago

R ominger's attempt started badly; on his first practice run he entered the banked turn too quickly, lost control and crashed heavily to the ground. Two days later he had recovered sufficiently and was ready to try again. Riding faster than he had ever done in his life before, Rominger on his new Colnago with its aerodynamic frame, futuristic handlebars and two lighter lenticular wheels, shattered Indurain's month-old record by covering the incredible distance of 55.291 kilometres (34.356 miles), a winning margin of 800 metres (2,625 feet).

Colnago. The bike on which Tony Rominger would break the world one-hour record in 1984.

Colnago's Success Story

What had helped Rominger break the record so dramatically was the aerodynamic handlebars of the Colnago that allowed him to adopt a sleek, streamlined riding position to minimise wind resistance. Unlike later Colnagos, this one was made of steel tubing with fork blades and seat tubes shaped as air foils. It also had wind-cheating lenticular wheels. Stung by Rominger's success, Miguel Indurain decided the following year to try again, this time using a carbon-fibre frame. He even went to the rarefied high atmosphere of Columbia for the attempt but failed to improve on Rominger's record which would stand until Chris Boardman finally broke it in 1996.

Rominger's relationship with Ernesto Colnago had been preceded by that of the Italian high-end racing bike builder with Eddy Merckx. Colnago had started his business near Milan in 1954 after a bad crash had ended his own racing career. Colnago's company, along with that of Ugo De Rosa, soon gained a reputation for high-quality steel-framed bicycles and later for innovation in design and for experimentation with such new and diverse materials as carbon fibre. From the very start the quality of his machines was apparent to everyone in the sport and he was also much in demand as a racing mechanic. Eventually he was appointed chief mechanic of the Molteni team, where he met the Belgian cycling legend Eddy Merckx.

Ernesto Colnago.
A worldwide reputation
for making high-quality
racing machines.

THE ACE OF CLUBS

Colnago was generally regarded as one of the builders of the world's best custom road race frames. He had found success at the Rome Olympics in 1960, when Luigi Arienti won a gold medal on a Colnago bicycle. A win on a Colnago in the 1970 Milan–San Remo race by Michele Dancelli for the Molteni team inspired Colnago to change the company logo to the now-famous 'Asso di Fiori', or Ace of Clubs, pictured left.

Merckx had recently joined the Molteni team and they formed a close and productive relationship. With a growing reputation from their racing wins, Colnago then decided to enter the production bike market. In the USA, the early 1970s witnessed a huge increase in bike sales and Colnago 'pumped out bikes as though the future of humankind was at stake'. The mainstay of the Colnago line in the 1970s was the Super, followed by the Mexico, named in honour of the successful hour attempt. Other models were added, including the Superissimo and Esa Mexico. While the finish on these early Colnagos was variable, they were great riding bikes and developed a cult-like following.

In the Frame

Yet Colnago was not totally free of criticism, particularly the complaint that his frames were not rigid enough. Ever the perfectionist, Colnago experimented with methods to change the behaviour of frame components. The result was that in 1983, he announced his new Oval CX with an oval-shaped top tube to stiffen the frame. He then went on to experiment with various crimped-tube frames that then became production models for his top-of-the-range frames. Continuing to experiment, Colnago built a frame made from tubing supplied by Columbas, the main competitor to Reynolds tubing in Italy. The resulting bike was used by Giuseppe Saronni when winning the world professional road race championship in 1982.

Production line at the Colnago company, with frames ready for building.

As new materials appeared on the market, Colnago was quick to incorporate them into his bikes. Throughout the 1980s he began using material other than steel including titanium, aluminium and carbon. Another advanced frame from this period, the Bititan, had a dual titanium down tube. An experiment with crimped and oversized tubes resulted in the Tecnos, one of the lightest production steel bikes ever produced. Similar oversized tubes and crimping were then used on the aluminium Dream frame.

Always at the forefront of research, Colnago, in 1981, produced the CX1 with a full monocoque carbon-fibre frame and disc wheels. Convinced that carbon fibre was the way ahead, the company worked with the car company Ferrari to develop the new technology. Ferrari also worked with Colnago on an innovative fork design. This led to Colnago's advanced Precisa straight-bladed steel fork. As other new materials arrived, Colnago experimented with multi-material frames, including the CT1 and CT2 constructed with titanium main tubes.

Although technically bold, Colnago's early attempts at carbon-fibre frames were not commercially successful. The lessons learnt, however, were always incorporated into their new products such as the C40 frame of 1994 and its successor, the C50. These carbon-fibre frames set new standards of excellence for the industry and were built using a modified form of traditional bike frame construction, substituting carbon-fibre lugs for micro infusion cast steel, and carbon-fibre 'tubes' for the complex steel tubes used for steel frame construction. Nor was braking ignored; Colnago launched a new era in bike design by introducing the C59 Disc bike with fully hydraulic front and rear brakes.

Colnago became famous for innovative fork design such as the Precisa straight-bladed steel fork.

Powerful and elegant. The Colnago C59 in grey.

41: Scott Addict RC
Carbon Special

The Scott Addict shows just how far carbon-fibre bike technology has come in the past decade. Launched as the lightest production frame in the world and weighing just 790 grams (1.74 pounds), it is a thoroughbred road bike with a top-class racing performance. It features race-inspired geometry with a short head tube, long top tube and slack seat angle. The bike also features carbon dropouts, front derailleur mount and cable stops. Its greatest claim to fame is its excellence as a hill and mountain climber capable of tackling the steepest inclines and yet maintaining the rider's comfort.

Year:
2000

Manufacturer:
Scott Addict

Location:
Switzerland

Carbon-fibre technology produced a new lightweight Tour de France contender: the Scott Addict RC.

The choice of carbon fibre was critical, because of its high potential strength and its versatility. Carbon fibre itself was first produced in 1963 in a process developed by W. Watt, L. N. Phillips and W. Johnson at the Royal Aircraft Establishment in Great Britain. It was a major development in the search for alternative raw materials as it is made from a petroleum pitch derived from oil processing. The great thing about carbon fibre is that it can be moulded into just about any shape; those shapes can then be used to add strength where needed. This makes a near-perfect material for bike building. The strength-to-weight ratio is excellent, which is why it is becoming vital in aircraft construction.

The disadvantage of carbon-fibre cycle frames such as the Scott Addict is that they are fairly expensive. Although mass-produced models have become affordable over the last few years, custom bikes are still relatively expensive to produce. The other uncertainty about them is their longevity and durability. It is common for a pro cyclist to break or crack a carbon-frame bicycle at least two or three times a year. Frames also seem to have a fatigue factor as they can lose rigidity after a few years. Some have also claimed that as carbon frames are built from a mould it is not a cost-effective way to build a custom bike frame, as the moulds cost a lot of money to make. With such a high-quality racing bike as the Scott Addict, this is not a problem.

Scott Sports SA

The Addict is made by Switzerland-based Scott Sports SA, formerly Scott USA, a winter sports, motor sports and general sportswear manufacturer. The founder was Ed Scott, an engineer and skier from Sun Valley, Idaho, who in 1958 invented a new type of ski pole made of aluminium that outperformed the traditional type made of steel or bamboo. This successful product gave Scott the financial security to branch into other sports.

In 1989, Scott introduced one of the most significant innovations in the history of modern cycling: the clip-on aerodynamic handlebar. This was used to great effect by the American rider Greg LeMond in his 1989 Tour de France win. Then, in 1991, Scott produced the first suspension fork, the 'Unishock'. Such innovations helped to establish Scott as a world-class contender on the international racing circuit and a consistent stage winner in the Tour de France. In 2000, the company presented the road-bike Team Issue with what was then the lightest frame available, weighing less than 1 kilogram (35 ounces), and he even beat that two years later with a 895-gram (31.5-ounce) frame.

The heart of Scott's cycling success remains the state-of-the-art carbon frame technology. The rear triangle, seat stays and seat tube of the Addict R3 are made using Scott's original tube-to-tube CR1 construction process, while the front section of the frame is moulded in a one-piece monocoque structure, as are the chain stays and the integrated fork design.

The Integrated Molding Process (details of which remain a secret) is claimed to shave 11 per cent of the material from the head tube intersection to produce a very light and fast frame. This determined approach to weight saving certainly produced results, with test riders impressed by the fast climbing potential of the bike. The 73.3-degree seat tube angle also makes it easier for the rider to jump out of the saddle for powerful efforts. Performance like this has attracted top-class riders, among them Mark Cavendish, who when riding for Team HTC-Columbia on a Scott Addict won six stage victories in the Tour de France in 2009 and five more the following year. Increasingly, the bike was seen as the benchmark in carbon construction for professionals. Not only is it light enough to climb fast; it is also stiff enough to win the sprints.

PURE GENIUS

The Scott success continued in other biking disciplines too, with the company producing the lightest full-suspension mountain bike in the world. This machine, the Genius, was a new concept of a full-suspension bike with the shocks adjustable into three different modes: lock-out mode, all-travel mode and traction mode. The success of the Genius bike was highlighted by Thomas Frischknecht's victory in the marathon event at the World Championships in 2005.

42: Pro Fit Madone
Lance Armstrong

Between 1999 and 2005, Lance Armstrong completely dominated the sport of cycling. His recent fall from grace is all the more spectacular given his many achievements, not least winning seven consecutive titles in the Tour de France. In 1997, the American Trek bicycle company had helped sign Armstrong for the Trek-sponsored United States Postal Service Pro Cycling Team. Riding a Trek 5500, Armstrong won his first Tour de France in 1999, so becoming the first American to win the Tour in an American team and riding an American-made bike. He went on to win six more, all of them on Trek bicycles.

Year:
2005

Manufacturer:
Trek

Location:
Wisconsin

An American champion. The Trek was a combination of the latest technology with great rider appeal.

T rek Bicycle, established at Waterloo, Wisconsin, by Richard Burke and Bevil Hogg, started manufacturing steel touring frames in 1975. The company grew until, without doubt, Trek became the most successful American racing cycle maker of all time. They implemented the latest materials and technologies in order to match and beat the long-established European makers. Much of this came from their Advanced Concepts Group, which they established in 1998. This was a group of highly skilled engineers and technicians constantly researching Trek's equipment. The bikes that resulted from this concentrated effort, including the original Trek Madone of 2003, named after the Col de la Madone near the French town of Menton, were then used by Lance Armstrong during his historic Tour de France wins.

Cycling Out of Adversity

Armstrong began life with many disadvantages. His mother was just 17 when she gave birth to him and his father abandoned the family when Lance was two and never saw them again. Surprisingly, Armstrong did not start as a pure cyclist but as a triathlete, a sport in which competitors swim, cycle and run. Good in the water and a fast runner, it was as a cyclist that his real talent obviously lay. So, abandoning the triathlon, he committed himself full-time to a cycling career. Success came swiftly; he won the USA amateur cycling championship in 1991 and then turned professional the following year. He won the World Road Race championship, triumphing by 19 seconds over Miguel Indurain, the USA National Road Race champion, and won his first stage victory at Tour de France all in the same year.

Already there were indications of the dark cloud that would later descend on Lance Armstrong. He tested positive for a banned substance during his first Tour de France win in 1999. This was explained away by saying it was the side effect of a prescription for a cream to treat saddle sores. From then on the doubts and rumours surrounding his exceptional performance refused to go away.

Then, at the age of 25 and at the peak of his racing career, Lance Armstrong's doctors told him that he had testicular cancer, the most common cancer in young men. If detected early, the cure rate was a promising 90 per cent. Yet like many others, Armstrong had ignored the early warning signs. Left untreated, the cancer had spread to his abdomen, lungs and brain. The prognosis looked grim, but the rider had some unusual weapons against the disease. First of all he was, apart from the disease, in excellent physical condition, had a strong support system and, above all, a highly competitive spirit. He took the challenge head on, declaring to the world that he was determined not to be a cancer victim but a cancer survivor. As he said at the time, 'Through my illness I learned rejection. I was written off. That was the moment I thought, Okay, game on. No prisoners. Everybody's going down.'

Lance Armstrong riding to victory before the doubts began.

'Through my illness
I learned rejection. I was
written off. That was the moment
I thought, Okay, game on.
No prisoners. Everybody's
going down.'

– Lance Armstrong (2011)

With his customary thoroughness he then researched every aspect of the disease and the treatment available. Armed with this knowledge and confidence in medicine, he underwent aggressive treatment and beat the disease. During this time and before he even knew his own fate, Armstrong created the LiveStrong Foundation, a charity for people living with cancer and a world representative for the cancer community.

Doctors had estimated that Lance Armstrong's survival chances were about 40 per cent, although they later admitted that privately they thought them far less. There were other problems, too, that resulted from his illness. His cycling contract was cancelled, leaving him unemployed and without health insurance. The treatment itself added to the indignity, robbing him of all his hair and leaving him without enough muscle mass to even pedal his bike up a small hill. At least he was alive and what he did next would be every bit as impressive as his recovery from cancer. For Lance Armstrong steadily regained his fitness, and just a few years later he won the first of seven Tours de France.

Doping Controversy

Armstrong was probably unique in being an athlete of world class who returned from having serious cancer to become a champion again. His iconic status, however, was to be deeply compromised by his involvement with a drug scandal. In August 2005, Jean-Marie Leblanc, director of the Tour de France, claimed that Armstrong owed the cycling world an explanation after French sports paper *L'Equipe* reported that erythropoietin (EPO), a performance-enhancing drug, had been found in his blood sample from the 1999 Tour. Armstrong immediately denied the accusation, a position that he maintained for many years. Unfortunately, such secrets are hard to keep and some of his ex-teammates began speaking of 'secret code words, clandestine phone lines and furtive conversations' regarding human growth hormone, all connected with the use of drugs.

In February 2011, Armstrong announced his retirement from competitive cycling, while facing a USA federal investigation into doping allegations. He returned to his first love, the triathlon, competing as a professional in several events. Then, in June 2012, the United States Anti-Doping Agency charged Armstrong with having used illicit performance-enhancing drugs. The drug-taking accusations had been fully investigated by the agency and 11 former teammates of the USA Postal Service Pro Cycling Team had given evidence against him.

On 24 August 2012, the USADA concluded that a 'doping conspiracy' had indeed existed and that Lance Armstrong had personally orchestrated 'the most sophisticated, professional and successful doping programme that sport has ever seen'. As a result it was decided to strip him of his seven Tour de France titles and to ban him from the sport for life. That same October, the International Cycling Union (UCI), the sport's governing body, announced its decision to accept USADA's findings. Faced with such overwhelming evidence, Armstrong chose not to appeal the decision to the Court of Arbitration for Sport. Finally, in January 2013, Armstrong went on American TV and admitted in a television interview with Oprah Winfrey that he had, in spite of his many previous denials, taken performance-enhancing drugs. Still the public found it hard to accept that a man who had shown such courage and strength of character could have lowered himself to cheat in such a public arena. Perhaps he should have stuck to his own promise made years earlier: 'It can't be any simpler: the farewell is going to be on the Champs-Élysées.'

Such was Armstrong's determination not to be beaten by anything that even while his future as a cyclist was being decided he began a new career in the triathlon, a sport he had not pursued since his teenage years. The USADA were not pleased by the news and banned him from competitions. A suspicion that Armstrong was bad news, whatever the sport, had developed. As one leading USA triathlete commented, 'Lance's participation was definitely positive in bringing more attention to the sport but the cycling community has a tainted reputation, and at the end of the day, we don't want to go down that road.'

Lance Armstrong has been almost universally condemned as a cheat, but some feel that it was the culture of the sport that really led to his downfall. As the great French rider and five-time Tour winner Jacques Anquetil had famously said in the 1960s, 'it is as impossible to ride the Tour on mineral water... you would have to be an imbecile or a crook to imagine that a professional cyclist who races for 235 days a year can hold the pace without stimulants.'

Armstrong on a drip. Public opinion changed from enthusiastic support to growing suspicion of a sporting enigma.

43: The Velib
City Hire Bikes

One of the features of urban life in recent years has been the rapid spread of bike-hire schemes in cities throughout the world. These provide a service in which the cycle is made available for shared use to those who want to transit quickly through the crowded urban streets. The main purpose is not to make a profit but to cover costs while reducing motor traffic on the streets. Today, in many cities the presence of the hire bike is obvious, with long rows of matching cycles appearing in central areas, such as outside the main rail and metro stations and near public monuments and parks.

Year:
2007

Manufacturer:
Mercier

Location:
Hungary

These bicycles sit there waiting to be used by anyone who needs to get from place to place swiftly and at low cost and is prepared to do the pedalling. Not that this is too strenuous, as most of the world's cities are historically located in low-lying areas, usually on rivers. There is a charge to use the service, of course, for as yet no publicly owned and administered bicycle-sharing programme has been able to consistently operate as a self-funding enterprise.

Often painted in bright colours for easy identification, city hire bikes are almost always steel-framed and have a simple hub gear, chain case, and other features. This makes them heavier and more difficult to ride than the lighter road bike used by most commuters. Steel-framed machines are also cumbersome to carry and store. For this reason, the steel hire bike type of

All in a row. The Velib city bike soon became part of the Paris street scene.

machine has not sold well to the general cycling public. Nor would they be first choice for commuters who have to carry their bicycles on and off public transport or for those commuters living or working in multi-storey buildings. But the heavier steel bike does have one great advantage in that it can be easily locked in a rack and stored outside even in the heart of winter.

The First Bike-Sharing Schemes

The first bike-sharing projects began in 1965 as an initiative by local community organisations. Some were charitable projects intended for use by the socially disadvantaged, but most were an attempt to promote bicycles as a non-polluting form of transport in increasingly polluted cities. It was important to locate the cycle parks where they could easily be found by potential users, so favourite location points became where people arrived or left the city or went to work. The obvious places were bus and train stations. From the start the big problem was theft and how to stop the machines being stolen or not returned by the hirer. This had to be done in a way that did not deter possible users. A lesser but still important problem was to try to limit the vandalism that the bikes would inevitably attract. This is a puzzle that has still not been solved. For this reason virtually every bike-sharing scheme now requires the user to put up a monetary deposit or some other form of security before riding off on their bike. However, theft rates in many bike-sharing programmes still remain high, as most shared-use bicycles have value only as basic transport and can be stolen and then resold to unsuspecting buyers after being cleaned and repainted. In response to this threat, some large-scale bike-sharing programmes have designed their own distinctive-looking bikes using specialised frame designs and other parts to prevent resale of an obviously stolen machine.

'The invention of the Velib has proved that a bicycle can be a serious means of transportation, not just a weekend hobby.'

– Member of the public, *Le Parisien* (1965)

The mileage covered by a single city hire bike is impressive and has increased significantly since many schemes encouraged one-way riding. Under this, a hired bike can be picked up at one location and returned at another. This has been made possible by the smart card. It has been calculated that a single bike may be taken on 10 to 15 rides a day, each with a different user. The total distance covered in one year by such a bike in the city of Lyon was an impressive 10,000 kilometres (6,200 miles).

That city bike hire has become such a success is all the more surprising given that the first attempt in 1965 was a near total disaster. The scheme was started that summer in Amsterdam by Luud Schimmelpennink in association with the anarchist group called Provo. This so-called White Bicycle Plan provided free bicycles that were supposed to be used for one trip and then left

City bikes have had a growing influence on traffic flow and road regulations in cities across the world.

for someone else. Within a month, most of the bikes had been stolen and the rest were found floating in nearby canals. Years later, Schimmelpennink admitted that the scheme was never viable from the start, not least because it only had ten bicycles, and that all the bikes that were left were seized by the police within a day. Amsterdam was not alone in facing a hire bike disaster. Much later, in 1993, the English city of Cambridge started its own Green Bike Scheme with a fleet of some 300 bicycles. Within a year the great majority of the fleet had been stolen, and the Green Bike Scheme was quietly abandoned.

The French city of La Rochelle had better luck than Amsterdam when it launched a free bike-sharing programme in 1974. Called the Vélos Jaunes or Yellow Bikes scheme, it featured unisex bicycles on a free-to-use basis. The public were much more positive in their response than the Amsterdammers. Today it is recognised as one of the first successful bike-sharing programmes in Europe. The Vélos Jaunes still run, although security has been tightened and hire charges applied.

The Velib Success Story

The honour of being the capital city to have the most successful bike-hire scheme goes to Paris. It was here that the world's pioneering Velib cycle-hire scheme was introduced by Mayor Bernard Delanoe in 2006. It was an instant success, as Parisians took to the streets on bicycles in numbers not seen since the Second World War. Today, over 20,000 Velib bikes are available at hundreds of stations right across the city. Along with the Velib, the local authorities have greatly expanded the number of bike lanes throughout the city. The system is very simple. Racks of bicycles are placed at popular locations in the city centre. People can take the bikes out for a period ranging from just 30 minutes to a few hours. They ride to their destination and then drop their machine at the nearest bike parking lot. This makes a popular alternative to walking long distances or dealing with crowded buses and subway cars.

The rental bikes have proved their worth, particularly for short trips. Like all cities, Paris has horrendous traffic problems. Cars still crawl along the boulevards at walking pace but cyclists, with a little effort, can cover about 5 kilometres (3 miles) in just 20 minutes zooming past the gridlocks with ease. There were some early problems with the Velib, such as where to find the bikes and what vacant parking space to return them to, but these have largely been solved. New technology has helped as there are now more than a dozen free smartphone applications, including 'Open Bike', 'Cycle Hire' and 'molib', that are able to direct Velib riders to the nearest available parking space.

BORIS BIKES

One of the most successful bike-sharing schemes has been the Bixi project in the Canadian city of Montreal, which was used as the model for the Barclays Cycle Hire scheme in London opened by the extrovert mayor, Boris Johnson, in 2010. Not surprisingly, the cycles were soon nicknamed 'Boris Bikes'. The machines used in London were very similar to those in the Montreal scheme. Once the hirer has paid a £1 a day access charge, the first half an hour's rental is free and he or she can make as many 30-minute trips in the day as they wish without paying more. Although this seemed reasonable, some early viewers complained that, unlike the Parisian scheme, the London hire cycles did not have baskets and inbuilt security chains. As in Paris, there were significant financial penalties if the bikes were misused. If a bike was returned late after the access time had expired, the hirer faced a punitive charge of £150. Even worse, if the bike went missing or was damaged, the hirer had to pay up to £300 to cover the total cost of the loss. Fortunately, punctures were considered fair wear and tear.

Boris Bikes. The London version of the city bike was introduced by the city's colourful mayor.

The success of Velib has been truly astonishing, for since its launch seven years ago over 140 million trips have been recorded. The effect on Parisians themselves has been equally dramatic, especially on their attitudes to mobility. A few years ago it was unimaginable that a businessman in a suit or an elegantly dressed woman would dare to mount a bike, but today they are a common sight on Paris streets. Two-wheeled travel in Paris has become increasingly popular and affordable for

Commuter special. There is hardly a city today without a bike rental scheme.

those willing to pay an annual 29 euro membership fee. For that, they get the first half-hour on the bike free of charge. After that, the hourly rental rate becomes increasingly expensive, underlining the intention of making the Velib a cost-effective alternative to car, bus and the metro. The only problem that Velib users faced was that they were charged large sums if they failed to return their bikes correctly.

Today, over 110,000 Velib trips are made daily in Paris, half by people travelling to and from work, and the number of cyclists in Paris has increased by 41 per cent. Moreover, the Velib has raised the general popularity of cycling too and people are now more inclined to use their own bikes to get about the city, accounting for a total of 200,000 trips of all sorts every day in Paris. Perhaps the effect on commuting in other French cities has been the most significant of all, as 700,000 French workers throughout the country now commute to work by bicycle.

CYCLING SAVES LIVES

There are other reasons for the success of bike-hire schemes, not least the beneficial effects on human health. There is general agreement that cycle rental schemes save lives by increasing physical activity levels among city dwellers, and that they should be expanded. Barcelona was one of the first cities to introduce a scheme in 2007 and has more than 180,000 regular users. A Spanish study analysed the health impact of the scheme by comparing cycling with driving. It found that every year as a result of the benefits of increased physical activity 12 deaths had been avoided in the city. Cycling also diminished the risk of obesity, stroke and heart disease. The report concluded: 'Our work has shown that low-cost public bicycle-sharing systems aimed at encouraging commuters to cycle are worth implementing in other cities, not only for the health benefits but also for potential co-benefits such as a reduction in air pollution and greenhouse gases.'

Bike-Sharing Schemes Worldwide

The popularity of the Paris and London schemes has encouraged many other cities throughout the world to follow suit. Most large European cities such as Brussels, Rome and Vienna have similar operations. The trend has spread to smaller ones too and Poitiers, Bordeaux and Avignon as well as Oxford and Cambridge now have them. Because of the small size of the country, with its many congested urban areas, Britain has been particularly keen on adopting bike-hire schemes. The OYBike company already operates such systems in Cardiff and Reading and is planning a third in Farnborough.

The USA has been equally keen to adopt urban bike hire. The country's most ambitious bike-share plan to date has been the installation of 10,000 bikes at more than 400 stations across Manhattan and Brooklyn in New York City. An experiment on the Amsterdam model was attempted in 1994 at Portland, Oregon, by civic and environmental activists. They simply provided a number of bicycles on the streets for unrestricted use. Although the scheme provided plenty of publicity, it proved unsustainable due to theft and vandalism of the bicycles. A similar project was attempted two years later in Tucson, Arizona, by a homeless association inspired by the Bikes Not Bombs movement. Using public funds they put 80 bicycles in downtown Tucson. Although painted bright orange they were all either stolen or vandalised within a few weeks. Madison, Wisconsin, tried bright red rather than orange for their bike scheme the same year but had no better luck. The riders were required to leave their Red Bikes

A city bike, whatever the colour. Bike rental is a major global business.

outside and unlocked, and thus available for any passer-by. After a surge in bicycle thefts and vandalism, the programme was modified to require a valid credit card and $80 in security deposits for both the bicycle and the now-mandatory bicycle lock. Like the other free schemes, this had again proved that a financial deposit must play some part in a bike scheme if it is to succeed.

City bike hire is now far more than a USA or European phenomenon; there are low-price urban bike rental schemes throughout the world, including in China.

Their popularity in tourist destinations is easy to see, as they offer a means of transport appropriate to leisurely sight-seeing. In May 2011 there were around 136 bike-sharing programmes in 165 cities around the world, making an estimated total fleet of 237,000 bicycles. Of these the Hangzhou Public Bicycle programme launched in 2008 in China is the largest bicycle-sharing system in the world. It has around 61,000 bicycles and over 2,400 stations.

44: Cervélo S5
Modern Classic

One of the bicycle-making companies that has fully embraced the latest carbon-fibre technology is Cervélo. In recent years it has attracted such world-class riders as Tyler Farrar. For a top-class sprinter like Tyler Farrar, even the smallest differences in aerodynamic drag can make a big difference to performance when travelling at speeds of around 70 km/h (43.5 mph). At these speeds, drag is the most significant force that the rider must overcome when a time difference of just 0.002 seconds represents a winning distance of half a wheel.

Year:
2008

Manufacturer:
Cervélo

Location:
Canada

The Cervélo S5 represents a new breed of aerodynamic road bike that combines the geometry and handling of a road machine with the special low-drag features that evolved from the disciplines of time trialling and triathlon. The most obvious aero feature of the Cervélo design is the seat tube that comes with a cut-out for the rear wheel to smooth the airflow through the bike. Carbon-fibre frames are expensive to develop, but offer the best combination of a slippery profile to cut through the wind and also the stiffness required to harness the rider's power.

Cervélo S5. A low-drag, world-class racer favoured by top sprinters.

In Search of a Faster Time-Trial Bike

Cervélo was part founded by a Dutch engineer, Gérard Vroomen, who took his skills to Canada to research bike dynamics at McGill University. In 1995, together with Phil White, he founded Cervélo Cycles in Canada – the name Cervélo being a combination of *cervello*, the Italian word for brain, and *vélo*, the French for bike. Phil White and Gérard Vroomen set up the company after a top Italian cyclist approached them to help design a faster time-trial bike. The cyclist felt that his current sponsor was only able to develop traditional bikes using off-the-shelf tube sets; he felt that he wanted more. He approached Vroomen in the hope of finding a brand new, innovative aerodynamic design that was specifically for time trials. The result was the Cervélo Barrachi, which proved a radical departure from the average bike with its full carbon frame that used a beam saddle design, radical deep aero section front and an integrated bar/fork/stem design.

The following year Cervélo launched with two road bikes and two trial or triathlon bikes. Their technology was so radical that professional cyclists were at first hesitant to try them. They had become used to the bike they currently owned and did not want to start compromising their potential wins by testing the new bike. However, in 2000 new rules were brought in regarding equipment

Cervélo: as successful on the road as they are on the track.

by the International Cycling Union that made many of the bikes currently being used illegal. This was a golden opportunity for Cervélo and a turning point for the company fortunes as they had already built these changes into their designs. In time for the new rules they released a new model line that complied totally with the new regulations.

Another stroke of good fortune was that a few triathletes began riding Cervélo frames with great success and then a couple of big name professional cyclists started using Cervélo frames for time trials, with their sponsors' bike logos on the frames. After this good fortune sales took off. Many successful designs later, Vroomen sold his stake in Cervélo in

Cervélo was particularly popular with triathletes before it was taken up by time-trial professionals.

2011. The company continued to flourish and was later acquired by Pon, a Dutch company that also owns the famous Gazelle brand and Derby Cycle, who own Raleigh, Univerga and Focus Bikes. The success continued and Cervélo took its place among the world's leading racing marques.

THE 'OPEN' MOUNTAIN BIKE

Having established a reputation as one of the world's finest makers of racing bikes, in 2011 Cervélo decided to launch a range of mountain bikes under the brand name 'Open'. The first model, the 74-centimetre- (29-inch-) wheeled O-1.0, was claimed to be the lightest 29-inch hard tail frame available, with a weight of just 900 grams (31.7 ounces) that included the large-sized frame with all of its accompanying hardware. A great deal of time was spent testing the prototype before the model was officially launched, for as Gérard Vroomen said:

'You can do a lot of work on the computer, but in the end you have to build it, test it and see how it works.' The bike was then submitted for testing by the German company EFBe in their mountain bike testing process. The result was approval as the lightest frame that the company had ever had pass their tests. The limited production model now comes with a no-holds-barred build that includes ENVE wheels and Acros hydraulic shifting. The bike may weigh only 8.62 kilograms (19 pounds), but costs a hefty $12,000, with the frame alone setting the new owner back $2,700.

'You can do a lot of work on the computer, but in the end you have to build it, test it and see how it works.'

– Gérard Vroomen (2011)

Racing Success

From the start, Cervélo was interested in establishing a reputation in cycle racing and in 2003 provided the bikes for the Team CSC. Although Team CSC was ranked only 14th in the world rankings, the cycling world was impressed as Cervélo were by far and away the smallest and youngest bike company to ever supply a team at this level. The investment paid off, for Team CSC became the world pro cycling team champions for three years. When that partnership ended, Cervélo in 2009 became the first bike manufacturer in the modern era to have its own cycling team at the highest levels of racing with its Cervélo Test Team. The sporting success culminated in 2008 with Carlos Sastre winning the Tour de France, while, at the Beijing Olympics, Cervélo bikes were ridden by more than 40 Olympic athletes, resulting in three gold, five silver and two bronze medals – a record.

This combination of racing success and high-tech research helped the company to become the world's largest manufacturer of time-trial and triathlon bikes. Throughout this period the company continued to refine its bikes with improvements always based on research. It even used wind-tunnel testing at a variety of facilities including the San Diego Air and Space Technology Center, in California, to track its bikes. Today, as carbon-fibre frames are probably as light as current technology allows, the company is concentrating on refining other aspects of the bike. For instance, one improvement made by Cervélo in the S3 over other bikes in the range is in the use of advanced internal cable routing.

With racing performance resulting from high-tech research, Cervélo are now producing mountain bikes.

45: The Gazelle
Nation on Wheels

Gazelle is the most historic and famous of all Dutch cycle brands. It was founded by Willem Kölling in 1892, who then joined forces with Rudolf Arentsen. They chose the name Gazelle having been impressed by the speed of a wild deer that raced across their path during a country walk. Their cycles sold well and from the 1920s to the 1940s, Gazelle successfully exported their bicycles to the East Indies. Today, Gazelles are much sought after by collectors, with many still being found in Indonesia.

Year:

Manufacturer:
Gazelle

Location:
Dieren

Gazelle went on to make a collapsible delivery bicycle in 1930, followed by a tandem in 1935. In conjunction with the Philips electrical company, an innovative early electric bicycle was produced in 1937. Then, in 1954, Gazelle became a public company, having just built its millionth bicycle. Other developments continued, including a first three-speed grip-shift gear system in 1959. By the mid-1960s Gazelle had established a specialised racing division at their Dieren factory making hand-built frames. Gazelle was then the first Dutch bicycle manufacturer to introduce the 'Kwikstep', a folding bicycle, in 1964. The front-hub drum brake was developed in 1968 and is still in production today.

The stately Gazelle. A favourite of Dutch cyclists since the 1930s.

A NATION OF CYCLISTS

No wonder the Dutch are thought to be cycling mad – the Netherlands is the only nation in the world with more bicycles than people! In a country with a population of just 16.5 million people, there are approximately 18 million bikes. That means 1.1 cycles for every single person. Amsterdam alone has over a half million, yet only 215,000 motor cars. Cycling has become one of the most important forms of travel for Dutch city-dwellers, with 26 per cent of all journeys taking place by bike, the highest in the EU. They are used to seeing people of all ages, shapes and sizes on bikes: from builders, bakers and bankers, to elderly statesmen and even royalty. It is not uncommon for a senior government minister to pull one up at a traffic light in The Hague.

No other nation depends as much on the bike, day or night, as the Netherlands.

Over the past 119 years Gazelle has grown from a small two-man operation into a leading international business; from precisely three bicycle sales in 1892 to the biggest bicycle brand in the Netherlands, with annual production of 350,000 bicycles. The centenary celebrations in 1992 coincided with the production of the 8-millionth bicycle. Furthermore, Princess Margriet of the Netherlands awarded the 'Royal' title to Gazelle in honour of the company's centenary. The success continued and the 13-millionth Gazelle rolled off the production line in 2008. Without a doubt, the Gazelle is the iconic Dutch bike.

An Enduring Love Affair

Why the bicycle became so successful in Holland may appear to be a mystery at first, particularly compared with Germany, where much of the landscape is similarly flat as in the Netherlands. The answer lies with the different class system, for in Germany the bike became very popular with the working class while the rest of society rejected it as a low-class means of transport. In contrast, the Dutch, workers and middle class alike, took to the cycle with enthusiasm and it became an accepted, reliable, solid and, above all, classless means of transport. It also suited the way in which the Dutch saw themselves as a practical, sober and hardworking people. Showing off on fancy machines or horses did not fit the Dutch character. As a result, bike ownership grew. In 1910 there were some 450,000 bicycles owned in the Netherlands and within a decade that figure had doubled. Much of this growth was due to the style of bicycle that became the top seller, known in Germany as 'das Hollandrad'. By 1919 the 'Dutch bike' had been perfected for practical, everyday transportation and incorporated features such as an upright riding position, a sturdy frame and components, robust luggage rack and mudguards.

> 'When I bike in Holland, I get the sense that the road was designed with bikes and cars in mind from the outset... I feel respected as a cyclist, and therefore I'm more likely to respect the traffic rules.'
>
> – Frank de Jong (2012)

There was to be a second impetus for the Dutch love of the bicycle when a massive popular reaction against the automobile began. People thought that the sheer number of cars was encroaching even more on the crowded Dutch streets and demanding more than their fair share of parking space. Street planning departments now began an offensive to limit the encroachment on the bicycle and one of the first new regulations in the 1920s was a law that ordained that every new house must have a shed of some kind for bikes. Even flats had to have a similar provision.

The idealised image of cycling as a respected, mainstream mode of transport means that there have to be strict regulations. Laws concerning lights, bells, bikes on trains, as well as compulsory cycle paths, are rigorously policed in Holland. Taking a bike on a train is expensive and requires a ticket in addition to the cyclist's fare, a significant cost for regular leisure riders. Many bicycle deaths are the result of getting hit by a car. Even so, with 49 deaths per million people a year in the Netherlands, the nation has the best road safety record in Europe. Many think this has more to do with the entire country being stuck in a traffic jam 12 hours a day.

It is no accident that the Dutch are so in love with the bike, for nowhere else in the world is there such a strong cycling culture that begins almost in the cradle. The first thing a Dutch child learns after walking is how to ride a bicycle. They ride to school, first with their parents and then on their own. At the age of nine they are expected to pass a cycling proficiency test and gain a diploma. Later, as teenagers, they use their bikes to go out on dates, cycling along with their boy- or girlfriends on bikes, partly because they are not allowed to drive a car until they are 18 years old. When they get a job and commute to work, most of them do it on a bicycle. Even high-ranking business people and civil servants of all ages commute to work on a bike. The Dutch police patrol on bikes and cycling holidays are common for families of all ages. Few other countries have such a landscape that seems almost designed for the bicycle. For the most part, the Netherlands, having once been partly submerged beneath the North Sea, is flat, except for the low, rolling hills in the province of Limburg in the extreme south of the country.

Over the years everything has been done by the Netherlands' government to encourage the use of the bicycle. Laws and above all the road systems are bicycle-friendly. The national infrastructure is dedicated to cycling, with over 29,000 kilometres (18,020 miles) of bike paths throughout the country and hundreds of dedicated cycle bridges, tunnels and cycle ferries to cross the many rivers and canals. Most urban roads have bike paths running alongside them and there are separate traffic lights for cyclists at virtually every intersection, with the bicycle symbol appearing in red, yellow and green. The infrastructure is totally geared towards cycling, making it a serious mode of transportation and an integral part of Dutch society. Yet the safety of having separate lanes for cyclists has often been questioned. Though there are many variables, and conclusions are contested, most studies suggest that separate paths, if anything, can often make cycling more dangerous as junctions – where most accidents occur – are more complicated.

Even in a country so devoted to accommodating the bicycle, the Netherlands must eventually run out of the space for the 5 million riders who take to the road every day, turning major city commuting into a nightmare. In Amsterdam alone 490,000 freewheeling 'fietsers' take to the road to cycle a staggering 2 million kilometres (1,242,742 miles) every day, according to statistics released by the city council. The result is that around major stations such as Amsterdam and Utrecht Central, tens of thousands of bicycles parked legally and illegally hog public space and restrict pedestrian access, while cyclists struggle to remember just where they parked their bike.

More bicycles per head than anywhere else in the world; the Dutch are a nation on two wheels.

THE MULTI-STOREY BIKE PARK

Parking, the major problem for most cities throughout the world, is made easier for the Dutch cyclist as there are 350,000 bicycle storage spaces at train stations throughout the Netherlands. The largest is at Amsterdam's Central Station, which has a massive, three-tier bike garage. Referred to as the world's first bicycle warehouse, it currently has space for up to 3,000 bikes. Close by are many other cycle parking areas, offering a total of over 10,000 spaces. If the other Amsterdam train stations are included there are about 30,000 bicycles parked each day in central Amsterdam. Nor are provincial cities neglected; Utrecht, a university town in central Holland, has spaces for as many as 20,000 bikes. For car drivers it is a far different situation, with meagre spaces and very high parking charges. Amsterdam, in fact, has among the highest parking fees in the world.

46: The Madsen
Cargo Bikes

One of the finest examples of a modern cargo bike is the American-designed Madsen. As its inventor Jared Madsen said, 'As soon as we built our first prototype with the load in the rear we overcame the problems of front-load cargo bikes.' What the new design offered was a ride just like a regular bicycle, able to handle rough conditions. Although the rider cannot see the cargo or passengers behind, he or she is a great deal more in control and is able to jump curbs, ride down stairs, and negotiate potholes safely.

Year:
2008

Manufacturer:
Madsen

Location:
Salt Lake City

 adsen are catering for a growing trend with individuals and businesses to use bicycles not just for personal transportation, but also to move heavier cargo of all kinds, including children. For instance, one of the latest Madsen machines can carry up to four small children (using a bucket with a removable bench seat and two seatbelts) and has a load capacity of 272 kilograms (600 pounds). Madsen's inspiration for founding his company was the feeling that in modern society, the bicycle should have more than just one function. Having lived in Holland for two years he saw that it should be seen as an everyday tool and not just as a weekend toy. This was indeed one of the cycle's original purposes when it first appeared.

Complete with bucket. Modern cargo bikes like the Madsen are gaining popularity fast.

The First Cargo Bikes

Ever since the bicycle was first invented, people have sought to find a practical use for it, other than to transport a rider. One of the first practical uses of a cycle as a goods carrier was in 1881 in Britain. This involved an early tricycle made by Bayliss & Thomas. It was based on the velocipede and was used by the Post Office for urban letter and package deliveries. Bayliss had proved that the tricycle was a far better load-carrier than a bicycle for the obvious reason that three wheels gave better stability than two. When stopped, it also needed no propping up or complicated parking. For this reason, and after the diamond-shaped frame was established, most manufacturers had a basic load-carrying model in their range – usually available only in black!

When Bayliss & Thomas began making their machines there were already two regular tricycle post rounds operating in Coventry, a city that was then the home of the UK cycle industry. The prospect of prestigious and lucrative contracts with the Post Office throughout Britain led to a boom in experimenting in cargo cycle design. Some of these new machines set out to extend the load-carrying capacity of existing tricycle design by adding an extra wheel, so turning the tricycle into a quadricycle.

'Every other butcher, baker and candlestick maker in the Kingdom finds use for the cycle... they are to be seen everywhere in the thick of London traffic.'

– Bicycling World (1885)

Within a decade the cargo tricycle had been redesigned so that a large basket or a container could be located between the rear wheels rather than in front. Shopkeepers found such machines so useful that they became commonly known as 'butchers' bikes' or in Germany as 'bakers' bikes'. Such was the demand for the cargo bike in Britain that *Bicycling World* claimed that 'every other butcher, baker and candlestick maker in the Kingdom finds use for the cycle... they are to be seen everywhere in the thick of London traffic.' Other less basic trades followed suit; the Quadrant Cycle Company produced a cargo trike that was specially customised for the use of the travelling photographer, who was able to carry his heavy camera and tripod and all his accessories.

AN 'IDEAL' SOLUTION?

One innovative machine was the 'Ideal' designed by a Horsham architect in 1882, featuring a large central driving wheel surrounded by four small stabilising wheels. The bike came with an ingenious mechanism that lifted it off the ground once in motion. Other European countries followed the British example and began experimenting with cargo tricycles. The Austrian postal service, for example, began using them in 1888.

Pedalling Postmen

Postmen in particular remained the prime target for cargo bike makers. Following early trials, British postmen were offered a curious scheme. They would be given a weekly allowance for providing their own cycle on their delivery rounds. As ordinary working men, few of them at the time could afford the cost of a cycle. For this reason the scheme was abandoned and the use of delivery cycles increased only gradually. In 1895 there were still only 67 machines in use, but the following year the British Post Office abandoned the tricycle and ordered 100 of the new safety bicycles for their telegraph boys. This helped spur the demand for cargo bikes and by the turn of the century there were many cycle manufacturers making trade bicycles and tricycles for all manner of deliveries.

Postal services have always been regular users of the cargo bike for letter and package deliveries.

Another boost to the cargo bike came in 1904 when each individual British Post Office was allowed to buy as many of them as it thought justified for local usage. With so many different machines and components now on the market, confusion arose. The solution came in 1929 when a Standard Post Office Cycle was introduced for use all over the country. The fleet began to grow significantly and by 1935 it numbered 20,000 machines. Together, the fleet covered a combined annual distance of over 193,000,000 kilometres (120,000,000 miles). A report of 1953 shows just how much the Post Office specifications had changed over the years, with the introduction of 26-inch wheels, a woman's frame and a lower riding position that made it easier for the postman to dismount.

One of the British companies that has successfully produced cargo bikes since the early days is Pashley. In the 1930s, Pashley made almost every component of their cycles in their own factory; it was only the tubing and lugs that were bought in. Frame building, brakes, wheels, sheet metal work, polishing and enamelling were all carried out in the works. With their commercial success from pedal cycles Pashley expanded the range they offered by producing motorised delivery tricycles, ice-cream carts, railway station trolley and specialist units for the dairy and catering trades.

By the late 1970s, Pashley was supplying bikes to the Post Office. The original designated mail machine had a single speed and rod-operated brakes. Eventually the company became the sole suppliers of this machine. This virtual monopoly appeared to be threatened when an international competition was held for the supply of Royal Mail bicycles. Pashley nominated its new 'Pronto' model with its step-through frame design, and won.

With the coming of email and online shopping, the pattern of postal shopping has changed and postal deliveries have become more dependent on carrying goods and packages rather than letters. To meet these new challenges the Netherlands, Denmark and some of the other traditional cycling countries of Europe have responded by adding trailers to postal delivery bicycles and tricycles and introducing the extended bicycle to their delivery fleets.

BABY ON BOARD

Postal deliveries have been the main but not the sole use for cargo bikes throughout the twentieth century. An entirely different market has grown up for using the cargo bike as child carrier. Even as early as 1891 the British cycle designer Dan Albone had thought of this idea. He made a wicker child carrier that fitted over the front wheel of a safety bicycle, which itself had been invented only six years before. Today it is mainly in Holland and Denmark that people use the bike as a child carrier. In these countries it is common to see a father or mother cycling to school with two children strapped to a carrier on the front of a bike or an old lady pedalling back from the local shops with bags of groceries in a carry-box on the back of her tricycle. This use of the bike as a shopping vehicle seems particularly relevant at a time when petrol prices make short journeys by car impractical. It is claimed that two weeks' shopping for a family of four could easily fit on most cargo bikes.

Great for bringing home the shopping, or even the children from school.

A Global Phenomenon

The use of cargo bikes was not confined to Europe and the USA. In 1910 the American vice consul in Yokohama reported that 'bicycles are in general use throughout the Empire' and that many of them were not imported but now made in Japan. The same was true of China, where the adapted cargo bike was put to a thousand different uses as a low-cost freight transporter. Yet it was all to change. As the motor van came to dominate the delivery system after the Second World War, the humble freight or cargo bike was relegated to factory floor duties and serving as small mobile shops, such as ice-cream bikes. Yet in the rest of the world they continued to be manufactured and heavily used.

Cargo bikes are a feature of street life throughout every city in the East.

Then in the 1980s in Europe, and the 1990s in the USA, there came a renaissance for such machines. As society became more ecologically aware designers and small-scale manufacturers returned to the market with updated and more sophisticated machines. This was the time when the 'longtail' bike appeared. With its very long wheelbase, it has space behind the rider for a luggage rack. The strong frame and wheels allow it to carry more weight on and around the rear wheel, so avoiding the problems of steering linkage found on cargo bikes with their front loading cargo area. Most importantly, it is far more stable due to its long wheelbase.

Many feel that for the modern cargo bike, the time has come. Yet apart from enduring the pollution, noise and traffic of modern cities there is also the element of physical risk to the rider. Big lorries on narrow city streets are involved in a disproportionate number of

THE DAILY SERVICE BICYCLE

In the USA cargo bikes had developed along with all the other types of cycle so that in 1910 the Pope Manufacturing Company launched its Daily Service Bicycle. This was a machine specifically designed for such people as postal deliverers, policemen, firemen, messengers and road workers.
Advertisements claimed that it answered a demand for 'a vehicle possessing greater strength and

durability to stand up day in and day out'. The greatest use for this type of machine remained, as in Britain, the various urban postal services. One of the largest, Western Union, bought 5,000 bikes annually then ingeniously sold them at a discount to their messengers. It was a novel and low-cost form of having a company car. The messenger boys were as young as ten and were paid by the mile travelled.

serious accidents, especially concerning cyclists. In London, an estimated 50 per cent of cyclist fatalities in recent years came in collisions with lorries. With more cargo bikes speeding to and fro, such hazards can only increase. But when faced with growing urban traffic congestion they do offer a way ahead to hard-pressed delivery companies. Firms such as TNT, FedEx and DHL are all known to be experimenting with cycle delivery.

Given the state of the world's traffic and the promising developments in cargo bike design, representatives from governments and industry met in Copenhagen in May 2011 to share ideas for altering the system of goods delivery in European cities. The emphasis in the future should be away from motorised delivery and towards using the pedal cycle and other non-polluting means of transport. For this reason, the conference agreed that businesses that use cargo cycles are being environmentally responsible as well as having a better chance of delivering their goods on time.

Nowhere has this been more relevant than in China. In large cities with dense populations, millions of bicycles and cargo tricycles are being employed for daily transportation of people and goods. Whether transporting garbage, fruit, a mini-barbecue, stacks of chairs or hay, the Chinese have been creative in using cargo bikes in any way to help them with their business or wherever they need to go, perhaps showing the way ahead for the rest of the world.

Cycle rickshaws are an important means of transport throughout Asia.

47: Specialized Tarmac SL3
Future Winner

In recent years the Specialized company has become a leading American contender in the quest for the perfect carbon-framed racing bike. Over the years it has established a reputation for producing bikes with precise handling and drag-racer acceleration such as the Specialized Tarmac SL3. Specialized is now one of the largest bicycle brands, just below Trek Bicycle Corporation and Giant Bicycles, and is tipped for even greater racing success in the future. Specialized's brand of hippie capitalism has lifted the company to an estimated $500 million in sales of bikes and accessories.

Year:
2010

Manufacturer:
Specialized

Location:
California

S pecialized was founded in 1974 by Mike Sinyard who, on a cycling tour of Europe, bought some Cinelli handlebars and stems and took them back to sell in the USA. This launched his career as an Italian bike parts importer at a time when such components were hard to find in America. Two years later Sinyard started producing his own bike parts, beginning with the Specialized Touring Tire. The business took off and in 1979 Specialized progressed to producing its first complete road bike, the Allez, although this was manufactured in Japan. Over the past 30 years the company has grown to become one of the world's leading bicycle and accessory manufacturers,

Aiming for carbon-fibre perfection. The Specialized Tarmac SL3.

whose products over the last 30 years helped transform the sport from cult pursuit to mainstream participation and Mike Sinyard from an obscure cycling geek into what many consider to be the industry's equivalent of the late Steve Jobs.

Faced with a fast-growing market, in 1981 Specialized launched the Stumpjumper, the first major production mountain bike in the world. The design was inspired by a Fisher/ Ritchey mountain bike and was produced in Taiwan. Over the years this highly successful machine has constantly evolved and is now made with a full suspension system. With its introduction in the early 1980s, the Stumpjumper helped turn cycling from the preserve of high-end road elitists into an accessible way of life available to the mainstream. So significant was the original Stumpjumper that one of the first prototypes is on permanent display at the Smithsonian Institution in Washington, D.C.

Fine component detail on the Specialized Stumpjumper mountain bike.

In the 1980s Specialized took a close interest in the development of carbon-fibre frames, eventually introducing the Epic, the world's second mass-production carbon-fibre mountain bike. A decade later the company came up with the Globe range of urban cycles. Sinyard hired a group of consultants, who advised him to stop focusing on performance and innovation and concentrate on selling more bikes. This ability to exploit new and growing markets became characteristic of the company.

The Stumpjumper in its natural environment, high on a mountain trail.

In 1995 Specialized overreached itself by launching its Full Force brand. This was intended to capture the lower end of the mountain bike market. The bikes were intended to be sold through sports stores and cut-price discount retailers such as Costco. The move proved a disaster. Quality plummeted as, in Sinyard's words, the company 'lost control of inventory management', alienating discerning riders without attracting the masses that it coveted. The move so angered established Specialized dealers that the company abandoned the Full Force line and Mike Sinyard wrote a letter of apology to all the dealers. Full Force proved a costly mistake; by the end of 1996, Specialized had lost 30 per cent of its bike shop sales and, according to Mike Sinyard, 'came within a few hundred dollars of declaring bankruptcy'.

Yet the company bounced back and in 2001, Merida Bikes of Taiwan bought into the company as Specialized continued to establish its racing credentials by sponsoring such high-profile teams as Quick Step and Saxo Bank. In return, Specialized gained valuable feedback from the team riders that proved invaluable for product development. For example, when the Tarmac SL2 was being designed, Tom Boonen, who won the World Road Race Championship in 200, asked for more frame stiffness; Specialized's

DESIGNING BIKES FOR WOMEN

Specialized has become involved in areas that few other racing cycle makers have bothered to cater for, such as women's bikes. The result of the research has been the Amira – the women's version of the Tarmac. This has been specially built with female proportions in mind. It comes in five different sizes for women while the male Tarmac comes in six, significantly more than produced by any other bike company. This led the Giant CFO team rider Bonnie Tu to claim that no other company is designing bikes for women. Whatever the truth of the matter, Specialized's commitment to women is arguably deeper than that of any other bike company, with four road models and five off-road models available.

The Amira range is specially designed for both women riders and racers.

The versatility of Specialized bikes was well demonstrated during 2004–7, when the British TV adventurer Rob Lilwall rode a Specialized Rockhopper (nicknamed Alanis) over 50,000 kilometres (31,068 miles) from Magadan, northeast Siberia, back home to London, via Australia and Afghanistan. Along the way, he rode his bike through the −40°C tundra of Russia, carried it through rivers and jungles in Papua New Guinea, and dodged through military checkpoints in Tibet.

response was to stiffen the SL2's platform as well as reducing the overall weight by another 100 grams (3.5 ounces). Later, this ability to listen to riders' requests based on actual performance led Specialized to move in the opposite direction and later models show a move away from the uncompromising rigidity of the SL3.

Specialized has one of the most impressive histories in the cycle industry from the production of the very first mountain bike, the Stumpjumper, to the development of the ultimate sports road bike, the Roubaix, named after the gruelling Paris–Roubaix race that it has won three consecutive times. In the late 1990s the company started working with Mario Cipollini, one of Italy's top riders. This involvement with racing soon began to produce results, with Fabian Cancellara winning the 2010 Paris–Roubaix race on a Specialized Roubaix and the world time trial in 2010 on a Specialized Shi. The top two finishers in the 2010 Tour de France, Alberto Contador and Andy Schleck, both rode Specialized Tarmacs. Three of the world's top pro teams switched to Specialized bikes; Team Astana, Saxo Bank and HTC-Highroad. A new Specialized racing bike, the Venge, was co-designed with McLaren, the Formula One motor racing team, and the world's top sprinter, Mark Cavendish of HTC, rode a Venge in the 2012 Tour de France.

The Amira is constantly updated, like all other Specialized products.

48: The Pinarello
Wiggins Machine

That an Englishman could win the Tour de France was, for the average English cyclist, a fantasy that would forever remain unfulfilled. That is, until a small, determined man with great cycling talent and a very odd name came along. For in 2012 Bradley Wiggins turned that dream into a reality by becoming the first Briton to win the Tour de France in its 109-year history – and he did it riding a Pinarello.

Year:
2011

Manufacturer:
Pinarello

Location:
Treviso

(F) or the final day of the race that finished, as usual, on the Champs-Élysées, Wiggins chose a special custom-painted Pinarello 65.1. But for most of the race he had been riding a Pinarello Dogma 2. The frame shape of the 65.1 remained the same as the Dogma 2, characterised by Pinarello's famous asymmetric design with its wavy fork, seat and chain stays. The main difference was that the 65.1 used a 65Ton HM 1K carbon-fibre frame that Pinarello claims was more rigid and more reactive than the Dogma 2 as well as being lighter at a claimed 920 grams (32.4 ounces). Wiggins, a cycling perfectionist, had been closely involved in the preparation of the machine.

The Sky Team Pinarello is the result of hands-on involvement from such team members as Bradley Wiggins.

Yet for the rest of the 3,218-kilometre (2,000-mile) race it was the Dogma 2 that Wiggins relied upon. With its entirely hand-built carbon-fibre frame the Dogma 2 had such personally chosen features as kinked chain stays and a personalised seat post. True to his maverick reputation, Wiggins insisted on using an unusual asymmetric chain ring. While the ring that carries the pedals is normally round, Wiggins's was egg-shaped. This, he is convinced, maximises pedalling efficiency when the rider's legs are at the peak of the stroke. Equally advanced was the electronic Dura-Ace Shimano D12 gear set that he chose. This system means that all gears are shifted electronically, so producing an effortless, lightweight and easy-to-maintain gearing system. The rider has much of the strain of changing taken off his hands throughout the race.

Pinarello: A Leading Racing Brand

Bicycle manufacturing by the Pinarello family can be traced as far back as 1922 when Alessandro Pinarello began making bicycles in a small factory and winning a gold medal at the prestigious Milan Bicycle Fair of 1925. In 1952, as his professional career came to an end, Alessandro's cousin Giovanni joined him in opening a factory in Treviso, where Pinarello is still based to this day. But the opening of the factory owed rather a lot to a major disappointment. Giovanni was forced to give up his place in his country's national tour, the 1952 Giro d'Italia, to a promising young Italian rider, Pasqualino Fornara. His sponsor, Bottechia, offered him a small fortune of 100,000 lire, if he would agree. Giovanni took

Founded in 1922, Pinarello still retain the character of a family business.

THE PINARELLO DOGMA 2

Wiggins's Team Sky had been riding Pinarello's Dogma 2 since the 2011 Tour de France. It is a bike characterised by asymmetrical frame design; as a bike has the transmission on the right-hand side of a frame, the frame should be stronger and stiffer to handle chain forces on the side where they are greatest. Using finite element analysis and lab testing, Pinarello studied the forces acting on each side of the frame. The design of the new Dogma reflected this research with tube shapes and carbon

fibre lay-up tailored to handle the forces acting on the frame. With its advanced construction technique the Dogma 2 was certainly a sleek machine. While the moulding process for most carbon-fibre frames involves using a rubber bladder to pressurise the structure from the inside, the Dogma 2's multiple layers of carbon fibre are laid over a polystyrene form and pressurised from the outside. This makes for a smooth inner surface that helps strengthen the frame.

A 1951 Pinarello shows the classic engineering of the era before the advent of carbon fibre.

the money and invested it in the Treviso factory. After years of steady progress the company's fortunes suddenly took off when Fausto Bertoglio of the Jolly Ceramica team won the Giro d'Italia in 1975 on a Pinarello. This victory was significant in establishing the Pinarello name as a leading racing brand. More successes came in the 1980s when Pinarello confirmed itself as one of the world's leading bike manufacturers by winning some of the top races, including the 1981 Giro d'Italia and Vuelta a España; the 1984 Olympic road race in Los Angeles; and in 1988 the biggest of all bike races, the Tour de France, thanks to Pedro Delgado.

At the time of the racing success in 1980 Pinarello expanded with the backing of Inoxpran, an Italian world-class leader in the development of stainless steel for domestic products. Inoxpran finance helped revitalise the Jolly Team that was now led by Giovanni Battaglin. For the first time since Pinarello had begun sponsoring professional teams, the Pinarello logo was now seen alongside that of Inoxpran. The reorganisation helped the team become highly successful internationally. The following year, 1981, proved an extraordinary season: Giovanni Battaglin conquered both the Giro d'Italia and the Vuelta a España, using a super-light Pinarello Tre Cime for the steepest climbs. The Pinarello team also captured both the Vuelta di Spagna and the Giro d'Italia.

'Everything just feels so smooth. There are absolutely no speed wobbles, no matter how fast we are descending, and the balance of the bike is second to none. Those aspects really boost your confidence.'

– Team rider Chris Froome speaking about the Dogma 2 (2011)

More success followed; in the 1984 Olympics the USA rider Alexi Grewal won a gold medal on a Pinarello and later Banesto, which included the Spanish champion Miguel Indurain, made the Pinarello the team's bicycle. Indurain went on to ride a Pinarello to victories at five Tours de France, two Giros d'Italia, plus an Olympic victory, a world time-trial championship and the world one-hour record. Now the name Pinarello was associated with success and the company formed partnerships with many other professional teams such as the Del Tongo team from 1988 to 1991 and the Mercatone Uno team from 1992 to 1995.

In 1993, Miguel Indurain's time-trial stage wins on the new Pinarello Chrono Indu carbon-fibre time-trial machine were the key elements in his overall victories in both the Giro d'Italia and the Tour de France. His choice of road bike for these events, however, remained a lugged steel Pinarello. Indurain continued his dominance in time trials and, in 1995, this steel TT bike brought him to his fifth straight Tour de France victory as well as the rainbow jersey of world time-trial champion. Another Pinarello carbon pursuit bike carried Andrea Collinelli to the Olympic pursuit gold medal in 1996 in Atlanta as well as to the team pursuit world championship in Manchester. This occurred just before the UCI banned the 'superman' riding position. The success of Pinarello was then reconfirmed in 1997 with the sixth consecutive victory in the Tour de France by Jan Ullrich before he went on to collect the road race gold medal in the Sydney Olympics of 2000.

Given this pedigree it was no wonder that Team Sky chose Pinarello's new Dogma 2 for their riders in the 2011 Tour de France.

Radical beauty. Miguel Indurain's Chrono Indu carbon-fibre time-trial machine of 1993.

Wiggins's Rise to Victory

The Dogma 2 and Bradley Wiggins were to prove a winning combination, although it was Wiggins who faced the tougher climb to the top. Born in April 1980 in Ghent, Belgium, the son of an Australian professional cyclist, Wiggins had a tough childhood when his father left the family when Bradley was two years old. Wiggins had obviously inherited his father's talent for racing as he won the individual pursuit title at the 1998 Junior Track World Championships in Cuba, aged just 18. That same year he represented England at the Commonwealth Games in Kuala Lumpur.

Man and machine in full flow. A determined Bradley Wiggins powers along on his Sky team Pinarello.

Wiggins's career continued successfully until he won the gold medal in the men's 4,000-metre (4,375-yard) individual at the 2008 Beijing Olympics. After that triumph, he took a break from the track to focus on the road. Initially seen as a time-trial specialist, he concentrated on improving his overall performance and was rewarded by fourth place in the 2009 Tour de France. Two years later Wiggins rode a flawless race for the first six stages of the Tour and was lying sixth overall, just 10 seconds behind the leader, when he crashed; a broken collarbone forced him to abandon the race. The stage winner that day was his teammate Mark Cavendish, who commented: 'I'm gutted for him, he was probably in the best form of his life.' Wiggins's time was yet to come.

THE GENTLEMAN

Late in the 2012 Tour de France Wiggins demonstrated his maverick nature. On Stage 14 a spectator threw carpet tacks on to the narrow road at the top of the Mur de Péguère climb. Several riders suffered punctures, including Cadel Evans, the defending champion, who lost almost two minutes while his team repaired his bicycle. Wiggins and his fellow Team Sky members did not suffer a single puncture. Believing that a puncture resulting from the actions of a saboteur should not disrupt the true course of a race, Wiggins intervened. He persuaded his teammates and the rest of the peloton to slow down until Evans and other affected cyclists had caught up. The peloton then stayed together for the rest of the race, resulting in little change to the general classification. Wiggins's action was seen as a generous act of sportsmanship and he was immediately nicknamed 'The Gentleman' as a result.

He began the 2012 season by finishing second in the opening time trial of the Paris–Nice race. The next day he took the lead and held it to the finish, so becoming the first British rider to win the race since the late Tommy Simpson in 1967. Then he went on to the Tour de Romandie in April where he won the final time trial, despite suffering a dropped chain, to take the overall victory and become the first Briton to win the race in its 65-year history. It was an omen of what was to come.

In the 2012 Tour de France, Wiggins and Team Sky steadily asserted their dominance, winning the stage 19 time trial. Going into the final stage they held a lead of 3 minutes 21 seconds and Wiggins helped his teammate Mark Cavendish achieve his fourth consecutive victory and confirmed his own overall victory in the process. With this victory Bradley Wiggins became the first, and only, person in history to win the Paris–Nice, the Tour de Romandie, the Critérium du Dauphiné and the Tour de France in a single season.

Yet he was not finished for the year. At the London 2012 Olympics, Wiggins on his Pinarello won gold in the time trial, so becoming Great Britain's most decorated Olympian with seven medals – four of them gold. His achievements that year earned Bradley Wiggins a Guinness World Record. He had become the first cyclist to win an Olympic gold medal and the Tour de France in the same year. The last person to win both was, appropriately, Wiggins's boyhood hero Miguel Indurain.

Wiggins, head down, riding a time-trial stage during his historic Tour de France win.

49: The Libbey
Electric Bikes

The birth of the purely electrical bike is generally credited to an American, Hosea W. Libbey of Boston, who invented a successful electric bicycle propelled by what he called a double electric motor. This bears a striking resemblance to the hub motor, which was to be the dominant drive system in electric bikes until less than ten years ago. Within two years, Libbey had applied for a patent that had the motor built within the hub of the crankshaft axle, which has more than just a passing resemblance to the 'mid-drive' or 'crank-drive' systems used today.

Year:
1897

Inventor:
Libbey

Location:
Boston

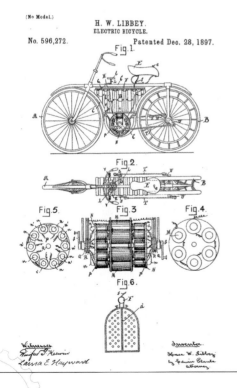

ibbey's design used a series of lead-acid battery cells under the saddle with a hub-mounted electric motor powering the rear axle via a twin-pushrod system. The bike had two motors, two batteries and two wheels. On a flat road, only one battery would work; when climbing a slope the second battery would also come into action. This is probably the first form of electric bicycle controller in history. It was a promising development and the basic design would be imitated a century later in the Giant Lafree electric bicycles of the late 1990s.

The Search for Power-Assisted Propulsion

Since the invention of the bicycle, inventors had been obsessed with producing some form of power-assisted propulsion. Steam engines were the only generating system available and were totally inappropriate for mounting on all but the heaviest cycle. The alternative would have to be something much larger. The first motorised bicycle is generally considered to be the French Michaux-Perreaux steam velocipede of 1868. It comprised a small Louis-Guillaume commercial steam engine attached to a Pierre Michaux iron-framed pedal bicycle. It was more like an early motorbike than a power-assisted pedal cycle.

Designs for the original Libbey electric bike from 1898.

A year later the USA produced a rival with the Roper steam velocipede. Neither machine was commercially successful. Only with the arrival of the gasoline-powered internal combustion engine in the 1890s did a practical solution seem possible. One of the first of these was the French Millet motorcycle of 1892 that had both pedals and a fixed-crankshaft radial engine in the rear wheel. Then in 1896, E. R. Thomas of Buffalo, New York, began marketing gasoline engine kits for propelling ordinary bicycles, followed by a complete motor-assisted bicycle known as the Auto-Bi, which is generally considered to be the first American production motorised bicycle.

The following year saw a return of interest in the purely electrical bike with Hosea W. Libbey's double-electric-motor cycle. Progress continued and in 1898 a rear-wheel drive electric bicycle using a drive belt that ran along the outside edge of the wheel was patented by Mathew J. Steffens. A year later, John Schnepf lodged a patent that used rear-wheel friction to power an electric bicycle. Yet again Schnepf's early proposition would reappear in the future as the inspiration for G. A. Wood Jr's device in 1969 that used four fractional horsepower motors connected through a series of gears.

Yet it would be almost a century before real progress was made in developing a practical electric bike. Only when battery technology had improved sufficiently could enough power be stored on board to provide reasonable acceleration and cruising speed. The development of torque sensors and power controls in the late 1990s showed the way ahead. More sophisticated prototypes began to appear and in 1992 Vector Services marketed the Zike. This was an electric bicycle with nickel-cadmium batteries built into a frame member and included an 850-gram (12.3-ounce) permanent-magnet motor. For some time this remained one of the few practical electric bicycles available.

The key to commercial success still lay in developing a lighter, more powerful, battery. Some of the less expensive electric bicycles still used bulky lead-acid batteries but improved technology was at hand. New batteries, NiMH, NiCd and Li-ion, now became available. These were lighter, denser-capacity batteries offering better performance in both speed and range. This dramatically increased both interest and sales with electric bike production between 1993 and 2004 increasing by an estimated 35 per cent.

Power in an electric bike depends on the efficiency of the battery on board.

By 2001 the new terms e-bike, power bike, pedelec, assisted bicycle, and power-assisted bicycle were now commonly used to refer to electric bicycles. At the same time the terms electric motorbike or e-motorbike had begun to be used to refer to more powerful models that attain up to 80 km/h (50 mph).

Today there are two types of electric bike: power-on-demand motorised bikes and power-assisted. Power-on-demand bikes are throttle- or gear-activated. These machines can do all of the work and can easily propel the rider up a hill. They are ideal for those who need to travel a longer distance. Whenever the rider tires the power can be brought in to take over from the pedalling.

The other primary type of electric bicycle is the power-assisted or pedal-activated bike. This can take over about half of the workload at any time, so allowing the rider to cover twice the distance for the same amount of effort. Power-assist electric bikes are particularly useful for those who travel around cities or towns. They make a good alternative to a second car or overcrowded buses and subways. As they require some physical effort they can help improve a rider's physical fitness. Some are known as 'pedelecs' and incorporate a torque and a speed sensor with a power controller that kicks in only when the rider pedals.

Charging points for electric bikes are becoming ever more numerous in cities and towns worldwide.

A Bright Future

Although the electric bicycle has become increasingly popular in the towns and cities of the West, it is in China that it has really found a home. There are five times more electric bikes on China's roads than cars and the nation is now the world's leading producer of electric bicycles. Each year it manufactures and sells 18 million machines and they now make up over 25 per cent of all two-wheeled vehicles on Chinese streets. By 2020 China expects to produce 75 million units per year, which will mean that a third of China's population will be self-sufficient for commuting and local transport. Most of China's electric bikes are low-powered units of 200 watts, fitted with reusable lead-acid batteries. They typically cost 2,400 yuan, less than US$ 400, the average monthly pay of a Chinese worker. They are basic utility machines that run at 20 km/h (12.4 mph). The workforce typically travels 50 kilometres (31 miles) a day on single charge, usually from home to workplace, and is said to save 150 million worker hours each day. By contrast, the USA motorbike market is 82 per cent for recreation with low average bike runs of 1,600 kilometres (1,000 miles) per year, against 19,300 kilometres (12,000 miles) per year driven by the American car user. This shows the importance of the bicycle as workhorse in the

Chinese economy. Other emerging economies will soon follow China's example. The market potential for the electric bike is enormous, as the world's five largest motorcycle markets are China, India, Indonesia, Brazil and Vietnam. Between them they have three billion people in need of low-cost, eco-friendly vehicles for daily commutes. Further worldwide growth for the electric bike can be expected as solar batteries replace lead-acid, lanthanum and lithium ones. Yet even lithium batteries have been reduced in weight by 70 per cent in recent years and have doubled their charge range. There have also been significant improvements in charging technology such that recharging periods are typically half what they were in the recent past. Battery cycle life, an important cost factor that directly bears on cost per mile, is now triple what is was just three years ago.

So the future looks particularly bright for the electric bike. In 2010, the world produced 60 million motorbikes that ran on fossil fuel and 32 million electric and hybrid two-wheelers. With a near average yearly growth of 20 per cent, electric-powered units will close the gap by 2015, with both categories expected to be producing 70 million units individually by that time.

Each year ever smarter and more advanced electric-powered bikes appear at the world's bicycle shows.

A SMOOTH RIDE

Today the e-bike even has potential outside the city. Rough and even rocky terrain need no longer be a deterrent to cyclists, even the elderly. New, completely computerised suspension systems can be provided by an intelligent electric-powered shock system. The rear suspension is adjusted in response to motion sensors detecting bumps in the front fork. Another advance has been automatic transmissions, now adapted for e-bikes, that shift automatically in response to pedal speed. One continuously variable transmission developed by the USA company Fallbrook Technologies is so smooth the cyclist doesn't even notice the shift. Advanced electronic technology offer other benefits such as an integrated immobiliser that is able to recognise its owners by communicating with their smartphones. Locking the bike will also be a semi-automatic process, operating much like car key remotes. An electronic key blocks the bike by altering magnetic fields in the electric motor, so preventing potential thieves from cycling away with it.

50: A Square-Wheeler?
Futuristic Designs

Since the latter part of the eighteenth century cycling has always embraced innovative technology as the invention of the pedal and gears has shown. That process continues today, but now with almost infinite possibilities given the development of such relatively new materials as carbon-fibre technology. The future looks even more exciting, with the bicycle moving into new areas of possibility.

Year: 1997

Manufacturer:
Bridge

Location:
Sheffield

Crazy or a bike with a future? Even square-wheelers have been considered.

Who in their wildest dreams could have imagined the possibility of a square-wheeled cycle, a concept so outrageous as to defy the imagination? But that is exactly what Phil Bridge has produced. His low-cost, eco-friendly bike really does have square wheels and performs surprisingly well as long as the bike is on a straight line and can maintain a constant velocity on an even road.

Origami Bikes

If a square-wheeled bike is a concept hard to swallow there is also another radical version of the city commuter – the circular bike. Josef Cadek's 'Locust' folds into a circular central frame, making it ideal for carrying onto trains and buses. Such a compact format is particularly appropriate at a time when space increasingly comes at a premium. This trend towards compactness is certain to be important in designs for city bikes of the future. One of the most radical solutions is that of the Chinese designer, Chang Ting Jen. The production version of his Backpack bike weighs just 5.4 kilograms (12 pounds) and folds neatly into a backpack that measures just under 60 centimetres (2 feet) in length. It is so compact that it can be easily picked up, slung over the shoulder, carried onto buses and trains, and up and down stairs and escalators.

There's even the Locust, a bike that folds up like a garden hose.

There are also contemporary versions of such relatively recent classics as the folding bike. With the increasing demand for flexible, fold-away city bikes, designers have been taking a close look at the established Moulton and Bickerton classics and seeing if they can improve on them. Among the most extreme innovations must be Yirong Yang's 'Rotation', a revolutionary type of city cycle. The 'Rotation' is fully adjustable so that the rider can choose the best position for the handlebars and saddle. Even the distance between the front and rear wheels can be customised to suit the individual rider. What makes the 'Rotation' even more unusual is that it is two different vehicles in one: it can be used as either a bicycle or a unicycle, and in both formats it can be folded up after use.

Unconventional Propulsion

Even the long-established mechanics of cycling are being questioned, including propulsion by pedals. For instance, the 'Hyper Bike' by Body Rite does not rely on the power of the legs alone. It makes use of a whole-body climbing, swimming motion to propel the machine forward as if the rider is on some kind of strange unicycle. The rider twists his or her torso, contracts the stomach and back muscles, and alternately extends the arms up and down as in a foot pedal motion. This is not easy, for at the same time the legs must be co-ordinated to produce the best push-and-pull movement from the lower pedals. Just propelling it along needs plenty of space, as the rider must be strapped in. It must be hazardous on the road too, as it is apparently capable of speeds up to 80 km/h (50 mph) and has monstrous wheels 2.4 metres (8 feet) in diameter. The whole contraption looks in many ways like something Leonardo da Vinci might have designed on an off day.

Another machine that uses unconventional propulsion has been developed by Michael Killian in Ireland. He decided that what the world needs is his Sideways Bike, a machine that uses the same body movements as if on a snowboard. It is a two-wheel bicycle with independently steerable wheels that travels sideways. This steering arrangement affords a unique and distinct motion much like the motion of a snowboard. Basically it is a fun machine that is best suited for children from age seven and up. Although it may be weird, it is still a recognisable bicycle.

Try riding sideways. It can be done on this improbably experimental bicycle.

A Bike for Every Occasion

A more practical design is the Cannondale CERV, the Continuously Ergonomic Race Vehicle, intended for riders who want to go fast and hard over varying conditions. It can be swiftly customised to meet varying conditions. Although stability and safety are maintained by an unchanging chassis, it has a cockpit that can be adjusted to provide a lower centre of gravity. The length of the top tube can also be increased or diminished to ensure maximum performance during climbing, descending or negotiating tight corners. Other features include a front wheel that leans into the turns to help when taking tight corners; fast, rim-mounted disc brake rotors to control speed and aid stopping power in all conditions; full-frame suspension, and a virtually maintenance-free enclosed chassis and drivetrain with push-button shifting.

The GT Melenio QR is a versatile cycle designed for navigating crowded city streets and suburban trails. The main attraction of this bike is its quick-release front-end design and an e-dock mounting pocket at the head tube. This transforms it from a human-powered commuter bike into a fully electric cargo-loading, grocery-shopping power machine in minutes. Almost instantaneously, the electronic gear shifter becomes an electronic throttle and the left brake lever goes from disc to front and rear internal hub drum

BACK TO BASICS

As carbon frames become ever more sophisticated there is even a return by some designers to more traditional and basic materials. One attractive example is Yojiro Oshima's design for a wooden bicycle. This is an all-wood machine in which almost everything, even the wheels, handlebars and saddle, are made of wood. The bike incorporates the benefits of a beam frame and a standard frame, so the short cantilevered seat beam is designed to minimise impact, while the seat stay and the chain stay remain conventional in order to maintain the rigidity of the bike. As well as being mechanically sound, the wooden bike is also unusually pleasing to look at with its wooden handlebar with integrated armrests and wooden baton spoke wheels with an arc between the spokes and rim to soften the ride.

The future of cycle design will have to concentrate on meeting the growing needs of the urban cyclist. More and more people are using the bike in town. To meet the demand New York has added 555 kilometres (345 miles) of bike paths in the last ten years with plans for an additional 745 kilometres (463 miles) and 6,000 bike racks in the next. Portland, Oregon, the city with the most comprehensive bicycle infrastructure implementation in the USA, has seen a six-fold increase in cycle usage since 1990. Today, 18 per cent of the city's population uses bikes as the primary or secondary mode of transportation. So with this changing pattern it is good to see one of the great names from cycling history playing a full part in its future.

Schwinn, founded by a German emigrant to the USA in 1891 and the maker of many iconic models in the nineteenth and twentieth centuries, has produced a new bicycle tailored to this future market, the Urban Velo. It starts out full-size but folds into a compact carry-on within seconds. Unlike most foldables, it also looks elegant. It says a lot for a company that it is still there and relevant and pedalling after 118 years.

brakes. Other innovative design elements include front fork and wheel storage under the cargo cart, independently turning front wheels for maximum manoeuvrability and safety at high speeds, and an electronic touch-control dashboard that toggles through information such as navigation and battery level. The motorcycle styling and waterproof under-seat storage big enough for more than just a maximum-security chain lock makes this bike the ideal commuter of the future. As a combination of conventional powered bicycle and e-bike it could well show the way ahead.

When engineering merges with architecture. The Two Nuns sprung steel bike, one of the most improbable bikes of the future.

Further reading

Abt, Samuel, *Greg LeMond: The Incredible Comeback*, Random House, 1990, USA.

Abt, Samuel, *Season in Turmoil: Lance Armstrong Replaces Greg LeMond as U.S. Cycling's Superstar*, VeloPress, 1995, USA.

Ballantine, Richard, *Richard's 21st Century Bicycle Book*, Overlook Press, 2001, USA.

Bathurst, Bella, *The Bicycle Book*, HarperPress, 2012, UK.

Beeley, Serena, *A History of Bicycles: From Hobby Horse to Mountain Bike*, Studio Editions, 1992, USA.

Bell, Trudy, *The Essential Bicycle Commuter*, McGraw-Hill, 1998, USA.

Berto, Frank, *The Dancing Chain: History and Development of the Derailleur Bicycle*, Van Der Plas Publications, 2012, USA.

Berto, Frank, *The Birth of Dirt: Origins of Mountain Biking*, Van Der Plas Publications, 2012, USA.

Bobet, Jean, *Tomorrow We Ride*, Mousehold Press, 2008, UK.

Buzzati, Dino, *The Giro d'Italia: Coppi vs. Bartali at the 1949 Tour of Italy*, Velopress, 1998, USA.

Dauncey, Hugh and Hare, Geoff, *The Tour de France 1903–2003: A Century of Sporting Structures, Meanings and Values*, Routledge, 2003, UK.

Dodge, Pryor, *The Bicycle*, Abbeville Press, 1996, USA.

Embacher, Michael, *Cyclepedia*, Thames & Hudson, 2011, UK.

Fife, Graeme, *Tour de France: The History, The Legends, The Riders*, Mainstream Publishing, 2012, UK.

Fitzpatrick, Jim and Fitzpatrick, Roey, *The Bicycle in Wartime: An Illustrated History* (revised edition), Star Hill Studio, Australia, 2011.

Fotheringham, William, *Fallen Angel: The Passion of Fausto Coppi*, Yellow Jersey, 2008, UK.

Fotheringham, William, *Put Me Back On My Bike: In Search of Tom Simpson*, Yellow Jersey, 2007, UK.

Garcia, Leah, *Cycling for Everyone: A Guide to Road, Mountain, and Commuter Biking*, Knack, 2010, USA.

Goddard, J. T., *The Velocipede: Its History, Varieties, and Practice*, Hurd and Houghton, 1869, USA.

Griffin, Brian, *Cycling in Victorian Ireland*, The History Press, 2006, UK.

Hadland, Tony, *Raleigh: Past and Presence of an Iconic Bicycle Brand*, Van Der Plas Publications, 2011, USA.

Heine, Jan, *The Competition Bicycle*, Rizzoli International Publications, 2012, USA.

Henderson, Bob, and Stevenson, John, *Haynes Bicycle Book*, Haynes Publishing, 2002, UK.

Henderson, Noel, *European Cycling: The 20 Greatest Races*, Vitesse Press, 1989, UK.

Herlihy, David V., *Bicycle: The History*, Yale University Press, 2004, USA.

Hindle, Kathy and Irvine, Lee, *Thorough Good Fellow: Story of Dan Albone, Inventor and Cyclist*, Bedfordshire County Council 1990, UK.

Hume, Ralph, *The Yellow Jersey*, Breakaway, 1996, USA.

Kossak, Joe, *Bicycle Frames*, Anderson World, 1975, USA.

Lovett, Richard, *The Essential Touring Cyclist: A Complete Guide for the Bicycle Traveler*, McGraw-Hill, 2000, USA.

Macy, Sue, *Wheels of Change: How Women Rode the Bicycle to Freedom*, National Geographic Society, 2011, USA.

McConnon, Aili and McConnon, Andres, *Road to Valour: Gino Bartali: Tour de France Legend and Italy's Secret World War Two Hero*, Weidenfeld & Nicolson, 2012, UK.

Mulholland, Owen, *Cycling's Golden Age: Heroes of the Post-war Era 1946–1967*, VeloPress, 2006, USA.

Obree, Graeme, *The Flying Scotsman: The Graeme Obree Story*, Birlinn Ltd, 2004, UK.

Pignatti-Morano, Lodovico and Colombo, Antonio, *Cinelli: the Art and Design of the Bicycle*, Rizzoli International Publications, 2012, USA.

Rapley, David, *Racing Bicycles: 100 Years of Steel*, Images Publishing Group, 2012, UK.

Roche, Stephen with Walsh, David, *The Agony and the Ecstasy*, Hutchinson, 1988, UK.

Rodriguez, Angel and Black, Carla, *The Tandem Book*, Info Net Publishers, 1998, USA.

Rubino, Guido P., *Italian Racing Bicycles: The People, the Products, the Passion*, VeloPress 2011, USA.

Sarig, Roni, *The Everything Bicycle Book*, Adams Media Corp., 1997, USA.

Sharp, Archibald, *Bicycles and Tricycles: A Classic Treatise on Their Design and Construction*, Dover Press, 2003, USA.

Simpson, Tommy, *Cycling is My Life*, Yellow Jersey, 2009, UK.

Vanwalleghem, Rik, *Eddy Merckx: The Greatest Cyclist of the 20th Century*, VeloPress, 1996, USA.

Wheeler, Tony and Janson, Richard, *Chasing Rickshaws*, Lonely Planet, 1998, USA.

Wiggins, Bradley, *In Pursuit of Glory*, Yellow Jersey, 2012, UK.

Witherell, James L., *Bicycle History: A Chronological Cycling History of People, Races, and Technology*, McGann Publishing, 2010, USA.

Worland, Steve, *The Mountain Bike Book*, J. H. Haynes, 2009, UK.

Index

Leblanc, Jean-Marie 178

Lefèvre, Géo 85, 87

Lemoine, Henri 103

LeMond, Greg 151, 175

Lessing, Hans-Erhard 9

Libbey 210, 211

Lilwall, Rob 203

Lister, R. A. 77, 79

'Locust' 214

Longo, Jeannie 110

'longtail' bikes 198

Lotus 108 166–9

Lucas bicycle lamps 72–3

Maclean, Craig 119

McClure, Sam 52

McGann, Bill 133

McGurn, J. 63

McLaren 203

McNamara, Mike 111

Macmillan pedal bike 22–3

Madsen 194

Malvern Star 80–1

Marinoni, Augusto 9

Martin, Gardner 103

Masurier, M. 11

Matsushita, Konosuke 72

Mecredy, R. J. 61

Merckx, Eddy 133, 148, 152–5, 171–2

Merida Bikes 202

Meyer, Eugene 34

Michaux, Pierre 24–6, 27

Michaux-Perreaux steam velocipede 210–11

Michelin brothers 61

Miller, Mrs Libby 68

Mills, Ernie 119

Milne, A. A. 66, 67

Mochet Velocar 102–5

Mockridge, Russell 83

Moore, James 29, 30

Morales, Bob 163

Morand, Paul 103

Morel, Charles 141

Motta, Gianni 153

Moulton Standard Mark 1 140, 142, 143–5

mountain bikes 156–61, 188, 201

multi-wheelers 46–7

Murray 51

Mussolini, Benito 97, 99

Nellis, George 51

Nelson, Frankie 71

Novara-Reber, Sue 110

Olivier brothers 25

Oppernam, Sir Hubert 83

Ordinaries 32–7, 48–53 dwarf Ordinaries 42–5

Oshima, Yojiro 216

Ovenden, Mr 11

Ozanam, Jacques 9–10

Paraskevin-Young, Connie 110–11

Pashley, William Rathbone 128

Pashley cargo bikes 196–7

Paul, Bill 119

Pavesi, Eberardo 133

Peake, Maxine 111

Pedersen, Mikael 67, 76–9

Pélissier, Henri 96, 97

Pennell, Joseph 91

penny-farthings 32–7, 48–53

Peracino, Enrico 154

Petersen, Jan 168

Peugeot 138, 142 PX-10 146–51

Peugeot, Armand 135

Peyton and Peyton 31

Piccini, Alfonso 99

Pinarello 204–9

Pland, Gaston 148

pneumatic tyres 58–61

Pon 188

Pope, Albert A. 48, 49–53

Pope Manufacturing Co.: Daily Service Bicycle 198

postal services 195–7

Pothier, Lucien 89

Prince, John 110

Pro Fit Madone 176–9

Quadrant Cycle Co. 195

Raleigh 65, 91, 92, 143–4

recumbent bikes 102–5

Reilly, William 91, 92

Reynolds, Debbie 71

Richard, Dr Elie 10

Richard, Maurice 104, 119

Ritchie, Andrew 33

Ritchie, Tom 158, 159

Rockhopper 203

Rominger, Tony 170–2

Roper steam velocipede 211

Ross 51

'Rotation' 215

Roubaix 203

Rough Stuff Fellowship 157

Rover 34–5, 38–41, 53

Ryan, Michael B. 142

Salisbury, Harrison 139

Salsbury, Edward 72

Salvo quadricycle 46–7

Salvo Sociable 66

Saronni, Giuseppe 172

Sastre, Carlos 189

Sawall, Walter 115

Schleck, Andy 203

Schnepf, John 211

Schoeninger, Adolph 53

Schrader, August 61

Schulz, Jacques 116–17

Picture credits